P9-DHA-333

Why Quit Our Own

by
George N. Peek
with
Samuel Crowther

"Why quit our own to stand upon foreign ground? Why by interweaving our destiny with that of any part of Europe, entangle our peace and prosperity in the toils of European ambition, rivalship, interest, humor, or caprice?"

*Washington's Farewell Address,
September 17, 1796*

New York: 250 Fourth Avenue
D. Van Nostrand Company, Inc.
1936

Published in part in the *Saturday Evening Post*
under the title "IN AND OUT."

PRINTED IN U. S. A.

PRESS OF
BRAUNWORTH & CO., INC.
BUILDERS OF BOOKS
BRIDGEPORT, CONN.

PREFACE

This book has been conceived and written not in a partisan spirit but solely in an effort to take the question of national prosperity and well-being out of the realm of mere words and theory and to discuss them on the sure basis of fact.

I have started with the assumption that we as Americans have as our primary interest the welfare of the American people.

I have also assumed that our national well-being depends upon the ability of the various groups of our population freely to exchange man hours of labor on a basis of reasonable equality. This implies a balanced economy—without any large, submerged sections of population. It also implies an American price system. To preserve an American economy, there must be an American price system that will be insulated so far as is humanly possible from outside influences.

The farm sections of the nation have been depressed and out of balance for a long time—I have been calling attention to that danger since 1921. Foreign trade policies are inseparably bound up with attaining and preserving a balanced domestic economy. They are a part of farm policy. They are equally a part of labor policy. Organized labor has recognized the dangers of cheap, immigrant labor. But that labor entering as goods is even more dangerous, for the goods are not consumers and the immigrants are.

The attaining of a balanced domestic economy must proceed from a determination of the bookkeeping facts: it is not a matter of rhetoric. It may be necessary to debate certain policies after the simple bookkeeping facts are in hand. Certainly there is no point in debating without the facts.

But for some curious reason it has seemed best to those who have shaped both our farm and our foreign policies to proceed not only without facts but also in a spirit of antagonism to facts. In my capacity of Administrator of the Agricultural Adjustment Act and later as Special Adviser to the President on Foreign Trade, I tried to initiate policies based on the arithmetic of the facts. The Roosevelt Administration rejected arithmetic and policies alike. Consequently I retired.

Since the writing of this book, a trade agreement with France has been promulgated. It is no better and no worse than the others. It completes the lowering of our general liquor and cheese schedules (except for Italian cheese) and gives to France unlimited access to our markets at lower rates. It does nothing to meet the essential export needs of our own country, and the increase in quotas of American goods which may be imported by France is trivial.

It is interesting to note that the agreement ignores the capital transactions with France and the great gift which this country has made to France by writing up the value of her gold. During the six years 1928 to 1933 inclusive, 70,096,275 fine Troy ounces of gold were transferred from the United States to France at $20.67 an ounce. Under the gold-buying policy of President Roosevelt, our Treasury bought from France during 1934 and 1935 a total of 34,136,660 ounces at $35.00 an ounce. The dollar value of the six-year shipment was $1,448,898,508; that of the gold bought back was $1,194,-783,000. Of the American gold taken by France, 35,959,615 ounces still remain in France and this gold now has a value of $1,258,586,525. In other words, the Roosevelt Administration, by its dollar devaluation and gold-buying policies, has made a gift to France of about a billion dollars based on the price for gold fixed by the Administration. The Treasury bonanza gold buying still continues and the perils to our national economy daily grow greater.

The facts which I have given on the amount of foreign investments in our country have, since the writing of this book, been officially substantiated by the Department of Commerce in a brochure, "Foreign Investments in the United States," by Amos E. Taylor, which is a public document.

About one-half of this book appeared in six articles in the *Saturday Evening Post* under the title "In and Out." I desire to acknowledge the courtesy of Mr. George Horace Lorimer in permitting the inclusion of that material in the book.

George N. Peek

CONTENTS

Chapter I

Broken Promises

I went into the Roosevelt Administration because I saw a chance to do something for agriculture and, through agriculture, for the nation. I got out when I saw that I had no chance there to do anything either for agriculture or for the nation. I am in politics for agriculture—not in agriculture for politics.

The Administration has committed itself, by a distortion of the lately deceased Agricultural Adjustment Act, to a policy of socialized farming. It has committed itself, by a distortion of the Reciprocal Trade Agreements Act, to a low tariff policy which has all the worst features of that free trade which the nation has always turned down at the polls.

Both these policies are utterly destructive. They can add nothing at all to the wealth and prosperity of the United States. They can only subtract from what we have, shift jobs from American to foreign workers and transfer to foreign nations the control of what we have left. Exactly that has been happening. The facts are very clear. I shall present them without prejudice or passion.

The facts as exhibited by the official records mean little to many in this Administration. The major policies of agriculture and foreign trade are in charge of men who have never earned their livings in industry, commerce, finance or farming and who have little comprehension as to how such livings are earned. Presenting facts to them is a sheer waste of time. They are long on theories but short on simple arithmetic. They are full of very big thoughts. These thoughts are so big that the United States is not a large enough field for them to operate in.

They would remake the United States as an incident to remaking the world. For instance, one highly placed official, at a time when crop surpluses were bothering us, came forward with an elaborate scheme for a world corporation which would pool all surpluses everywhere and distribute them to the poor of the world. He actually succeeded in calling a conference of departmental officials to consider his scheme. Another bright young man, who prided himself on the breadth of his views, was going to solve everything by having the United States forcibly guarantee the peace of the world. No one will ever know how many fantastic schemes were in the air. Many of them crossed the border line of sanity, but anyone who attempted to apply elementary common sense was denounced as an obstructionist. It was heresy to assert that two plus two had to equal four.

I had left the Republican Party to support Alfred E. Smith in 1928 because he promised to put into effect the farm program which I had been working on as far back as 1922. I worked for the election of Franklin D. Roosevelt because he seemed to comprehend the farm situation and promised to try to solve it along the lines a group of us had been steadily advocating. I entered what I thought was a Democratic Administration, not because it was Democratic but because it was pledged to a certain course of action. I eventually found that I was not in a Democratic Administration but in a curious collection of socialists and internationalists who were neither Republicans nor Democrats.

They, fanatic-like, believed that their objectives transcended the objectives of ordinary human beings and therefore they could not allow themselves to be hampered by the codes of ordinary mental honesty, by platform pledges, by the Constitution, or by any other of the ordinary rules of human conduct.

There were two broad general groups—the socialists and

the internationalists. The socialists or, more strictly, the collectivists seemed—for nothing was in the open—to be headed by Felix Frankfurter, Rexford G. Tugwell, and Jerome Frank. They gained the mind of the Secretary of Agriculture and had a good deal of sway throughout the Department. The internationalists ruled the State Department and were headed by Secretary Hull and Assistant Secretary Sayre. Those within the groups had many divergent aims. Secretary Wallace, who has an elastic and fantastic mind capable of any stretching, alone managed to be in both groups.

The collectivists tolerated the internationalists and avoided any open clash because the more astute undoubtedly knew that the chief obstacle to a planned and regimented economy in this country is our high standard of living and widespread ownership of property. They must have known that lowering the tariff was the surest method of breaking down the American standard of living by mingling it with the international standard of living. The outstanding and only common characteristic of both groups was their willingness to make the interests of our country and its people subservient to the practice of their theories and to substitute personal government centralized in Washington for our traditional state and local governments. The tactics pursued were unpleasantly reminiscent of those followed in the setting up of totalitarian governments in Russia, Italy and Germany. Both groups have blind spots where the interests of the United States are concerned.

These are serious charges and I do not make them lightly. I intend to prove each point. But first I want to make my relations with the Administration very clear. I entered the Administration on my own terms. I did not want a job or political preferment of any kind. My salary as Administrator of the Agricultural Adjustment Act I turned over to private counsel whom I retained to advise me independently of the A.A.A. counsel—in whom I had no confidence.

The Agricultural Adjustment Act was a hodgepodge of conflicting notions compromised into a bill which had to be passed in order to get action. In supporting the Act, I thought that it would be used for constructive purposes and I did not have the slightest idea that in its administration it would become principally an instrument to regiment the farmer through acreage control. I had not the slightest idea that it would not be used for the purposes which through the years we had discussed—to open our foreign markets, to sell our surpluses, to improve distribution at home and to pay proper benefits independently of acreage control. I thought that before taking office I had made my views abundantly clear. I have no doubt now but that I did. But others had other views—and they were willing to wait until they could make them prevail.

Through all my life I have been steadfastly against the promotion of planned scarcity. On this point Secretary Wallace and I disagreed sharply while the bill was in the making. That I shall take up in detail in a later section. The point of importance now is my understanding with the President as a condition precedent to taking office. Here are some entries from my diary for April 5th, 1933—the Agricultural Adjustment Act was passed on May 12th.

I talked with Wallace. I told him I was going up to the Hill for a while (meaning Senator Smith's Office, to review my testimony). Upon arrival at Senator Smith's office a messenger from the Secretary's office came for me and said the Secretary wanted me to come to the Department right away, which I did. He said the President wanted us to come to the White House at 4:15, and asked what my answer would be to the President. I told him that depended upon the President's decision as to policy, which I would discuss in our interview. We spent twenty minutes with the President, who asked me if

I would take the administration of the farm bill. I said that I regarded the problem as more industrial than agricultural, and that B. M. [Bernard M. Baruch] was the best man in the country for the job. He said he had talked with Baruch and that he could not take it but had strongly recommended me. I said that I came down here at Wallace's request, and had tendered my services to be helpful but that I could not take the job without a lot of things being understood because I felt that he [the President] alone must outline the policy, as in my opinion the success or failure of his whole administration and the recovery of the country depended upon the successful administration of this Act; that all that he had done about the banks and other things would be of no avail if this failed. I said that

First, the form of the bill itself as it came through the Senate must be considered in connection with its administration.

Second, that his policy toward it must be known.

Third, that responsibility must rest with the Secretary and the Administrator, who jointly must have direct access to him, with no one else permitted to run circles around them to him.

Fourth, my 5-point program represented my views. I left it with him. He congratulated me upon getting them all upon one page.

We told him Lowden [Governor Frank Lowden] would be here Friday and he asked that we get Baruch to come too, that we should get together for a general discussion. The President referred to Raskob's change of heart between the 1928 convention and the 1928 campaign, and said that R. had first been opposed to the farm plank and later agreed with it, to show how reasonable it appeared when explained.

The President asked me again if I would administer the bill and I said that my views were in conflict with those of the Secretary and that a general understanding was necessary. Wallace confirmed my statement of the difference in views. The interview ended, to be renewed Friday.

This is a copy of the "5 Points" I left with the President:

1. Situation to be Corrected.

The policy of attempting to expand industrial exports, regardless of the effect upon agriculture, is a demonstrated failure. It has been attempted by previous administrations, supported by leaders in business and finance, and by Government itself, but the plan collapsed when we could no longer continue to lend money to other nations to enable them to buy our wares.

Agricultural exports are more important to the nation than are industrial exports. In the 23 years from 1910 to 1932 the total income from all exports averaged 7.45 per cent of the whole national income, but the proportion of agricultural income attributable to agricultural exports was 17.86 per cent, while the proportion of industrial income attributable to industrial exports was only 5.21 per cent. The importance to industry itself of buying power in farm areas has been demonstrated and now is admitted generally.

2. American-owned Foreign Plants.

Many of our processors have foreign plants which to a considerable extent take care of their trade outside of the United States. Our aim should be to ship products of the farm in manufactured form from plants within the United States to increase employment and stimulate activity at home. (If discrimination is to be practiced, American manufacturers without foreign plants should be favored, and in this event due regard should be given to economic distribution and location.)

3. Centralized Control or Supervision of Exports and Imports.

Such control is suggested in order to benefit industries, localities and labor within the United States. This suggestion of control may be extended to industries other than those manufacturing the raw products of the farm in order that both exports and imports may be selective.

4. Competition for the Consumer's Dollar.

This competition exists generally in all industries, but I refer to the food industries in particular. Price cutting and other trade practices due to such competition are among the primary causes of the present depression as well as of the disparity in prices between farm commodities. Large volume business is sought with the result of ruinously low prices to the farmer and at the expense of net profits even to the processor and distributing agencies.

We have an over-capacity of industrial plants for profitable operation, as well as of farms. This over-capacity must be liquidated in an orderly manner to a point where production of industrial products may be more nearly balanced to domestic demand and potential foreign markets.

5. Policies Regarding Domestic vs. International Trade.

We cannot follow both at the same time. My view is that we should favor the former and adjust our tariffs and perhaps the foreign debts by reciprocal agreements to encourage, in the national interest, exports of farm products, preferably in manufactured form, in exchange for non-competing farm products and selected industrial products. This selection should be so made as to do the least possible violence to our industries. Eventually we may be required to lower tariffs generally but I think this should be accomplished selectively and gradually.

Continuing the diary:

(April 7, 1933—Friday). Lowden, B. M. B. and I went to the White House at 3:30 for a conference with the President. We spent nearly an hour there. The President said he had read my 5-point memorandum and was quite in accord with it. He and I disagreed on the question of restricted production as a national policy. He said that it was likely the international wheat situation would be discussed at Inter. Conference on April 21. B. M. B. went over his objections to the bill and the President agreed to send for him before the bill went to conference, after it passed Senate. I argued strongly for one hundred million appropriation, Treasury to be reimbursed by tariff duties on agricultural imports, especially fats, oils and blackstrap molasses. Governor Lowden supported me in this view and the President said he would not object. I argued the injustice of asking processors to pay the expenses of a retreat from our traditional land policy. [I felt processors should be compelled to pay the farmers fair prices, and if they would not do it, I favored taxing them and paying the farmers a benefit payment to insure parity prices on the domestically consumed portion of the crop. I felt that it was not fair to ask them to pay for the retirement of acreage.] It is clear that further understanding is necessary, including freedom of action in selecting assistants.

. . . The conference was of far-reaching importance, as both B. M. B. and Governor Lowden agreed to be of any help they could in an advisory way.

B. M. B. told me he had a conference with the Cotton Ex. people in response to my suggestion, and they said they did not see how it could be worked out (i.e. separate foreign and domestic prices). He said he told them that there was no point in talking about it, that they had to do it, and to go figure out how. [I had asked B. M. B. to discuss with the New York Cotton Exchange authorities the possibility of changing their practice of quoting cotton prices upon the single level of world prices to quoting on two levels—foreign and domestic.]

(April 22, 1933—Saturday). By request went to see Secretary Wallace yesterday evening. Did not discuss details of administration of bill. Urged him to get comprehensive data on all exports and imports with each country for the purpose of determining expansion of agricultural exports. The Secretary expressed himself as of the opinion that we should go on through with the deflation now, adjusting supply to demand, and has not given up his idea of taking acreage out of production, although Earl Smith and Gregory shocked him considerably in a talk they had with him earlier in the day about the bad effect of his bureaucratic tendencies. Smith [Earl C.

Smith, president of the Illinois Agricultural Association] and Gregory [C. V. Gregory, editor of "The Prairie Farmer"] asked me if Ezekiel [Mordecai Ezekiel, a bureau economist], and who else, was responsible.

(April 26, 1933—Wednesday). Suggested to Wallace yesterday the possibility of disaster if commodity prices were to rise sharply while unemployment continued, wages were reduced, and people continued to be laid off. Urged that some general industrial and municipal activities be encouraged. He asked me to see Ickes. Wallace said later that a committee had been appointed by the President of three men: Ickes, Wallace, and Dern.

(May 3, 1933—8:30 P.M.) F. D. R. at White House;
Wallace
Tugwell
Wilson (M.L.)
Appleby

H. Cummings
Roper
Perkins
Woodin
(Asst.) W. Cummings
Farley
(Asst.) Moley
(Dir. Budget) Douglas
Morgenthau

Other assistant Secretaries and attaches.

Very spirited debate over policy, and organization. President finally settled matter of organization by marking Department chart. After adjourning meeting about midnight he detained Wallace and me to decide matters of organization. [This chart suggested an administrative organization as follows: The Secretary and the Administrator, and Divisions of Processing and Marketing, Finance, Information and Publicity, and Production; the six heads to form an administrative council. The Office Manager, General Counsel, Statistical Division, and the World Trade Representative were to report to the Administrator as staff assistants. Wallace said he would like to have Rex a member of the council; the President said "no."]

On May 15th, 1933, upon taking office as the Administrator of the Agricultural Adjustment Act, I issued a statement which said in part:

In the first place the sole aim and object of this act is to raise farm prices. Generally speaking, it is to raise them to a point where farm products will purchase as much of industrial products as they did before the War, and to keep farm prices at that level. This is just what farmers through their organizations have been demanding for a dozen years.

With Charles J. Brand as co-administrator, an organization for the administration of the A.A.A. was put together. Mr. Brand had organized the Bureau of Markets of the Department of Agriculture, and was thoroughly familiar with government procedure—which I was not. He was then engaged in private industry. Mr. Brand was a most able and loyal associate. We got the best men we could and as quickly as we could. Generally we were fortunate in our own selections. But everything was in confusion and we found ourselves saddled with many more whom we did not choose and did not want.

A plague of young lawyers settled on Washington. They all claimed to be friends of somebody or other and mostly of Felix Frankfurter and Jerome Frank. They floated airily into offices, took desks, asked for papers and found no end of things to be busy about. I never found out why they came, what they did or why they left. Perhaps all of them expected to be hired, and some of them were hired. I only know that in the legal division were formed the plans which eventually turned the A.A.A. from a device to aid the farmers into a device to introduce the collectivist system of agriculture into this country. This was due to Jerome Frank—probably acting as a spearhead. He was a lawyer who had practised in Chicago and New York and had come to Washington, so he told me, at the request of Felix Frankfurter. Dr. Tugwell brought him to Agriculture.

The case of Mr. Frank is somewhat peculiar. I found that I knew him—I had met him at a time when he was counsel for a group of banks.

He told me that he had more recently been with Thomas L. Chadbourne's firm in New York. He was a good lawyer but, as I later discovered, was more concerned with social theory than with law and was so certain of his cleverness that he thought he could frame new laws or interpret old laws in such a manner as to carry out the theories he held. Practically all the young lawyers who swarmed into Washington dangling Phi Beta Kappa keys were enveloped in the delusion that they carried with them the tablets containing a new dispensation. They were going to inform the established lawyers and the Supreme Court what the law really was. Mr. Frank was slated to be solicitor for the Department of Agriculture. Mr. Farley killed that projected appointment. Shortly after I had accepted the position of Administrator and Brand had agreed to act as Co-Administrator, we went to the White House with Secretary Wallace to discuss procedure with the President and to arrive at a starting point. During the conversation I objected to Jerome Frank acting as General Counsel for A.A.A. I advanced among other reasons the thought that he had had no experience with farm organizations and farmers, that he had been a city lawyer, and that his personality was such as not to inspire the confidence of the farm leaders. In all of this Brand concurred. After discussing the subject for a few minutes, the President agreed with our point of view and told Wallace in our presence that he had better get rid of Frank by having him transferred to some other department, and suggested Justice. Upon our return to the office, Wallace sent for Brand and me, and when we arrived at his office we found Frank there. Wallace said he had told him what the President had said, and we thought that the matter was settled. The next morning Wallace sent for me again. He was in great distress and appealed to me to retain Frank in the face of what the President had said. Wallace said in effect, "If you force Frank to resign, I will also have to resign; it will interfere with all of our plans."

I never knew what he meant. Against my better judgment, I yielded to his appeal. As a precaution, I retained Frederic P. Lee as private counsel. We shortly discovered that Mr. Frank and his division were more concerned with matters of policy than with questions of law. They appeared to be proponents of the puppet system of government and very anxious to extend government control as a prelude to government ownership. Contracts and arrangements which did not have Mr. Frank's approval for social rather than legal reasons seemed, no matter what their urgency, to get pigeon-holed in his office. He always claimed that he did not have enough assistants to put things through promptly—although for a while he succeeded in getting over a hundred lawyers on his staff.

I have the suspicion that Dr. Tugwell had influenced the appointment of Mr. Wallace as Secretary to suit his own purposes, and that Mr. Frank was part of a deliberate set-up to use the A.A.A. to further collectivism. On September 30th, 1933 Mr. Brand resigned. In December an article appeared in a New York newspaper to the effect that there was a split in the A.A.A. between the radicals headed by Mr. Frank and the conservatives headed by me and that the young liberal lawyers, not only in the A.A.A. but throughout the Administration, were about to walk out. It was written by a reporter who was close to the President and to the left-wing lawyers. Unfortunately it was not true.

The President, on December 11th, asked me to see him and, without going at length into the differences which had developed in the A.A.A., said that he had some special and important work for me to do in connection with foreign trade and, since it was directly in the line of my Five Points, he felt that I could do more in that field than in the position I had. This was equivalent to asking for my resignation from the office of Administrator.

I left for Chicago that afternoon to address a meeting of the American Farm Bureau Federation. I made it very plain to that meeting that I was not in sympathy with the talk about abolishing the profit system and radically changing our institutions. I said in that speech:

Now for the final part of my talk: about the profit system, and its detractors. All through this land there is constant discussion of the so-called new functions of Government, of Government plans for this or that, of what the Government is going to do next. What is Government?

This is what has been going through my mind. Our Government is not some mysterious device handed down from above or dug up from below. It is of our own making. In setting up our original Government our forefathers followed the English guild system of local self-sufficiency. As local governments expanded and interests crossed, overhead governments were set up, resulting in county and State governments.

The Federal Government was supposed to intervene only in such matters as could not be settled by the States themselves. The foundation of the whole structure from the first has been a respect for private property rights, and the sacredness of contracts.

There is great apprehension in the minds of many business men today about the relations of government to business. There is grave concern over the expressions of a few ultra-liberals about the Government taking over private business. If you want my opinion—personally, not officially, mind you—I would say that this apprehension is unwarranted. Unless it hustles, the Government has more hay down now than it will get up before it rains.

Legitimate profits have always been regarded in this country as a proper reward for individual initiative, industry, and thrift. I know of no substitute for such traits. I am in favor of the profit system; but I am in favor of starting with the farmer.

There is abroad in the land a propaganda of more or less importance for doing away with the profit system. This means no more and no less than doing away with the institutions under which we have all grown up and prospered more or less. I am against the racketeers of high finance as much as I am against the racketeers in the underworld. But the remedy lies not in destroying our institutions. It lies in reaching those racketeers in high places under the laws of our land. If those laws are inadequate, they should be revised and extended so that no guilty man shall escape. I am dead against the malpractices of the so-called monopolies; I say "so-called" to differentiate between "malefactors of great wealth" and the millions of heads of business, large and small, performing a useful service. I am not committed to any one method of farm adjustment. I have not yet seen the perfect system either for the farmer, for the laborer, or for industry. I feel that fundamental plans should be discussed and understood before adoption; that new methods of social control should be clearly outlined, and that the people as a whole should have the right and duty to make the ultimate decision.

On my return from Chicago I found that the White House had issued a press release announcing

. . . "a Temporary Committee to recommend permanent machinery to coordinate all government relations to American foreign trade. . . . The report of a committee and final action thereon is expected within two weeks. George Peek, Agricultural Adjustment Administrator, having completed the organization period of the A.A.A., is designated to head this committee as special assistant to the President on American trade policy.

"As far back as last March, in his discussions of the agricultural policy, the President discussed with Mr. Peek the possibility and advisability of reopening foreign markets for agricultural surpluses. It was decided at that time that the immediate domestic supply should be restricted, in view of the fact that foreign markets were closed temporarily by tariffs, quotas, etc., so that the immediate task was to restrict production until the machinery for the limitation of burdensome surpluses could be put in operation.

"Now the time has come to initiate the second part of the program and to correlate the two parts, the internal adjustment of production with such effective foreign purchasing power as may be developed by reciprocal tariffs, barter, and other international arrangements.

"Mr. Peek will head the new organization when it is created."

I resigned as Administrator of the A.A.A., setting out in my letter to the President that it was at his request. I felt that the A.A.A. was headed for trouble, for it was developing into an agency for permanent and wholesale acreage control from a central point and without due regard to local conditions.

Such a program is wrong in theory and is difficult, if not impossible, to administer in a democracy. I could not then or now willingly be a party to seeing control of the land of the farmers taken from them and put at the disposal of a Washington bureaucracy. As the A.A.A. began to expand as a social reform instead of as a farm aid, it became inevitable that in time the farmers would own their farms in name only and that in fact they would be the hired hands of Washington.

I had the choice of getting out of the Administration or staying in and seeing what I could do about foreign trade. I chose the latter course—albeit with misgivings and some sacrifice of spirit. I felt that eventually the proper development of foreign trade could effect a disposal of some surplus crops and in that way aid the domestic program—perhaps it might even be developed to a point where it could be used to kill off the acreage limitation and regimentation movement.

On December 30th I filed a report with the President recommending a foreign trade administration and a United States foreign trade corporation. The arrangement that I proposed is not to be confused with any of the numerous corporations chartered with the public funds to put the Government into business. I had in mind something more in the nature of the British Board of Trade which would act as a clearing house for statistical information and set up double entry books on the whole of our foreign trade so that we might distinguish between foreign trade and finance conducted at a profit to the nation as a whole and that trade and finance conducted only for the profit of small groups and at the expense of the nation as a whole. I had a suspicion that proper accounts would show that our foreign trade and foreign lending from the war period through to the beginning of the depression had been merely draining our resources.

The President at that time was apparently in accord with my position—which I had already presented to him in the Five Points. On February 2nd, 1934 by Executive Order he established the Export-Import Bank and asked me to serve as president. The purpose of this bank was to help finance trade with Russia, but, because of the misunderstanding concerning the Russian debt, it never did anything. On March 9th he established the Second Export-Import Bank. This was designed for trade with Cuba. Later the banks' activities were consolidated and their powers made general. (The life of the banks was later extended by Congress.) Both were under the authority of the National Industrial Recovery Act, and under that same authority on March 23rd, 1934 the President established the office of Special Adviser to the President on Foreign Trade. Four days later he extended the executive committee on commercial policy.

As Special Trade Adviser I took it as my function to find out what we had been doing on foreign trade through the years. When a man takes charge of a business, he first calls for an independent audit of the books so that he will know what he is expected to manage. The results of my audit were submitted in two comprehensive letters to the President. He discussed both letters with me, apparently approved my findings and ordered the documents printed as a part of the public records. It is enough here to say that the first thing I found out is that we had kept no books in the modern sense of the word. We had been keeping, in various places, records by a single-entry system, but with no real income statement or balance sheet. Statistics on foreign trade are filed in fifty or more different governmental agencies, committees or departments, all supposed to have something to do with the subject. The first part of the job was to assemble from these statistics an income account and balance sheet to show whether we had been doing business at a profit or a loss. This accounting showed, for the past thirty-eight years, an increasingly disadvantageous position, by reason of a large increase of debts owed us from abroad.

The next step in our investigation was to break down the debit and credit items into terms of goods, services—visible and invisible—and capital transactions, including gold and silver. This led to startling findings. For instance, in 1919, less than 9 per cent of our total dollar settlements was in capital transactions—investments, here and abroad. Seventy per cent was in merchandise and services, the remainder being for war debts, tourist expenditures, immigrant remittances and miscellaneous items. But in 1934 capital transactions between this and other countries accounted for 43 per cent of the whole international movement, and in 1935 preliminary figures indicate 53.7 per cent.

Having found out in a general way where the nation stood on foreign balance, it seemed in order to do something about it, but I began to find that government bookkeeping in foreign trade was not wanted. A considerable group, both in and out of the Administration, for various reasons preferred the old copybook theories of foreign trade to any policies based on factual information. Many bankers were against bookkeeping —in spite of the fact that most of them had no knowledge at all of the actual accounts and, as I shall subsequently show, conducted enormous international financial operations with practically no knowledge of what they were doing. The war debt cancellationists—and among them were practically all the League of Nations special advocates—did not want accounts, perhaps because the accounts showed plainly that the United States had in its hands the power to collect its war debts. The professional foreign trade boosters did not want accounts which might disclose that their policies at times ran counter to the public interest as well as to the interests of investors.

All of this opposition centered in the State Department. Secretary of State Hull is a very worthy gentleman who spent his early days as a lawyer and judge in Tennessee. Most of the time since 1907 he has been a member of Congress. He has been on a public payroll of one kind or another since 1903. Like most of his generation in the South, he grew up in the tradition of free trade. To him low tariffs are in the nature of a religion. He does not consider those who disagree with him and who ask for facts as being merely wrong. He believes they are heretics.

Mr. Hull has as his chief collaborator a very estimable gentleman, Professor Francis B. Sayre, who married a daughter of the late President Wilson. Messrs. Hull and Sayre were both appointed to satisfy a certain wing of the Democratic Party. Professor Sayre was left enough money by his father, a Pennsylvania manufacturer, to do more or less what he pleased and, graduating from the Harvard Law School, he has preferred to teach law rather than to practice it. His widest experience was during the years 1923-30 which he spent as adviser to the Siamese Government. He is a doctrinaire who believes in the brotherhood of man which is somehow to be brought about through the League of Nations and international free trade. If you do not agree with him, he thinks your motives must be bad because his are good.

It would not be fair to say that Messrs. Hull and Sayre would be willing to subordinate the interests of the United States to the furthering of their policies. It is fair to say that their mental processes are so rigid and their range of view so narrow that practically they might not know the interests of the United States when they saw them.

Messrs. Hull and Sayre represented the internationalist viewpoint within the Administration just as the Tugwell-Frank coterie with Felix Frankfurter on the side-lines represented the collectivist viewpoint. A collectivist believes in a planned economy. This requires a nationalist state and is directly opposed to internationalism. Secretary Wallace is, I am informed, the only human being who ever succeeded in being both a collectivist and an internationalist at the same time. He wrote a book "America Must Choose" which no doubt explained to his satisfaction how anyone can go in opposite directions at the same time.

However, the problem involved in attaching divergent pulls to the Chariot of State did not seem to bother these groups in the Administration. While the A.A.A. was seeking to raise farm prices so that agriculture could buy on an equality with industry, the N.R.A., through the President's Reemployment Agreement, was seeking to raise non-agricultural wages which would have the effect of putting industrial products out of the buying reach of the farmer. The Hull-Sayre program, as it developed, had as its objective the lowering of all import duties and thus knocking the pins out from under both the N.R.A. and the A.A.A.

The Executive Committee on Commercial Policy (established by the President on November 11th, 1933) believed that if the President were empowered to execute reciprocal trade agreements, granting concessions in duty if need be, our foreign trade might be stimulated. The whole world was doing that and we were being left out. Some of the discussions leading up to the drafting of the Reciprocal Trade Agreements Act inclined to the ludicrous. The planned economy experts got an inning and actually drew up a plan as to what American industries were non economic and should therefore be destroyed by permitting and even furthering foreign competition. Master minds were everywhere about us, but that project was killed off.

In June, 1934 the Reciprocal Trade Agreements Act was passed by Congress and became a law. In all my work as Special Adviser I found my every recommendation opposed by Messrs. Hull and Sayre, and when the Trade Agreements Act went through I found that they intended to administer it exactly as they chose and to the end of breaking down the American tariff system, in the fervent belief that somehow the affairs of the whole world would thus be bettered. Their method of doing this was very simple. Our country had what are called "unconditional most-favored-nation" clauses in its commercial treaties with a few countries. This was construed by Secretary Hull to mean that if in a special agreement a duty be lowered to Country A in return for certain concessions from it, the same lowered duty will apply to all nations without any concessions from them. The process of applying the lowered duties to every other country is called generalization and its effect is to make every tariff reduction in a so-called reciprocal treaty a general reduction. On this account practically none of the other countries of the world generalize their reciprocal concessions.

As Special Adviser to the President, I many times protested these interpretations. In my report of December 31st, 1934 I made formal protest and I also recommended abolishing my office and creating a permanent foreign trade board. My office as Special Adviser expired after the Supreme Court declared N.I.R.A. unconstitutional. It was impossible for me to discover whether the President agreed or did not agree with me. I determined therefore in July, 1935 to press the matter to a decision. On July 16th I wrote to the President in part as follows:

> As these studies progressed I was forced inescapably to the conclusion that our general depression and the financial collapse of 1931-1932 were traceable in very large measure to the commercial and financial policies pursued by the three post-war administrations in their relations with foreign nations. These policies rendered us vulnerable to the economic shocks which eventually overwhelmed us.
>
> This conclusion in turn led me to make to you two recommendations of major importance designed to correct the condition to which I refer.
>
> First, was the creation of a permanent foreign trade board to coordinate the various foreign trade activities of the Government under unified direction and to deal comprehensively with our foreign commercial and financial activities. The creation of such an agency appears to me vital if we are to develop adequate foreign trade policies and to administer them effectively. . . .
>
> Second, I have recommended that we abandon the unconditional most-favored-nation policy adopted under the Harding administration and return to the traditional American policy of extending conditional most-favored-nation treatment only on a quid pro quo basis.
>
> My objections to the unconditional most-favored-nation

policy are two-fold. In the first place, its use involves the progressive destruction of our bargaining power at a time when the conditions in international trade require that we retain the maximum freedom of action and bargaining power if our nationals are to compete on equal terms with the nationals of other countries in the markets of the world. In the second place, the result of the generalization of concessions under the unconditional most-favored-nation policy is to effect a general reduction of our tariff in return for scattered concessions from a limited number of nations. The limited safeguards surrounding the trade agreements already made leave the country apprehensive of what may happen next. The declaration of policy of the Reciprocal Trade Agreements Act does not suggest that Congress in passing it intended to delegate power to effect a general tariff reduction or appreciated that the authority conveyed might be used for that purpose. I believe that a low tariff policy is not an appropriate one for us at a time when our internal economic balance is in process of readjustment and when unemployment figures remain at their present level. I think that before we attempt general tariff reduction there should be a clear indication of policy from Congress on the subject.

My fundamental reason for taking this step is that I feel increasingly out of sympathy with the foreign trade policies now being pursued. I believe that national recovery will be impossible so long as these policies are continued.

I followed this a few days later with another letter in which I said, among other things:

As I have indicated to you on a number of occasions, a question of major policy is involved. For the past dozen or more years I have given the best in me to the subject of agricultural problems and remedies. The solution of these, which I regard as essential to national recovery, is dependent upon a proper foreign trade policy. I believe that the future of American agriculture and of industry also depends in large measure upon a revision of the present policy, which permits a continuing drain upon our liquid resources and our national wealth. To accentuate this condition through a program of what amounts to general tariff reduction is not, in my opinion, justifiable on either economic or political grounds.

Unless the issue is squarely faced and rightly settled within the Democratic party, it is one which may well become a major campaign issue in 1936, with results to our administration and the Democratic party which cannot now be foreseen. It can and should be settled, through free and open discussion of the principles involved, in the party councils and in Congress.

Then I presented my resignation as president of the Export-Import Bank—which was the only position I then held. The President in a letter to me suggested that, since he was going away on a long vacation, I withhold my resignation until after his return when we would talk everything over. On July 29th I replied, agreeing to withhold my resignation but making it very plain that remaining in the Administration must not be interpreted to mean that I approved its foreign trade policies or would refrain from public criticism. In that letter I said in part:

In view of your request that I remain at my post for the time being, I shall not now press the matter of my resignation, but will leave it for future events to determine. At the same time I repeat that I think that I have finished the job you asked me to do.

It is true that I am anxious to see certain policies rectified within a brief period. I regard the policies in question as unsound economically and politically. I cannot place myself in a position of endorsing them by remaining silent. Delay in revising them simply means a continuation and aggravation of the conditions created by the three preceding administrations. This is a point which political opponents are not likely to overlook.

It became increasingly evident that the State Department was using the Reciprocal Trade Agreements Act to further the fantasy that it was the high mission of our nation to promote world trade in the interests of world prosperity—regardless of the interests of the United States. Of course world trade is a consequence of world prosperity and not at all its cause.

The State Department went ahead making its agreements without any comprehension of the actual facts of trade or the importance of maintaining an American economy distinct from an international economy. A great deal more than tariffs is involved in the question. The tariff is only one of several means to an end. That I shall later bring out. At a later date, Dr. Henry F. Grady of the State Department and Chairman of the Trade Agreements Committee put into a magazine article what those of us who were following the situation already knew—but which the public did not know. He said:

> Our objective is the general amelioration of the world situation. . . . We have already lowered many rates, which have been generalized to other countries. When we shall have gone the rounds of most of the important countries of the world, reducing in each case the duties on commodities of which it is the principal source, we shall have lowered our tariffs on a great many items where the case for lowering is justified. As a result of extending these reductions to virtually all countries, we will obtain, it would seem, what the proponents of unilateral tariff reduction desire; but we will do it more carefully and scientifically than is possible by legislative action.

Later in a speech at Riverside, California, he said,

> This new policy is of an importance that can hardly be exaggerated. We are to a greater degree than ever before meshing our domestic economy into world economy.

The State Department, being entirely convinced that both Congress and the business interests of the country were quite too stupid to grasp what trade policies ought to be, went ahead. They set up a trade agreement mechanism which, in effect, excluded any conference with the practical interests and put the actual making of the agreements in the hands of college professors and men of only bureau training. If an American business man wanted to find out what was being done about any particular agreement, he had to go to a foreign embassy or send a representative abroad to talk with business interests.

None of the agreements gave any benefits to the United States commensurate with the concessions granted. I shall later discuss the various agreements to show what they actually mean as contrasted with what they are supposed to mean.

The State Department paid no attention at all to the protests of the representatives of the Special Adviser's office. They refused to make any agreements touching the recovering of public or private debts owing to Americans, while all the other nations, and especially Great Britain, in their agreements saw to it that the debts owing to their nationals were looked after. The State Department bound articles on the free list in such fashion as to destroy much of our bargaining power and to prevent the rounding out of a self-reliant United States. Also it limited the taxing prerogative of Congress. They made a duty cut, on the ground that American prices were too high—and again because they thought industrial salaries were unduly large. Whether they were right or wrong does not matter. Congress had not given to the State Department a mandate to pry into industry.

I talked with the President but got nowhere. I was under no obligation to keep silent. I spoke my mind before a luncheon of the War Industries Board Association in New York City on Armistice Day, 1935. I said:

> . . . our discussions have been predicated upon an American point of view and the development of an American policy, as contrasted with the internationalist point of view and the adoption of policies of foreign or international origin. This question is fundamental in times of war and peace alike. As our political parties are now constituted it is not a partisan question. Both of our political parties have wavered indecisively

between the two points of view. Nevertheless this question is basic and must be answered unequivocally if we are to build our national life and policy soundly and surely.

Which do we want: to take advantage of our position of geographical and economic security and contribute to world peace and prosperity by developing our own country and by attending to our own affairs, or to contribute our resources and our markets to a common pool in the management of which ours will be but one voice and not the controlling one. In other words, are we willing to dilute our strength with the world's weakness and thus reduce our standards of living?

An American point of view calls for one policy, the internationalist point of view for quite another. We have straddled long enough. For my own enlightenment I have drawn up a list of eight contrasting points. The "deadly parallel" is a graphic method of comparison. When we Americans choose —let us choose America.

AMERICA'S CHOICE

Which Shall It Be?

A Policy for Internationalists	*A Policy for America*
I	I
Relaxation of immigration laws and regulation of immigration by international agreements.	Rigorous tightening of immigration laws: (*a*) To reduce American unemployment. (*b*) To reduce alien influence in our domestic affairs.
II	II
General reduction of tariffs: (*a*) Laissez faire. (*b*) Unconditional Most-Favored-Nation.	Preservation of the American market, American price levels and American employment: (*a*) Selective imports and exports. (*b*) Tariff reductions only for specific advantages in individual foreign countries (i.e. reciprocity or conditional Most-Favored-Nation).

A Policy for Internationalists	*A Policy for America*
III	III
Stabilization of currencies by general international action (i.e. return to unregulated or foreign controlled gold standard).	Stabilization of American dollar at American price level—thereafter stabilization by agreement with individual countries or blocs where possible. (i.e. a managed currency based on national bookkeeping.)
IV	IV
Free export of capital and resumption of general foreign loans. Multiplication of branch factories and American direct investments abroad.	Control of export of capital: (*a*) To conserve national assets and resources. (*b*) To assist American trade, foreign and domestic. (*c*) To minimize foreign influence or control over American securities market and American enterprise.
V	V
Naval limitation by international agreement to meet the requirements of Great Britain, Japan, France, Italy and Germany.	Navy designed to meet American requirements including defense of the Panama Canal and the Pacific Coast.
VI	VI
Dependence on foreign shipping and communications.	Development of American shipping and communications systems.
VII	VII
Submission of disputes to decision of foreign dominated tribunals such as the World Court.	Settlement of disputes by arbitration confirmed by the Senate.
VIII	VIII
Automatic intervention in European or Asiatic political disputes, as under the Kellogg Treaty and Stimson Doctrine. Collaboration with League in naming "aggressors" anywhere in the world and enforcing sanctions.	In case of wars in Europe or Asia, strict neutrality and avoidance of "moral" judgments on belligerents. Cash and carry policy for direct or indirect trade with belligerents. For the Americas the Monroe Doctrine plus the Good Neighbor Policy.

I had a meeting with the President on November 19th. He asked me about the Canadian agreement which had just been announced. I told him that it was a very good agreement for Canada and some other countries but a very bad one for the United States and that I was preparing a factual memorandum on it. He asked me to send him a copy. Later in the day at a press conference he said that he had asked me to make a study. I left with him a copy of the Eight Points.

A New York newspaper picked up the parallel columns of my Eight Points and printed them in big type. The President saw that editorial and he wrote to me from Warm Springs a page and a half letter which showed both irritation and agitation. He denied that the policies labeled "internationalist" were the policies of his Administration. In that I profoundly differed from him, for to me the trend was unmistakable. I took the opportunity at once to resign.

I saw the President again on December 12th. Our meeting was cordial. He asked what I was going to do. I said:

"I am going out to continue the work that has taken most of my time for thirteen years."

* * * * * *

I know that I have fought for the truth as I have seen it; I have kept the faith as I have known it. In recording the struggle, I am seeking to tell my loyal associates and supporters in the long farm battle what the developments have been and what the portents are if present policies are carried through. In conscience I can do no less.

The American dream of a free, peaceful, and prosperous United States, resting on the foundations of a self-reliant home-owning agriculture, is not yet dead. It is worth working for and fighting for. It still lies within our power to make this dream come true.

Chapter II

The Lost Opportunity

The farm problem in the United States is primarily a tariff problem. It is a problem of the Republican Party—as the party of the protective tariff. It is a problem of the Democratic Party with its slogan of equal opportunity for all and special privilege for none. It was because the Republican Party failed to recognize not only its responsibilities but also its own best interests that many of us who had through so many years worked for farm equality supported Smith and the Democratic ticket in 1928 and Roosevelt in 1932.

Preserving the American industrial market for American-made goods has been the keystone of our industrial prosperity and progress. We have had American prices for American goods. The wage earners and the distributors of industrial goods, with their families, form the best market for American farm products. The American farmer is entitled to the exclusive occupancy of that market at American prices. He has had, at an American price, the American market for dairy and some other products. His home market is now being broken down by the monetary, the restriction of production, and the trade agreement policies of the Roosevelt Administration. Other products, such as wheat and tobacco, although they have been protected by the tariff, are world products, and that part of them which is sold abroad at a world price largely governs the domestic price. The farmer has had, until recently, the American market—but not at an American price. Many crops are not primarily export crops and the domestic market really matters most. Cotton is in a slightly different situation. But, because the world price of these products influences the domestic price, we have had the spectacle, since the war, of industry getting an

American price for its products and agriculture getting an international price. That has prevented a free exchange of goods and services within the United States between the two great groups.

We must have either a complete American price system or a complete international price system. An international price system involves free trade, and free trade might be all right if the whole world were on the same standard of living. But until the Orientals learn to eat wheat and meat or our people learn how to get along with a bit of dried fish and a handful of rice we are not going to have an international standard of living. Lowering the tariff on industrial products might or might not lower the prices of the industrial products which the farmer buys. The tariff does not necessarily increase the relative prices of many articles which can be made in quantity, even if it does restrict foreign competition. But if lowering the tariff did lower industrial prices to the farmer, he would not be helped greatly if at all. For the farmer must sell his products to the great home industrial markets, and, if the purchasing power of these should be wiped out, the farmer's market would also be wiped out. The Mid-Western farmers know that, and that is why they have been high-tariff Republicans and have distrusted low-tariff theories.

There is no real economic antipathy between agriculture and industry in the United States—although for their own purposes agitators are always trying to create an antipathy. The simple fact is that both the Republican and Democratic parties have failed to grasp the full meaning of the high protective tariff as an insurance of a balanced economy, and for that reason the farmers have suffered through the country being out of balance.

The war demands threw agriculture out of balance and the great and absurd loans, both war and private, to foreign nations—loans that were made not out of savings but out of artificially created credit—prevented the unbalance from being evident to everyone until the crash of 1929. I am not saying that the gap in exchange levels between industry and agriculture alone brought on the depression. There were many other causes—undue and illogical credit expansion being one of them. But I do say that, until the American price level applies to both agriculture and industry, this country will not realize its possibilities. It follows as of course that if the gears of the American machine are meshed with the gears of the international machine, the American machine will have to stop and start with the international machine and there can be no American price level. Therefore the question of our foreign trade and financial relations is one that reaches into every farmer's and every worker's home. As Sir Josiah Stamp once said to me: "The United States can go anywhere it likes and there is no limit to its material prosperity, but you cannot expect to have a distinctly American standard of living and at the same time try to be bankers for the world."

At the time, I did not know quite what he meant. But now, having studied our international accounts, I know only too well what he meant. The Republican Party failed to recognize, after the war and after the war loans had died down, that our country was no longer the food shop for the world and that something additional had to be done in order to make the American protective system apply to the farmers. If only that had been realized in time, we certainly should not have had so devastating a depression and we might have been spared the A.A.A, the N.R.A. and the Reciprocal Trade Agreements Act.

All these matters I shall later develop. I am here merely trying to sketch in the background, in order to give a quick comprehension of why the farmers shifted into the Democratic Party in 1932.

I shall not attempt to name all the good men with whom I

fought the farmers' battle from 1922 on. Our fight extended over a broad front. Here it is enough to say that we centered on the McNary-Haugen Bill and saw that bill twice passed by non-partisan votes in Congress, only to be twice vetoed by a Republican President. The principle of the McNary-Haugen bills—and there were several such bills—was an American price for the American market and a world price for the surplus sold in the international market. We made our last stand for a McNary-Haugen plank at the Kansas City Republican Convention in 1928. We lost our plank in the resolutions committee. Earl Smith, Illinois member of the Resolutions Committee, took it to the floor of the convention. In a great speech, Frank Murphy of Minnesota summed up our case. He said, in part:

The only controversy that resulted in a split in the Resolutions Committee, ladies and gentlemen, was the one relating to agriculture. And that is a tremendously serious one. These millions of organized farmers in these great agricultural States who made this fight do not believe in Santa Claus, and you act as though they did. They will take nobody's promise again unless it is definite and specific. And I want you to think, my friends, that the McNary-Haugen bill, five years or more before the bar of public opinion, before Congress, has never been challenged legislatively by any man in or out of Congress by a plan that would solve the problem of the surplus and make the tariff on farm commodities effective.

We do not want to borrow any of the Government's money. And we will not take and have not asked for a subsidy. We ask the right as conservative men and women of America's farms to pay our own way. And, ladies and gentlemen of the Convention, we reserve the right to do our own thinking, and you cannot and will not think for us. And I want to say with all respect to the men of the Committee who drafted the majority report, which was drafted by leaders in other groups, that agriculture proposes to write and urge its own bill. Agriculture understands its own problem. And what agriculture wants is a better price. Agriculture wants and will stay in the fight until it gets the benefit of existing tariff schedules.

We did not get our plank and so some of us left for Houston, where the Democratic Convention did give us what we wanted. That is why I left the Republican Party and supported Alfred E. Smith in 1928. That campaign is another story. I am not sure that Governor Smith ever fully understood the Middle Western farm problem, but at least he was willing to learn. Few people did understand it except the farmers.

The McNary-Haugen bill would be a sound measure today except in detail. It remains sound in principle—the establishing of a two-price system. Under our tariff and the condition of world markets and currencies, it is absolutely necessary to have an American farm price, as well as an American industrial price.

The question is not one primarily of surplus. We in the farm movement have talked so much about surplus that perhaps we have disturbed right thinking to such an extent that any sort of surplus is looked on as a curse. I am afraid that our desire to get rid of certain surplus production which temporarily hurts prices has been so great that we have been led into a position where we have seemed to advocate the abhorrent and un-American doctrine of scarcity. When I was a boy, that farmer was regarded as a rich and provident man who carried over a crib full of corn or a bin full of wheat. We gauged a man by the size and condition of his herd. That man had real wealth, he had something for a rainy day—he was insured against a bad crop. "As good as wheat in the bin" was our measure of real worth. Those principles must always hold good, and there never can be a solution of the farm problem—or any other social problem, for that matter—if plenty is held to be a curse. There has been too much talk of surplus. And

I can say that all the more positively because I have probably contributed to the talk.

There is no surplus over the years, and any system which assumes a continuing surplus and attempts production control as a regular measure is bound to fail. Controlling acreage as a method of controlling production involves a fundamental fallacy. This was conclusively pointed out by the Secretary of Agriculture in his 1927 report. He said:

> Variations in production from year to year are due to changes in acreage and to variations in yield. Since the latter come mainly from seasonal conditions, they are largely beyond the farmers' control. From 1905 to 1925 variations in yield per acre accounted for 60 per cent of the fluctuations in cotton production, with the remaining 40 per cent due to variations in acreage. Variations in production due to yield per acre of certain other crops were: corn 85 per cent; oats 63 per cent; and tame hay 47 per cent. It is obvious from these figures that fluctuations in production, with resulting variations in prices, are a hazard of farming, which is to a large degree unavoidable.

After the 1928 campaign was over and Herbert Hoover elected, I felt that I had done everything that I could do and that it was high time to give attention to my own affairs. But before I left politics, Chester C. Davis—who had been closely associated with me in the farm fight since 1925—and I drew up and circulated a memorandum on farm relief which set out the positions of the respective parties and the measures which had the support of the bulk of Mid-Western farmers. The document is interesting, not only because Mr. Davis followed me as Administrator of the A.A.A., but also as showing that the A.A.A., as it was worked out, ran directly counter to all the principal tenets of the farm organization platforms. The A.A.A. departed from the two-price system we had advocated and took up the limitation of production which had been a Republican policy. The paper is a long one. Here are a few extracts:

The burden of the post-War reversal in trade balances is certain to continue to fall with disproportionate weight on agriculture unless effective action is taken to permit farm export trade to be continued by enabling farmers to dispose of exportable surpluses abroad independently of the domestic price secured for that portion consumed at home. It will continue to react unfavorably on business and labor.

The Democratic platform said:

"We condemn the policy of the Republican Party which promises relief to agriculture only through a reduction of American farm production to the needs of the domestic market. Such a program means the continued deflation of agriculture, the forcing of additional millions from the farms and the perpetuation of agricultural distress for years to come, with continued bad effects on business and labor throughout the United States."

Surpluses in farm products cannot be disposed of by wishing them away or by turning the producers immediately to other lines:

(*a*) Agriculture is the only productive industry in which volume of production cannot be adequately determined in advance by adjustment of the physical plant or by the intentions of the producer. The Democratic platform says:

"The Democratic Party recognizes that the problems of production differ as between agriculture and industry. Industrial production is largely under human control, while agricultural production, because of lack of co-ordination among the 6,500,000 individual farm units, and because of the influence of weather, pests and other causes, largely is beyond human control. The result is that a large crop frequently is produced on a small acreage and a small crop on a large acreage, and measured in money value it frequently happens that a large crop brings less than a small crop."

(*b*) Agricultural surpluses constitute valuable national insurance. A serious shortage could hardly be avoided in some years if a successful attempt were made to cut the acreage of important crops down to the point which would, with average yields, barely supply the domestic need. The Senate and House Committees on Agriculture said in their reports to Congress last spring:

"There is a distinct difference between making wise crop adjustments, and deliberately adopting a national program which aims to do away with all national surpluses of important food products and raw materials.

"It would be difficult in practice, if not impossible, to cut down the farm acreage of the United States to the point where there would be no prospect of surplus production in a favorable season. From the consumer's viewpoint nothing could be more dangerous than to urge general curtailment of the supply of essential food and raw materials. Repeatedly representatives of the American Federation of Labor have indorsed legislation for agriculture such as is embodied in this bill, and have pointed out the serious danger to consumers of any policy to do away with crop surpluses. From the national viewpoint, the grave danger in such a policy is best pictured when one asks the question: 'What would have happened to the United States and to the allied nations in the late war if the agriculture of the Nation previously had been reduced to a domestic basis?' It was the fact that they were then on an export basis that enabled the farmers of the United States to supply quickly to the Allies food that was necessary in carrying on the war."

As an economic policy, it is impossible, by influencing the extent of planting or breeding, to determine in advance the volume of farm production. As a national policy, it is unwise to attempt to reduce toward the danger point the volume of the production of essential foods and raw materials. The problem, therefore, is control of supply rather than control of production.

We have built up in this country a vast protective system for the benefit of many of our major groups of industry, transportation, finance, and labor, which places agriculture at a disadvantage on its major cash crops of which we produce a surplus.

(*a*) The Democratic party made it perfectly clear in the recent campaign that it accepts the principle of a fair protective system, and thus to a degree eliminated the tariff as a point of partisan difference. It insisted upon equality of treatment between agriculture and industry.

The 1928 platform said:

"The Democratic Party has always stood against special privilege and for common equality under the law. It is a fundamental principle of the party that such tariffs as are levied, must not discriminate against any industry, class or section. Therefore we pledge that in its tariff policy the Democratic Party will insist upon equality of treatment between agriculture and other industries."

Governor Smith at Louisville, Kentucky, October 13th, said:

"I condemn the Republican party for leaving the farmer outside our protective walls. On import crops, he must be given equal protection with that afforded industry. On his other products, means must be adopted to give him as well as industry the benefit of tariff protection."

The Democratic party insists that if the protective system is maintained it must be extended to include agriculture, and proposed in its 1928 platform that provision be made through legislation for the producers of the major cash crops, "in order that the price of the surplus may not determine the price of the whole crop."

As a means to that end the Democratic party proposed to establish by legislation a device by which the surplus could be lifted and thus prevented from determining the price of the whole crop, the operating cost of such a device to be borne by the commodity benefited.

* * * * * *

Permanent and effective control, which would make the tariff operative for agriculture, can only be secured through legislation which embodies the principles recognized in the agricultural plank of the Democratic platform. No plan, whether it operates through stabilization corporations, export debentures, or otherwise, can be permanently successful if it departs from these principles.

* * * * * *

The one economically sound and permanent principle of dealing with surpluses in an effective manner is that which would require the commodity benefited to raise the necessary funds. Alternative proposals are either wholly ineffective or would involve such a degree of government subsidy and government in business that the public would not long permit it to continue.

During the Hoover Administration, little attempt was made to press the McNary-Haugen legislation, although its principles remained alive. The Farm Board did not seem to me to be a sound measure. I happened to spend Sunday with the late Alexander Legge, just before he went to California on a vacation whence he was called to act as Chairman of the Board. I told him that the Board would fail because the act contained no provision for selling off the surplus abroad at less than the domestic price without drawing upon capital. Mr. Legge lived to see this truth demonstrated.

When the Government backs a stabilization corporation, it must either be prepared to sell some of its stocks at a loss, while sustaining the domestic price, or it must be prepared to hold a long time until prices rise. In the first case, the loss falls on the taxpayers at once. In the second case, the holding may extend over so long a period that interest and storage expenses take the cost to a figure where only an abnormal price will clear the sheets. The Canadian Wheat Pool demonstrated that, before the Farm Board started to give another demonstration. The "Ever Normal Granary" plan of Secretary Wallace without a two-price system only repeats the Farm Board principles. The extent to which disaster will overtake it will depend entirely on the extent to which markets are kept open.

The farm price question gets around to extending the tariff protection to the farm products or not extending it. The two-price system is the only one that fits into the tariff policy. And the tariff policy is so fundamental that it ought not to be changed.

When a market is rising, the collective marketing or stabilizing organization takes the credit. In a falling market, such a corporation can dam the current for a while, but if it holds on long enough it will involve the finances of the whole country. That is the record of the Canadian Wheat Pool. The Farm Board was as well staffed and as well managed as any institution could be, but its fundamental theory was wrong and it could not meet the situation.

By 1932, the impotency of the Farm Board method became apparent. Early in April, General Hugh S. Johnson wrote to me saying, among other things:

"This is the time to put over our farm relief. I know whereof I speak. Why don't you get busy?"

I had known General Johnson since war days and we had been associated in business for a time. We had both worked on farm relief. General Johnson has a good brain and is an indefatigable worker. At the time of writing to me, he was engaged with Bernard M. Baruch investigating various problems, private and public. I replied from my Chicago office:

I will answer your question first. During the period of my public activity on the farm question from 1924 to 1928 inclusive I was in a position of recognized standing. First, as president of the American Council of Agriculture, second, as chairman of the executive committee of '22 and third as chairman of the Smith Independent Organizations Committee. In each capacity my position was such as to justify me in insisting on being heard. Since the election of 1928 I have been a private citizen and have not made a single public statement except the one before the War Industries Board Association last Armistice Day. At this time I represent no organization.

I do not desire to inject myself into the limelight although I will be very glad to lend my fullest cooperation to a responsible movement which has for its purpose a correction of the agricultural situation which I feel is responsible to a very great extent for our present economic plight. . . .

I do not know what you may have in mind in the way of this procedure but I believe you will agree that the condition and the trend of affairs will brook no delay. My thought is that the time has arrived for the Democratic Party and all others interested in the welfare of America to act. I wonder if it would not be good procedure for Senator Robinson, the recognized leader of his party in the Senate, to make a speech drawing heavily on the substance of Governor Roosevelt's radio address last night and of Mr. McAdoo's address and offer a resolution requesting the agricultural committee of the Senate immediately to conduct hearings, to summon a limited number of the leaders of agricultural thought and then to prepare the necessary legislation addressing the cause. I believe that the heads of the three big farm organizations already have gone on record in a joint statement to the committee for the equalization fee, debenture or some other adequate method. These heads are O'Neal, president of the Farm Bureau, Taber, president of the Grange, and Simpson, president of the Farmers' Union, and they should not be overlooked in any new call. . . .

A new crop of wheat will start to market in about sixty days and if present prices or anything like them prevail, and similar prices for other farm crops, I hesitate to predict the effect. Among other things I foresee is repudiation of indebtedness simply on account of inability to pay to such an extent as to threaten our entire structure of government. In such a case the rich will not be immune.

General Johnson brought up some additional points in his answer and on April 13th in reply I wrote:

I have your note of the 11th inst. What you say about the word in Washington that the farmers "no longer want relief of this kind" is pure bunk. You know I heard that same statement over and over again for a good many years while I was active in the farm fight in Washington, and such a remark belongs in the class of "farmers can not agree among themselves, etc."

You will recall that I told you in my recent letter that the Presidents of three major national farm organizations recently appeared before the Agricultural Committees in Congress and presented a joint statement demanding the equalization fee, debenture, or some other method of accomplishing the purpose. I do not know what better evidence they want in Washington. Even if there is no such howl about this legislation as there was a few years ago the business and financial interests would do well to promote the idea themselves. I mean the idea of "an American price for American consumption, independent of the world price for the surplus." I do not care about the method. . . .

The situation, as I see it, is that unless something is done immediately, before many months have passed the present tendency toward repudiation of debt, payment of taxes, etc., will grow to such an extent that the whole house of cards will be down on our heads. . . .

It will be remembered that the Democratic Party held the legislative power in 1932. The House was Democratic, and in the Senate the Progressives held the balance of power. The late Henry T. Rainey was the Democratic leader in the House of the 72nd Congress and he felt that the Democrats, being practically in power, had the responsibility of doing something for agriculture and that it was not patriotic to let the farmers suffer just to promote agitation for the Presidential campaign. He put his country above his party.

Mr. Rainey got hold of Earl Smith in Washington and wanted to know if a bill could not be drawn of an emergency nature which would lift the farmers out of the hole on that year's crop (1932). Earl replied that of course something could be done and that he would consult with me. He wired me and we met in Chicago. He told me what Mr. Rainey was after and asked whether I thought it was possible to draft anything which could be made effective for the current year's crop. I answered:

"Yes, but we will have to wipe out of our minds all we have tried to do in previous legislation and make a fresh start."

We called Fred Lee from Washington to Chicago, and, after a good deal of discussion, drafted what was afterwards known as the Rainey Bill. Then we got in Chester Davis, Alexander Legge, Clifford Gregory and a few others whose judgment we respected. They all approved the draft.

Taking the bill to Washington, we presented it to Mr. Rainey. He at once introduced it into the House, and Senator Norbeck introduced it into the Senate. The Senate passed it by a non-partisan vote. The bill went to the House as S. 4940 and there it was quietly shelved by Speaker (now Vice-President) Garner.

The provisions of that bill are important. It contained, for the first time in any farm bill, a processing tax levied as an excise tax in what we believed then and I believe now was Constitutional fashion. No regimentation or bureaucratic control was involved. The bill empowered the Secretary of Agriculture to determine what percentage of the estimated production of cotton, wheat and hogs of the current year would be domestically consumed. He was to base his estimate on the average of the Department of Agriculture statistics for five years past. Each producer, on marketing his cotton, wheat, or hogs, would be entitled to receive a negotiable adjustment certificate redeemable after thirty days by the Treasury. These certificates would cover such portion of the lot so marketed as it was estimated would be domestically consumed and at the rate of five cents a pound for cotton, forty-two cents a bushel for wheat and two cents a pound for hogs. It was contemplated in the administration of the bill that the local buyer would issue a purchase ticket which would be given to the farmer; the farmer in turn would take this ticket to the duly authorized government representative in the locality who would issue a negotiable adjustment certificate; further, it was contemplated that a list of these certificates would be published in the local papers at regular intervals in much the same manner as tax assessments are published. The money to pay these certificates was to be raised by an excise tax on processors in the same amount. In Mr. Lee's brief is the following clear and direct explanation:

To illustrate the working of the Bill, take wheat, as an example, and assume that the Secretary of Agriculture has determined that three-fourths of the production will be domestically consumed. Then, for every 100 bushels of wheat marketed by the farmer during the life of the Bill, he will be entitled to a certificate covering 75 bushels at the rate of 42 cents a bushel. These same 75 bushels, when subsequently processed, will be subject to a processing charge at the rate of 42 cents a bushel which will go into a special fund for redeeming the certificate. Thus each commodity finances itself without any permanent drain on the Treasury, and the farmer receives a direct benefit, equivalent to an adequate tariff protection, on so much of his production as does not constitute exportable surplus.

The present price at which the farmer sells his commodity —in most cases the world price—is in no wise interfered with. The price at which the farmer sells or at which the buyer buys is not fixed, nor are the present customary channels of marketing in any wise altered. Production is not stimulated, for this year's acreage is already established. Without attempting to provide additional means, such as equalization fees, debentures, or stabilization operations, or disposing of or controlling surpluses, the farmer is directly given benefits on that portion of his marketed crop that is entitled to domestic protection, to the same extent as if such surpluses were adequately and effectively disposed of and controlled.

It will be noted:

(1) That this bill, with the processing tax, would have given the relief to the 1932 production. It was direct in its application.

(2) That it set up no bureaucracy.

(3) That it contained no political pap for anyone and was designed solely to help the farmer.

That bill was passed by a non-partisan United States Senate. It was allowed to die in a Democratic House dominated by the present Vice-President. The responsibility is clear and unequivocal.

Those who defeated that bill must therefore accept a part of the responsibility for the final collapse.

Chapter III

The Pledges of 1932

Being entirely out of politics, I kept busy with my own affairs. The time that I spent in Washington and the help I gave on the Rainey Bill were in no sense partisan. The British have taken the farm out of partisan politics, and we are not going to effect any permanent American solution until we do likewise. I felt that the Republican Party was committed to a course of action that involved the restriction of production and marketing through a stabilization corporation. The restriction of production by governmental edict is more than wrong. All wealth must come from productive effort.

The farm situation could not, I was convinced, await the outcome of the national election and the convening of a new Congress. This caused me, on April 30th, 1932, to write to Governor Roosevelt at Albany. I had known him slightly in the 1928 campaign. I felt that he had a grasp of the farm crisis. In my letter I said in part:

I should like to have you consider immediately making some such statement on agriculture as is suggested in the following:

The Democratic party in 1924 and again in 1928 promised the farmer an extension of the protective system to include him. This would require a mechanism to make the tariff effective on surplus crops which is necessary to insure him an American price for that portion of his crops consumed in America independent of the world price for his surplus sold abroad.

I believe in this principle, and pledge myself if elected President of the United States immediately to urge Congress to create a mechanism to put this principle into effect, the cost of which should be borne by the commodity benefited and not by the national treasury, and as President I would sign proper legislation. This is exactly the principle that the Republican party in convention in Kansas City in 1928 refused to accept and the last three Republican presidents have refused to accept.

The Republican party has demonstrated its incapacity and unwillingness to solve the agricultural problem and that its promises are but empty words. Its proposed remedy to restrict production to the demands of domestic markets, which was originally promulgated by the present incumbent of the White House, has proved ineffective as have the efforts of the Farm Board to enhance the prices by withholding and storing surpluses.

The failure of the Republican party to deal adequately with the post war collapse of agriculture has resulted in widespread bankruptcy beginning with the farm states and now extending generally through commerce, transportation, and banking.

There can be no recovery from this depression until the half of our population, living upon or directly dependent upon the farm, continuously receives a price for their products and services comparable with the return in the industrial field.

To this, Governor Roosevelt replied from Warm Springs, under date of May 19th:

I like many of your definite suggestions and without doubt I shall incorporate some of them when I speak. I am keeping out of the existing differences between various members of the Democratic party for the very good reason that they are only giving comfort to the Republicans and our principal objective should be victory in November.

I can assure you that I have given more study to this problem of agriculture than to any other in the whole country and I should like much to have a talk with you if you come East at any time. I expect to get back to Albany May 30th.

We had some further correspondence and I made available to Governor Roosevelt and Henry Morgenthau, Jr. some of the studies which I had previously prepared.

The platform as adopted by the 1932 Democratic convention was not as clear and specific on agriculture as was the 1928 platform. General Johnson, who had a good deal to do with the 1932 agricultural plans, agreed with me that it was unwise to bring up the McNary-Haugen Bill as such. The farm leaders were interested in a principle—not a method. The platform was, however, clear on

(*a*) obtaining for the farmer an American price for American consumption

(*b*) being opposed to restriction of production as a policy; and

(*c*) making reciprocal trade agreements which would actually be reciprocal.

The parts of the platform which most interested me were as follows:

We believe that a party platform is a covenant with the people to be faithfully kept by the party when entrusted with power, and that the people are entitled to know in plain words the terms of the contract to which they are asked to subscribe. We hereby declare this to be the platform of the Democratic Party:

The Democratic Party solemnly promises by appropriate action to put into effect the principles, policies, and reforms herein advocated, and to eradicate the policies, methods, and practices herein condemned. We advocate an immediate and drastic reduction of governmental expenditures by abolishing useless commissions and offices, consolidating departments and bureaus, and eliminating extravagance, to accomplish a saving of not less than twenty-five per cent in the cost of federal government, and we call upon the Democratic Party in the States to make a zealous effort to achieve a proportionate result.

We favor maintenance of the national credit by a federal budget annually balanced on the basis of accurate executive estimates within revenues, raised by a system of taxation levied on the principle of ability to pay.

We advocate a competitive tariff for revenue, with a fact-finding tariff commission free from executive interference, reciprocal tariff agreements with other nations, and an international economic conference designed to restore international trade and facilitate exchange. . . .

Extension and development of Farm Cooperative movement and effective control of crop surpluses so that our farmers may have the full benefit of the domestic market.

The enactment of every constitutional measure that will aid the farmers to receive for their basic farm commodities prices in excess of cost. . . .

We oppose cancellation of the debts owing to the United States by foreign nations. . . .

We condemn the extravagance of the Farm Board, its disastrous action which made the Government a speculator of farm products and the unsound policy of restricting agricultural products to the demands of domestic markets. . . .

Equal rights to all; special privileges to none.

Mr. Roosevelt as a candidate declared: "I am for this platform 100 per cent."

The strange decease of the Rainey Bill in the House, although presumably it had the support of leading Democratic members, had been disheartening—it meant putting off farm relief until the Short Session in the fall, by which time the crisis, in my judgment, would have so developed that probably no effective relief could be given in time to prevent a general collapse. Only those of us who lived out in the Mid-West among the farmers could know how desperate was their condition. I put down the failure of the Rainey Bill to some under-cover disagreements within the party and not at all to the candidate, for Governor Roosevelt seemed both anxious and willing to elaborate the platform into a very definite commitment along the lines I had been advocating. In his Topeka speech, he followed exactly our farm program. Here are some extracts from that speech:

I seek to give to that portion of the crop consumed in the United States a benefit equivalent to a tariff to give you farmers an adequate price.

I want now to state what seem to me the specifications upon which most of the reasonable leaders of agriculture have agreed, and to express here and now my wholehearted accord with these specifications.

First: The plan must provide . . . . a tariff benefit over the world prices which is equivalent to the benefit given by the tariff to industrial products. . . .

Second: The plan must finance itself. . . .

Third: It must not make use of any mechanism that would cause our European customers to retaliate on the ground of dumping. . . .

Fourth: It must make use of existing agencies and so far as possible be decentralized in its administration, so the chief responsibility for its operation will rest with locality rather than with newly created bureaucratic machinery in Washington.

Fifth: It must operate as nearly as possible on a cooperative basis. . . . It should moreover be constituted so that it can be withdrawn whenever the emergency has passed. . . .

I took an active part in Governor Roosevelt's campaign. I followed his speeches closely, picked up what appeared to be weaknesses from time to time and sent them on to General Johnson, who was at Democratic headquarters, and he saw to it that the points were covered in later speeches. I had some contact with Henry Wallace, who was then editor of "Wallaces' Farmer" at Des Moines and whose father I had known very well, both before and during the time that he was Secretary of Agriculture. The present Secretary of Agriculture had never been an active member of our farm group and had not gone through the days of battle. He had rather tended to specialize in the study of corn and was a dreamy, honest-minded and rather likable sort of fellow. He had a mystical, religious side to him, and, never having been in the real rough-and-tumble of life—for he simply went on the family paper as of course —he was apt to view clashes of economic forces as struggles between bad men and good men and not as between groups, all of whom believed that right was with them. Since Henry was always with the good men, he never quite got the whole of any picture. He believed in low tariffs, for instance, as a moral issue. Under date of August 29th, 1932 he wrote me this letter:

Dear George:

I wonder if you could loan me a copy of those 1925 hearings to which you refer in your letter of August 16. Murphy of Dubuque who is candidate for senator will be in Des Moines soon and I want to call his attention to this matter.

I had a luncheon conference with Governor Roosevelt about two weeks ago and among other things he inquired about you. He said that some folks in the Democratic party felt that you were overly optimistic as to what could be done with the farm vote in 1928. Morgenthau who happened to be the only other man present, as well as myself, came to your rescue and pointed out that many of us were deceived as to the significance of the religious issue. I told him that I knew you were because I had argued the matter with you in the summer of 1928.

Governor Roosevelt is a fine gentleman. If he becomes president, a lot depends on just who he looks to for advice. Professor Rex Tugwell of Columbia University seems to have the inside track at the present time with the Governor on economic matters. Tugwell is quite sold on the Domestic Allotment Plan but he is against the "honest dollar." Roosevelt at heart is, I believe, an inflationist but I doubt if he says much about the money affair one way or the other in this campaign.

I do not know precisely what Wallace meant when he said that Governor Roosevelt was at heart "an inflationist." Out in the farm country we were short of money and we could not transact business in the ordinary way. Business concerns—in default of money exchange—accepted corn and cotton in payment of debts and for new goods. It was the burden of debt that chiefly concerned us. I then thought with many others that it was possible to have a controlled inflation which could go under the name of "reflation." But I never took a great deal of stock in money tinkering as a long-range help for the farmer. The interesting point in the Wallace letter was the apparent divergence on monetary affairs between the views of the candidate and the principles laid down in the platform. Senator Glass had been insistent that the party stand for sound money.

I became the member for Illinois of the "National Progressive League for Roosevelt and Garner." Wallace became the member for Iowa, Frank Murphy for Minnesota, and Ralph Snyder, the president of the Kansas Farm Bureau Federation, for Kansas. Harold L. Ickes was the chairman of the league. In addition to directing the farm campaign in Illinois for the Democratic state organization, my contribution was to suggest the preparation of a pamphlet for general distribution among the farmers. This pamphlet I wrote with Henry Wallace and Ralph Snyder, and the first lot was run off on Wallace's press at Des Moines. It was devoted largely to the tariff and the obtaining of an American price for American consumption, and it consisted principally of printing extracts from Governor Roosevelt's Topeka speech in parallel columns with extracts from President Hoover's speech at Des Moines. The pamphlet contained also these two paragraphs as outlining the fundamental difference between the Hoover and the Roosevelt programs:

The fundamental difference between the Democratic party and the Republican party is that the Democratic party proposes to establish an effective control of the sale of exportable surpluses in order that the surplus alone shall flow at world prices and that the farmer shall receive the benefit of the tariff on the large proportion of his production consumed in the domestic market.

The Republican party and Mr. Hoover stand squarely opposed to this principle by which the farmer could get the benefit of the tariff on the proportion of these surplus crops consumed in America. Mr. Hoover for years has advocated starving out acreage, or, in other words, "restricting production to the demand of the domestic market," which is difficult in practice due to the effect of weather and pests upon crop production, and un-American in principle if at the same time we encourage expansion of our industrial exports as has been the case during his administrations as Secretary of Commerce and President of the United States. We would be drying up farm acreage in the United States while foreign exporting countries would be increasing theirs to fill the vacuum made by our withdrawal.

It will be noted that, as the Agricultural Adjustment Act was administered, it exactly reversed these positions, and that Mr. Wallace, when he came into power as Secretary of Agriculture, forwarded the very principle of acreage limitation which he and I in the campaign had emphasized as the chief reason why President Hoover should not be reelected.

The farmers became afraid that Governor Roosevelt, if elected, might lower the tariff. I relayed this to General Johnson, and Governor Roosevelt at Baltimore on October 25th and again at Boston near election time restated his faith in the tariff. The tariff fear was so great in the Mid-West that on November 5th I went on the air, largely to give tariff reassurance, and I repeated this paragraph from Roosevelt's Baltimore speech:

"Of course, it is absurd to talk of lowering tariff duties on farm products. . . . I promised to endeavor to restore the purchasing power of the farm dollar by making the tariff effective for agriculture and raising the prices of farm products. I do not intend that such duties shall be lowered. To do so would be inconsistent with my entire farm program, and every farmer knows it and will not be deceived."

And this extract from his Boston speech:

"I favor—and do not let the false statements of my opponents deceive you—continued protection for American agriculture. I favor more than that. I advocate measures to give the farmer an added benefit, called a tariff benefit, to make the tariff effective on his products."

Under the Reciprocal Trade Agreements Act, a policy exactly the opposite of what was then pledged is being followed in actual administration.

I am emphasizing these points because during my years in farm politics the farmers came to know that, whatever else they might think of me, I would keep my word. I do not know how many of them voted for Franklin D. Roosevelt on the promises I made in that campaign, but I want them to know that the promises I made were based on solemn representations.

After Thanksgiving I went to South Carolina, and on my way home I stopped in Washington. I went in to see Senator Pat Harrison. He greeted me:

"I suppose you came in to make me like the protective tariff."

"No," I replied, "just to show you how in this legislation you can get away from any mention of tariff."

I then explained the parity provisions.

He said, "First see Marvin Jones."

Mr. Jones of Texas was chairman of the House Agricultural Committee and an old and valued friend. We had worked on farm bills for years. He saw a big cotton crop coming along and he wanted to do something about cotton at once. We discussed emergency legislation and he asked me to be around when Congress met, in order to help frame a bill.

Arriving in Chicago, I found that Earl Smith had a letter from Congressman Rainey calling a meeting of farm leaders in Washington on December 12th and asking him to bring me. M. L. Wilson of Montana—the principal proponent of the Domestic Allotment Plan—dropped into Smith's office while I was there. He said that he was on his way by plane to Washington to attend a meeting called by Wallace and Tugwell who had just, so he told us, come from Warm Springs. A number of us who had been active in the farm movement had not been asked by Wallace, but that did not seem significant to us at the time. We did not know that the principles for which we had fought were soon going to be quietly shelved.

The months between election and inauguration were crowded. We in the farm group were given to understand that President-elect Roosevelt wanted a farm bill at the Short Session. It is impossible to say how we were given this understanding, but we all had it. And it was the logical course to be followed by anyone who really cared to help the farmer, for a bill passed in the closing months of 1932 or the early months of 1933 would have been well under way to catch the 1933 crops in ample time, while a bill delayed until after the meeting of a special session ran the chance of coming too late.

Professor Tugwell appeared to be the representative of the President-elect; I cannot say that he represented himself as speaking for Governor Roosevelt. I can say that he did nothing to destroy the impression that he was.

My diary is very full on this period. It is too long for complete presentation and also it contains many matters not of general interest. Therefore I shall shorten the story and give parts of the diary only when they seem pertinent.

On December 6th and 7th, I attended a meeting of the American Farm Bureau Federation in Chicago and we talked over various courses of action. We had no specific measures to advocate, for the whole program on which for years we had been working had been accepted by the President-elect and could not fail in a Congress which he already controlled. We had complete confidence that he would keep his word. Henry Wallace and M. L. Wilson arrived from Washington and told us that they had been working on a bill with Mordecai Ezekiel,

Chairman Marvin Jones, Henry Morgenthau, Jr. and some others. We called the group the "economists" as distinguished from the "farm" people. I arrived in Washington on December 9th. Fred Lee had been asked to make into a bill the suggestions of the "economists" and he brought a copy of his draft to me. It was not a bill setting up a two-price system to extend the benefits of the tariff to agriculture, but was essentially a bill to limit production by renting acreage and to tax processors for the necessary revenue. The bill was nearer to the Agricultural Adjustment Act which the next Congress passed than it was to the Rainey Bill or any of the previous methods the farm leaders had agreed upon. The attitude of leading Democrats and farm men towards the bill at that time is more important than the bill itself—for the bill contained the first suggestions of the big shift in the farm methods that was to come. Referring to my diary:

Monday (December 12, 1932—Washington). Farm leaders arrived, about forty of them, and Morgenthau, Tugwell, and others here, including Myers and Ezekiel, and M. L. Wilson. For two days and nights they were in continuous conference and I stayed in my hotel in communication with them. . . .

(December 15, 1932.) Smith, Wilson, and Lee came in at my call. After they explained developments I told them that I thought they should draft a farm bill irrespective of processors and then be in a position to sit down and discuss procedure with processors, if it could be shown that a proper bill from the farm angle was not entirely practical. I pointed out the great difference between foreign and American prices on wheat, hogs, lard, etc. . . . I suggested consideration of my "modified Rainey Bill" with the amendments I proposed. The meeting was rather stormy. . . .

(December 16, 1932). . . . I called Marvin Jones and told him there were some big holes in the draft of the bill now in preparation, and that there was some danger ahead unless care was exercised, but that it could be fixed up. He said he recognized that, and that it was his purpose to conclude the hearings and then perfect the bill with the assistance of "you and a few others." . . . Later went to see Smith [he was ill at his hotel] and had quite a serious conversation with him. He said he thought Tugwell represented Governor Roosevelt. Later he called me and asked me to sit in his place with the members of his committee. This I did, only to become more firmly convinced than ever that farm leaders were being led off by economists. The only contribution I made at this meeting was to take violent exception to Ezekiel's trying to clutter up the bill with reservations. . . . I demanded consideration of a bill in the interests of the farmers, on the ground that processors could take care of themselves better than farmers. . . .

(December 17, 1932). . . . Lunched with Smith, O'Neal, Gregory, and Lee and went with them to Congressman Jones' office. Jones told them their tentative draft was too complicated and must be simplified. Clearly indicated something along line of modified Rainey bill, with some provision for acreage payment on idle land was what he had in mind. . . .

Earl Smith made splendid statement. Earl and I then called on Congressman Rainey, and Earl outlined situation to him. . . .

By December 19th I was back in Chicago and in the midst of long distance calls and conferences. James F. Bell, of Minneapolis, was keenly anxious to have a small conference between representatives of the farmers and the processors, in order to decide upon some course of action away from the Washington economists. Here are some diary extracts which show the scene:

(Wednesday, December 21, 1932). Attended meeting, upon invitation, at Washburn Crosby office, Chicago, at which were present Messrs. Moscrip, Minneapolis, representing dairy interests; Bell, Anderson, and Wells, representing milling and grain; Wilson and Cooney, packers; Earl Smith and myself.

The following points were stressed as requiring immediate attention: debt, taxation, low commodity prices, foreclosures, and banking system. Word was received from H. S. J. [General Hugh S. Johnson] that representative of textile industry would be present Thursday and that tobacco representative could not be secured in time for this meeting. No difference of opinion developed about urgent necessity for action; decided differences developed regarding practicability of measure being considered by House Agricultural Committee. At seven o'clock meeting recessed until 10:30 Thursday A. M. Mr. Bell presided at the meeting.

(Thursday, December 22, 1932). Prior to opening of meeting at 10:30 I had half an hour with Bell and Anderson and pointed out to them Farm Journal article with stream line across front cover "British Growers Received $1.30 for Wheat"; item from Chicago Tribune today reporting from Hagerstown, Md., a sheriff sale upon property of Frank B. Statler, Green Castle, at which horses brought 5 cents each, cows and calves from 10 cents to 75 cents, and automobiles 60 cents each; also item reporting resignation of Wiggin as President of Chase National Bank, New York, with statement that John D. R., Jr. was the largest stockholder in the bank, and pointed out that it was well known that the R. interests controlled the National City Bank, thus leaving control of two of the largest banks in the country in R. hands. I asked them what they thought the reaction of the country would be to such news. I told them that it seemed to me that they must be convinced that the interest of the processors was with the producer rather than with those groups made up of bankers, speculators, and commission men; that it had seemed to me that they had affiliated with these groups and combined against the farmers' interests and that their reasoning in so doing was beyond my comprehension. I left nothing unsaid and they swallowed it without undertaking to refute a single statement I made.

The meeting convened at 10:30, and all present yesterday were there with the exception of Moscrip and Smith, who came in later. In addition we had today Mr. Sweet and Mr. Stevens, cotton textile manufacturers. No tobacco man was present. The cotton men said that a 5-cent tax on cotton in a pair of overalls selling at 69 cents retail meant an increase in the cost of raw material entering into production of 12 cents; but that the retailer might mark up that price of 69 cents to anywhere from 85 cents to $1.00. I called attention to the fact that it might be desirable for legislation to provide that the tax should be treated as an income charge rather than as an addition to the cost of material, to be pyramided. . . . Earl Smith made a splendid statement and was much less irreconcilable than I had been in connection with the necessity of getting all of the benefits back to the farmer at one jump. He stated the objects farmers were seeking, i.e., a fair exchange value for their products, and said that if there was any better way to attain these objects than had been proposed he would pledge his support to it, even though it might differ from any and every suggestion which had been made.

(Friday, December 23, 1932). . . . Went to Earl Smith's office. He had telegram from Lee saying (1) Agricultural Committee had deferred further consideration pending call of Chairman after January first, (2) Lee and Morgenthau to be in Chicago Wednesday for conference with small group which Smith was to select. Smith asked me to attend. . . .

I told Smith that he had better think about the position he was put in by ——— in Washington when he was allowed to go through that conference with the understanding that Tugwell represented Governor R., and that this should make him exceedingly cautious; . . .

(December 28, 1932). Spent all day with farm group consisting of: Smith, Huff, O'Neal, Winder, Kirkpatrick, and Fred Lee. Part of time Cowles and Wright, of I.A.A. were present. Lee emphasized great pressure for immediate action. During the afternoon Jim Bell telephoned me and emphasized critical situation in Northwest, urging particularly remedial action to meet condition caused by depreciated currencies in other countries.

(December 29, 1932). Called Fred Lee at A.F.B.F. He said he would come to my office shortly. Henry Wallace came in just before Lee arrived. Later C. C. D. came in. Wallace objected to acreage payment concurrently with processor's tax, although on December 10th he had concurred in proposal as substitute for other proposed legislation.

(December 30, 1932). Arrived at Washington. Charles Brand lunched with me. Said he thought my idea of state administration of farm bill correct and if acreage were to be restricted the place to start was, as I say, in states which produce the surplus, and further, that the idea of renting acreage in such states is sound. Met Jones by appointment in his office. He asked me to have Perley [of the House Legislative Counsel] put in his bill provision authorizing Secretary to publish benefits to farmer so Secretary could put consumers on notice against unjust increase in price; also provision for agreements with processors and associations of producers. . . . Said this legislation would have to go to conference and he wanted to get his bill out quickly and passed by House within next week or so. . . .

(January 2, 1933). Wallace and M. L. Wilson called at ten-thirty and spent half an hour going over matters. I went to Brand's office at eleven o'clock to prepare "Comments" and have it typed, and at three returned to hotel to meet Wilson, Wallace and Lee. I went over "Comments" and after much discussion they agreed my position was correct. . . . We then went to Jones' office and had long discussion with him. . . . Graduated benefits and tax on hogs decided upon by Committee—other commodities not immediately effective—my agreement provision turned down, and some minor changes. Bill will be introduced Tuesday, printed, and reported out Tuesday afternoon or Wednesday morning. We pointed out how little consideration hog section was getting. He [Jones] countered by saying he was entirely sympathetic with our whole point of view and suggested that we get provisions as we wanted them in Senate draft . . . . I told him I was delivering in person letter addressed to him with "Comments" and suggested that under the circumstances as he outlined them I thought I would ask Senator Harrison to take copy of December 31st print and "Comments" to Governor Roosevelt. He said he thought that was real sense and was in favor of it.

(January 5, 1933). . . . At Senator McNary's request I went to the Capitol to see him. The Senate was just adjourning, (2:00 P.M.), at the news of ex-President Coolidge's death. Met Senator Harrison. . . . He asked me about the Committee amendments. I told him that they modified but did not remove my objections, that McNary had sent for me and that I was going into the matter thoroughly with McNary. . . .

At this juncture Senator McNary came along and we went to his office and spent nearly two hours in conference. His comment on the House bill was so picturesque as to preclude detailed quotation. He wound up by saying that he took it home to study last night and found it so impossible that he consigned it to the scrap basket. He asked if I had seen it and I told him "yes" and that I had written a memorandum on it for Congressman Jones and had given a copy of it to Senator Harrison and Fred Lee. He asked for a copy and I went over it with him and left a copy. He approved of my position in every instance, but was much inclined to fall back on tariff benefits instead of ratio price. I explained to him how inadequate tariff benefits would be in this crisis, and he acquiesced. He said————had been to him with a simple plan for making the tariff effective and with Boots [Legislative Counsel] had drafted a bill which Senator McNary had intended to introduce this afternoon, but for the unexpected adjournment on account of Coolidge's death. I told him that I should like to get Fred Lee and draft a bill along simple lines, covering all that was in the House Bill that was worth saving, plus my suggestions in "Comments". He said he would be very glad to have me do this and would give me until Monday to complete the bill (three days), and to make myself at home around there, use the Agricultural Committee room, etc. . . .

(January 11—Wednesday). Called Fred Lee and discussed situation with him. Suggested he might desire to ask Jones to see McNary or Harrison. After a long discussion he thought they might as well have a test vote now in the House. Heald called me from the drafting service and went over numerous points in the bill they are working on, and said he would telephone me late this afternoon if they were ready with the draft.

H. S. J. called me from New York and said headquarters becoming much disturbed over situation with bill. . . . I said I thought it should pass and be fixed up in conference—that if it was a bad bill it was the fault of———— and the economists, who insisted upon it. . . .

(January 12). The House Bill passed at 6:00 tonight, 203 to 151, with seven commodities included—wheat, cotton, hogs, rice, peanuts, tobacco, butter-fat.

The bill was a composite of a variety of ideas contributed by Tugwell, Morgenthau, Ezekiel, M. L. Wilson, some other professors and economists and perhaps Henry Wallace. It was not the farmers' measure. It applied only to wheat, rice, cotton, peanuts, tobacco, butter-fats and hogs and provided for adjustment certificates issued for the portion of the crops going into domestic consumption on somewhat the same lines as the Rainey Bill.

But the great divergence from all previous farm bills was the acreage control vested in the Secretary of Agriculture. He was empowered to withhold certificates unless production had been decreased according to certain provisions. That was going directly against the campaign pledges. It was establishing the Secretary of Agriculture as the autocrat of farming. That ran counter to everything I had been taught was American.

Continuing the story from the diary:

(January 14—Saturday). Went to McNary's office between 10:30 and 11:00 o'clock. He was vicious in his comments on the proposed Senate draft, [which I had left with him the day before] although admitting he had not read it. I told him that if he did not want to take time to read the bill I hoped he would at least read the memorandum of it, which I worked upon last night. I repeated what I said Friday . . . . [i.e.] he could not afford to condemn it without informing himself what was in it. . . . He asked me if I wanted someone to introduce my proposed Senate draft "by request" and I said "no," that I had put in my time day and night for more than a week in making an honest effort to correct the shortcomings of the House bill and to do a constructive job, that if after reading it he did not think my efforts worth while, to throw the damn thing in the waste basket. He said he would read it today, aand asked me to come back Monday morning. . . . Senator Harrison called to me to come about 4:30, and I spent two hours with him. . . . Harrison suggested that I see Senator Smith, but I pointed out that since I had gone to McNary at his request and McNary had not yet turned down the proposal, I thought I had better wait until after I had seen McNary again before approaching Senator Smith. He agreed, but said that Governor R. had indicated that he wanted action on farm legislation. We discussed other aspects of the economic and political situation including Treasury and Agriculture in cabinet appointments. . . . This has been for me one of the most trying and important days I have spent.

We did not get anywhere. The Democratic leaders were anxious to please Governor Roosevelt, but they did not seem to know exactly what he wanted—even after conferences with him. Here are some random sidelights:

(January 25, 1933—Wednesday). Mr. Sherman Rogers came at 10:00 and spent the morning. He was very interesting and went into detail on Wall Street's attitude toward farm legislation. He said Wall Street paid no attention to farm difficulties before Farmers' Holiday demonstrations; that they thought interference with legal procedure should be met by sending troops. I observed that care should be taken in the selection of the troops, lest on arrival they take the side of the farmers. He asked if I thought any of the state legislatures would vote a moratorium. I replied that such action would do much less violence than if they took action toward repudiation of debts.

(January 26, 1933—Thursday). Mr. X came in and discussed the Wallace and Morgenthau situation and expressed great apprehension about the political results of M.'s connection with Agriculture and suggested I pay his expenses to go to see Farley. I declined to do so.

(January 27, 1933—Friday). X called about 6:00 and showed me a letter he had written Farley. Said he would call again Saturday, but that he was very apprehensive of Mr. M.'s identification with the Department of Agriculture.

(January 28, 1933—Saturday). X telephoned, and I urged him not to send the Farley letter. Told him I did not object to his discussing the situation with anyone, but thought he should not write such a letter except upon request of Farley. In the Carlton dining room met General Johnson and Alex

Legge at dinner with Clark Howell, who are here with B. M. B. and Al Smith on Railroad Commission. General Johnson said they had a very straight talk at Warm Springs and pointed out impossibilities of Allotment Plan in time to do any good this year. . . .

(January 29, 1933—Sunday). . . . I went to the train with B. M. B. at 4:00 o'clock. . . . I pointed out great responsibility of those who promoted the allotment bill for the Chief [F. D. R.]. He wanted to know what I thought of acreage rental and I told him "no good at this late date for this year." He asked my suggestions and I related substantially what I have in mind for Senate Committee amendments. He asked if I thought Hoover would sign and I said I had no idea, but I did not see how he could without stultifying everything he had said. B. M. B. pointed out that he might let it become a law without his signature, referring to campaign pledges of F. D. R. and election results, and then let the Democrats have the odium of administering it. . . . Charlie Smith came in, but had no definite news. . . . He was discussing Reciprocal Tariffs. He once heard Champ Clark say that when he first came to Washington Mr. Dingley gave him this advice: "Young man, tariffs are the whole of government. Study them."

(February 1, 1933—Wednesday). Fred Lee came in in the afternoon and said he thought farm organizations should raise the Devil and issue a statement against Senate Democratic leadership. He added that Mr. M. had been here today on his way back to New York from Warm Springs. . . . He said Governor R. was still insisting upon farm legislation at this session, and upon some sort of acreage control. Apparently it has not occurred to Mr. M. how impossible the House bill is. Lee said that Mr. M. and Tugwell do not jibe at all. . . . I told Lee that I criticize Mr. M. for letting the farm people get themselves into a position of going along with Tugwell against their judgment. . . .

(February 10, 1933—Friday). Received a telegram from the Senate Finance Committee to appear on Tuesday, February 14th, at 10:00 A.M.

(February 13, 1933—Monday). B. M. Baruch presented

an elaborate memo. before the Senate Finance Committee advocating getting people back to work by making money work. "To make money work we must balance the budget." . . . He also proposed a plan for farm mortgage relief by setting up a corporation which should issue debentures; (interest guaranteed by the Government), to take over farm mortgages from those who wanted to dispose of them on a basis of not to exceed 60 per cent of their value. My comment is best expressed by my own proposal drafted for presentation tomorrow. . . . Ed O'Neal, President of the A.F.B., spent the evening with us and was greatly pleased with the memorandum, which I read to him. "Boy," said he, "you have written the Bible of Agriculture! I am going to make speeches from it for several years."

Chapter IV

Making the A.A.A.

In the Short Session a new group, as I have noted, appeared in farm matters. The new group was led by Tugwell, Mordecai Ezekiel, Henry Morgenthau, Jr. and other men who had never been active in our farm fight. They had with them Henry Wallace and M. L. Wilson. It was this group that sponsored the House bill setting up the Secretary of Agriculture as the czar of farming.

It is impossible to say which one—if any—of the group actually represented the President-elect. It is entirely possible, however, that the legislation was in the nature of a trial balloon to see how far Congress would go in delegating the functions which by their oath of office the members had sworn to retain. The House passed the bill under the impression that it was doing what the President-elect wanted. Many Democratic members of the House were willing to do anything they were told to do, and they thought they had been told to pass this bill. I doubt if anyone had the authority actually to tell them. The Republican members did not care.

The Senate did care. It still preserved a sense of legislative responsibility. So, more for the purpose of making a record than of influencing the pending bill, I made a very complete statement before the Senate Committee on Finance and backed it up with a full series of carefully prepared tables giving a statistical history of the farm in its relation to the nation. I also proposed certain amendments which are important only as serving to show how completely the pending bill departed from all the principles that had been threshed out during the years. For the Agricultural Adjustment Act, later to be passed, was used to thrust to one side the two-price system of making the tariff effective by the removal of supplies to foreign markets. In my testimony I said:

Any plans for the restriction of agricultural production to the demands of the domestic market involving substantial curtailment of acreage, except occasionally in case of great emergency, as in case of cotton at present, should be considered in the light of our whole national and international economy, and should not be adopted as a permanent national policy. Our national effort should tend toward making the farm a satisfactory place for more, not less people. . . .

The importance of the processor must be recognized as he performs a necessary service between the farmer and the consumer.

Agreements should be authorized between the proper governmental bodies and existing agencies, including processors and associations of producers. The aim to be accomplished by these agreements should be to dispose of existing surpluses and to keep the channels of trade open through every instrumentality at our command; that is, governmental, producers, processors, and exporters (private or cooperative).

Prevention of burdensome supply in future should be provided for by decreasing prospective production before harvest in the areas where it is excessive, compensating the farmer for so decreasing production. Such action can be fully justified as a contribution to the general welfare.

Reduced production should be effected in areas of surplus production. Reduction should not take place in sections or areas where the particular products are deficient in supply. To do otherwise would be wasteful and uneconomic and would create dissatisfaction and unrest.

The Senators saw the point clearly. For instance:

Senator Harrison. The House allotment bill does not do that, does it?

Mr. Peek. No. It merely curtails acreage.

Senator Harrison. Yes; but it curtails acreage everywhere, whether or not there is a surplus in a particular product for a State. . . .

MR. PEEK. For example, why should South Carolina decrease her corn production when she imports corn and the surplus of corn originates in the Middle West?

I may say right there, I was in South Carolina the latter part of November. A gentleman with whom I talked had just shipped in a carload of corn for which he paid 62 cents a bushel delivered at Georgetown. The farmer in Iowa got 10 cents a bushel for that corn and the 52 cents was absorbed between the farmer and this man who bought it for distribution at 62 cents. Now why ask South Carolina to curtail its production of corn when the Middle West is producing it?

Senator SHORTRIDGE. Yes; it is perfectly absurd.

MR. PEEK. Or why should New York State reduce her wheat production of 5,000,000 bushels when she is forced to import millions of additional bushels each year, and the surplus is made in Kansas, North Dakota, and a limited number of additional States? . . .

Senator HARRISON. There would be no reason to make California, for instance, decrease her cotton supply when they do not produce a surplus out there?

The discussion before the Committee was free and open. Senator Harrison asked me to prepare some amendments and I submitted them with some additional analyses. The statements on the futility of acreage reduction as a farm aid have been abundantly proven by the history of the A.A.A. These sections of the memorandum seem pertinent:

The amendment contemplates that if, with the assistance of government, it is impossible to dispose of production and surplus at home or abroad, through every conceivable marketing channel and in manufacture, then the Government may step in during this emergency and offer to arrest the harvesting of a part of any commodity by paying to the farmer the local price, less the cost of completing the production, harvesting, preparation for and hauling to local market. In such event it will be possible for the Government to go into those production areas and States that are producing a surplus and control the supply there, rather than to have it mature and break down the price of the commodity throughout the whole country and in foreign markets. The amendment is so worded that it is possible to secure complete administration of this provision through State authorities with their cooperation. It provides that the Secretary of Agriculture is authorized to designate in each State a committee composed of the head of the State Department of Agriculture, the head of the Agricultural Extension Service of the State, and such person as is recommended to the Secretary by the Governor of the State, to administer this provision.

The cost of removing excessive supply is proposed to be met from the duties collected on imports of certain agricultural commodities as provided in the House bill. If the amount of money received from this source is insufficient, duties may be imposed on other agricultural commodities which now come in duty-free.

The futility of undertaking to control supply by renting acreage or by limiting planting throughout the United States instead of controlling excess supply when and where it is known to exist in a particular year is apparent. Attention is directed to the yield per acre, in recent years, of wheat, corn and cotton in a few of the farm states.

Wheat Yield per Acre—Bushels

	1930	1931	1932
North Dakota	11.0	5.3	10.7
South Dakota	11.9	5.7	13.5
Kansas	13.5	19.0	11.5
Oklahoma	9.5	17.0	11.0

Corn Yield per Acre—Bushels

	1930	1931	1932
Ohio	25.5	45.0	35.5
Illinois	26.0	37.0	43.0
Nebraska	25.0	17.0	25.3
Iowa	34.0	33.5	46.0

Cotton Yield per Acre—Pounds

	1930	1931	1932
All cotton States	147.7	201.2	162.1

The comment on my statements was very favorable. Some of it is instructive, in the light of what afterwards happened. It may be recalled that Edward O'Neal, reading the statement before delivery (Diary, Feb. 13th), said that he was going to make speeches on it for years. Here are some diary extracts:

(February 20, 1933—Monday). Went over memorandum with Charles Brand. Put finishing touches on memorandum with Fred Lee and delivered copy to Senator Harrison. He congratulated me upon my statement before the Committee and said that the exhibits attached were convincing. . . .

(February 23, 1933—Thursday). . . . Found . . . B. M. B. at hotel. . . . He said he and Johnson separately agreed that my memorandum to the Committee was a great document. . . . Found letters here from Cliff Gregory and Chester Davis complimenting me extravagantly on my presentation.

With banks closing everywhere and Congress marking time until the Session closed, I went back to Moline and Chicago to tend my own affairs. We all felt that we had laid the groundwork for quick farm action in the new Congress to be called into special session. Here are some further diary excerpts which carry on the events:

(March 2, 1933 — Thursday). Received letter here (Chicago) from Wallace, saying he would like to lunch today with General Wood and me. . . . At 11:00 o'clock Wallace telephoned saying he was leaving by plane immediately for New York in response to call. Discussed my proposed amendments briefly. He said he had them with him and would read en route. He asked when I would be in Washington and I said I did not know. . . . Met General Wood at the Chicago Club. He asked for fifteen copies of my statement immediately. He inclined to urge his Committee [U. S. Chamber of Commerce Committee] to back my suggestions.

(March 3, 1933—Friday). Gregory and Chester Davis lunched with me at the University Club. Discussed my statement and proposed amendments. Gregory very favorably impressed and said the Prairie Farmer this week is giving extensive comment to my paper. Said he would write Wallace and Morgenthau at once, as revised bill was being drafted for the new Administration.

The closing of the banks and the inauguration of Franklin D. Roosevelt as President served to flatten out the quibbling over the details of farm relief. But in the flattening the basic principles also got lost. With Henry Wallace as Secretary of Agriculture, Professor Tugwell as Assistant Secretary and Henry Morgenthau, Jr. as head of the Farm Credit Administration, the "economists" were definitely in the saddle. The emergency hysteria partially paralyzed the farm group. I had turned over to the group the services of Fred Lee—whom I had personally retained during the Short Session period. The farm leaders at a meeting in Washington with Wallace, Tugwell and others turned over the whole job and also the services of Mr. Lee to Messrs. Wallace and Tugwell. These gentlemen accepted the responsibility with alacrity. Tugwell knew what he wanted.

The President had promised legislation exactly along the lines which for years the responsible farm men had been advocating. When the critical time came, the farm leaders, although they had Mr. Lee ready at hand to draft a bill, muffed their big chance and left the field open to the professors. But, although I represented no one, I stayed in the fight!

(March 11, 1933—Saturday). Wallace called me at 8:45 and asked me to come down to his office right away. I got there shortly after 9:00 A.M. He was visibly excited and worried. Said he wanted to have a long talk with me when he could get time. I said I desired it, too, but business in hand must take precedence if we were to get anything by first of week and I wanted to help; that my principal interest was legislation. . . . He asked me to sit in with Fred Lee and Ezekiel in drafting it. I declined, but told him I wanted his permission to discuss everything with Lee. He said O.K. and to tell Lee that if he got into any difficult position on account of differences in opinion to come to him. He then said if we got the bill he wanted me to stay here and help draft . . . regulations. I told him I would. He said to be sure to tell Lee to get in Sections 19 and 20. I told him I thought the Committee recommendations broad enough to let them in. . . .

Fred Lee called me and asked me to go to Department of Agriculture tonight to review work done on bill. . . . At department with Lee until 11:30. Ezekiel came in about 10:30. We disagreed, as usual. Wallace called me about midnight. Said he was at Willard with Moley. Asked me what I thought about getting Hugh Johnson down here today to go over matter and bill. I said good idea. . . .

(Sunday A.M.—March 12, 1933). . . . Wallace telephoned 10:30. Had talked with B. M. and he (B. M.) . . . told him he was about to write him to tender his help. . . . I told Wallace B. M. could see through a stone wall.

. . . Went to Department of Agriculture at 6:00. Stayed until 11:30. Wallace had whole farm group there. I suggested international agreements for immediate exchange of commodities and tax on imports for acreage rental. Wallace asked me if I would come in and run the new job if law passed. I said "No" but would be glad to help him in whatever way I could by advice, etc., but I did not want any job. . . .

(Monday, March 13, 1933). I went to the Department and Wallace called B. M. B. . . . to tell him (1) about the legislation, (2) where money was coming from, (3) how he proposed to administer it. He discussed the situation with B. M. B. in about the order named. B. M. then talked with me and said Wallace had a big job and he wanted to be of help. . . . Wallace telephoned me to ask if I thought B. M. would come to meeting Tuesday of a few people. I said I thought he would, and suggested he call him.

(March 14, 1933—Tuesday). . . . Returned to hotel at 7:00 P.M. Met Johnson in lobby. . . . At 9:00 Johnson came upstairs with us. . . . Called Wallace at Johnson's suggestion. Wallace and Tugwell came to my room. . . . I suggested B. M. B. to head new job. Tugwell said repeatedly he would not take it. Tugwell said this bill was a new charter—temporary vs. permanent bill, etc.

(March 15, 1933—Wednesday). . . . Johnson called . . . Told him I was going to see Wallace at once. He wanted to meet me there.

He told Wallace and Tugwell processors cocky because they understood farm bill disapproved by President. I told Wallace I wanted to be present when processors met with him today. . . . I had told Bell, Wilson and Stevenson in Chicago that processors, bankers and speculators had been ganging the farmer. People had expressed their disapproval on election day. We had a New Deal. President could not lean two ways; one toward the farmer, the other toward the old gang. Tugwell said this kind of talk should be presented to the President. Wallace said he intended to find out this A.M. where the President stood. Asked Johnson to go with them to the White House. They left at 10:30. I came back to the hotel. Result of White House conference: President stands with Wallace.

(Thursday, March 16, 1933). I telephoned Wallace Johnson's position last night. . . . I told him I would bring Johnson right down. Bill not changed enough to meet Johnson's objections, so he sent his letter of protest to the President. Wallace and Tugwell went to the White House at noon. Result: President approves Wallace's procedure and at 4:30 sent message to House with the bill. . . .

The bill carried such a broad grant of power as to make everything dependent upon its administration. Pledges and promises could be fulfilled under it or they could be stultified.

It is not useful to go into the details of the House bill—it was broader than the "economists' bill" of the Short Session. I thought the real fight would come in the Senate—which had blocked the Short Session bill. Secretary Wallace was worried about the administration of the bill. Matters of administration never worried Professor Tugwell and his associates. They had had so little experience in administration that they did not comprehend the wide gap between writing something and doing something. Tugwell appeared to be quite satisfied that he was on the way to getting whatever he was after. The days were very full:

(Friday, March 17, 1933). Developed ideas on five points:

1. A policy re national vs. international trade
2. Competition for consumer's dollar
3. Foreign plants
4. Centralized control and supervision of exports
5. Advisory Council

(Saturday, March 18, 1933). Wallace telephoned me at 8:00 A.M. I told him someone should explain the bill so people would understand what was in it and what was intended in the way of administration. I telephoned Earl Smith and asked him about appointment with Secretary. . . . He telephoned Wallace we were coming right over. . . . Wallace said he had put up the proposition of inviting Baruch to take charge of the administration of the bill to the President but had not heard. . . . I told Wallace of suggestion of Advisory Council with Baruch a member. He was very receptive. Earl and I returned to the hotel. . . . We returned to conference with Wallace and [Thomas E.] Wilson at 2:00. Tugwell present. Wilson's attitude fine. He asked Wallace how he was going to administer the act. Wallace replied, in short, with the cooperation of producers and processors. Apparently Wilson much relieved. Wallace then called B. M. and invited him to head administration of the Act. Told him he had discussed the matter with the President, that if that was impossible for him to do, he wanted him to think over idea of Advisory Committee with which he would cooperate as a member. Tugwell obviously was not pleased with the trend of affairs. Wallace told Tugwell the President wanted memorandum Monday morning of how Wallace proposed to proceed with administration. Tugwell replied they would have to get busy and outline procedure. I interposed and said, "I can tell you in fifty words how you should proceed." Wallace said, "You write it." I declined, but suggested: Advisory Council to meet with each group of processors, producers, and the Secretary, and secure their views and suggestions regarding each commodity, then decide on procedure, but if possible do the whole job through the cooperation of the industries. (39 words.) In other words, follow War Industries Board precedent.

Tugwell objected. Said, "We must write the regulations."

I replied, "You know nothing of the intricacies of the business of different industries. No one is qualified except the processors themselves, but they of course must be supervised by the duly appointed administrative officers." Wallace asked me if I would serve on Advisory Council, and I said yes, if desired. . . . Tugwell very unhappy. . . . I showed Wallace my memorandum on five points. He was noncommittal but said finally, "This memorandum must go to the State Department." Tugwell said the President would never agree to Advisory Council.

(March 20, 1933—Monday). H. S. J. telephoned me. . . . Asked what I had done with memorandum he sent. Told him I had given it to Wallace, who called in Lee and we went over it together. He asked what Wallace was going to do about it and I said he had better ask him; that I did not know. . . . He asked why Wallace did not get a good lawyer. I said he had one. "Who?" he asked. I replied, "Lee." . . . Johnson . . . said Wallace . . . had asked B. M. to take charge, . . . that ——— was a damned Communist, and that the whole idea of benefit payments was communistic. . . .

While I was out to dinner Wallace called. I went over to see him and suggested that he see Senators Harrison, Robinson, and Pittman, Tuesday A.M., for if the bill passed the House it would be before the Senate immediately. . . . He said Wheeler had telephoned offering his cooperation. He again urged me to say I would take charge of administrative duties, but I told him no one should do that until the bill passed so that the form of the legislation was known and an agreement reached on procedure. He asked about Brand and C. C. D. [Chester C. Davis] I told him under the circumstances C. C. D. could not act as promptly as Brand, who is conversant with the whole problem and the Department. He said B. M. B. had telephoned him this afternoon again offering his cooperation. . . . Things cracking very fast. I urged Wallace to include other grains in basic commodity list and definite amount of appropriation. . . .

(March 22, 1933—Wednesday). Wallace called and asked me to ride out to Wardman with him. . . . Upon arrival at Wardman Hotel we ran into Senator Harrison, . . . Senator

Stevens [and three or four friends] . . . Wallace did not go with us to the room, but Harrison . . . suggested that Wallace get Robinson, McNary and Smith [Senator] to sit down with us and work the thing out. He said there were many violent objections to the bill as written.

Senator Stevens declared open warfare on the bill, particularly general curtailment of acreage; referring to the social aspect of turning people out of employment in the country to drive them into the city, et cetera. After he completed a fifteen minute discussion I told him he was quoting my paper before the Senate Finance Committee and I felt our views were not far apart. After explaining the necessity for broad powers I asked them whether, if they could be assured of sensible administration, advised by such men as Baruch, Lowden and Alf Stone, for instance, the opposition of senators generally would be withdrawn. They replied in the affirmative; although making reservation about slight changes in the bill.

. . . On my way home I stopped to see Judge Cooney at the Mayflower. Had a very good talk and laid my five points before him. He said he agreed 100 per cent with every point. In discussing them and the bill he said that chain stores especially broke prices but that seven packers, if allowed to agree, could correct this situation and bring prices to parity and keep them there. He did not want restriction of production. I asked him point blank if they would object to the bill if they felt they would receive sympathetic and business-like administration of it. He said "no," but that they shuddered at the thought of ——— and ——— . . . .

(March 25, 1933—Saturday). Senator Harrison telephoned at 9:30 and asked me to come right down to his office. Senator Stevens and Alf Stone there. Spent two hours discussing situation. Alf suggested idea of Advisory Committee, either in the law or by announcement of President or Secretary. Both senators agreed that if such a thing could be brought about many objections to legislation would be withdrawn. We discussed such men as Baruch, Lowden, Stone and others. Alf went to lunch with me. . . . I . . . told him . . . that no man with any sense would take the administrative job and have such men as Tugwell and Ezekiel in a position to run circles around him and perhaps around the Secretary, and appealing to the President. . . .

Stevenson, of cotton processors, came in and we had a friendly visit. He said processors could not agree among themselves. He said Senator Smith's feelings were hurt because he had not been called in to write the bill (although W. and Tugwell told me that Smith [Senator] had been over the bill with them and Marvin Jones while it was being drafted and had pledged his support. There is something behind the scenes that is not clear. . . .)

Fred Lee later came in and I put up to him the possible conception of the distribution of wealth as contrasted with the responsibility of Government for decreasing production since it had increased it previously, leaving the responsibility upon the processors to maintain prices only as indicated in my amendments to House bill before Senate Finance Committee. I discussed Jerome Frank more fully with Lee. Lee agreed as to necessity for Advisory Committee for purpose of inspiring confidence in administration of the bill.

. . . I urged Wallace to telephone both Hirth and Murphy and urge them to come down and to extend the invitation to any of the other leaders they desired. Wallace said he would act on suggestion at once. . . .

(March 26, 1933—Sunday). . . . Wallace telephoned three times during forenoon about Hirth, Murphy, and other matters. I urged him to invite B. M. B. down this week while processors battle is raging. He asked me to see Jerome Frank in afternooon. . . .

I came back to Carlton to meet Jerome Frank at 2:00. He stayed over two hours. Said he was a close friend of Felix Frankfurter and said it was through him that he came here. He said, "You have the full and complete confidence of the Secretary." We discussed many angles of the existing depression and the way out. He said he was going to try to get Frankfurter and Dr. Rogers down here, and asked if I would put in some time with them if they came. He said that many of them were of the opinion that another bank crisis would develop in a short time (a few months) unless something more is done than has been discussed.

(March 27, 1933—Monday). Went at 9:30 to Senator Robinson's office. Secretary Wallace came in soon after. Spent an hour there discussing situation in general. . . . Senator R. telephoned the White House and made appointment to see the President with Secretary this P.M. . . .

B. M. B. telephoned from New York and [said] . . . that he had had several hurry-up calls to come to Washington; . . . that nobody could get him into a jam with me, that if we disagreed he was going to leave town. I told him I felt the same way and I had told Wallace I would rather have his friendship than any job the Administration could offer.

I telephoned Wallace . . . and said B. M. had called me up and would probably be here tomorrow. W. said conference today at White House satisfactory, but things would be held up a couple of days pending development of farm mortgage plan. . . .

(March 28, 1933—Tuesday). B. M. B. came to town. . . . After putting in two hours with him we called H. S. J. into the conference. . . . I explained the politics of sticking close to the Administration proposal, and suggested we get Wallace and Lee with us. B. M. said, "All right." . . . I telephoned, asking Wallace and Lee to come over and asked W. not to bring anyone from the Department. . . .

Wallace came in at 5:00, Lee later, and we were in session until 11:00 P.M. Johnson and B. M. succeeded in convincing W. and Lee that there were some holes in the bill which should be plugged up. They conceded it. . . . Strenuous day.

(March 29, 1933—Wednesday). Secretary Wallace called up at breakfast time and asked me to come to the Department. He was worried about opposition amendments. . . . He wanted me to be available for Committee and suggested J. Frank go with me. I said no. . . . I then went to Senator R.'s office and told him what had happened yesterday. I talked very plainly about the confusion resulting from half-baked proposals being sprung before they were ready and pointed out that the party would be made or broken on the result of this winter's program, and that Agriculture is the most important spoke in the wheel. I spoke of my 5-point program and he asked for it. I told him that it represented my view of what our national policy should be, especially toward agriculture, and that it represented the conclusions of my 12 years study, merely as a basis from which to start procedure. He was much interested and indicated that he was in accord with what I said. I suggested he call a meeting of Administration leaders at once with the Secretary, decide upon what corrections should be made in Senate draft. . . . This afternoon he telephoned he had decided to act upon my suggestion and invited me to attend a meeting at his office tonight at 8:30.

At lunch time Secretary Wallace called up. In my conversation at his office this morning I told the Secretary no one would undertake the administration of such a job without having it understood that the Tugwells and Ezekiels could not run circles around him. . . .

In the evening went to Senator R.'s office for conference until midnight. The others were Senators Harrison and Bankhead, [Fred] Lee, and Secretary Wallace. Discussed many angles of legislation and agreed upon some amendments. Before conclusion of conference I asked Secretary Wallace and Lee if they understood they had met all of the objections raised in conference with B. M. and H. S. J. They said yes, but Lee referred to some exceptions such as direct appropriation and specific taxes.

(March 31, 1933—Friday). Went to W.'s office and he again emphasized necessity of my taking job with Chester. I assured him that I would not run away but would continue to help him, but that there were some things in connection with the whole matter that I must take up with him privately.

(April 1, 1933—Saturday). Wallace telephoned at 9:00, asking me to come right down to his office. Again he said I must administer the bill and he would insist upon C. C. D. [Chester C. Davis] or C. J. B. [Charles J. Brand] assisting. I laid cards on the table and said no self-respecting man could take it without a definite understanding with the President . . . that I felt the whole structure of Government was at stake and that no one could afford to take such a position under existing conditions who did not have the complete confidence of the President; that an understanding with the President was as essential to Wallace as it was to the man who undertook the administration of this job, and that if I had any influence with C. C. D. or C. J. B. I should advise them against getting into the position without a complete understanding.

Wallace's office called me in the afternoon and asked me to go to Senator Robinson's office at 9:30 Sunday A.M. for conference. . . . I told him [Wallace] the same men who had messed up legislation last December (i.e., Tugwell, Ezekiel and others) were doing the same things again with this new bill.

(Sunday, April 2, 1933). Met Wallace and Lee at Senator Robinson's office and reviewed Comm. situation and detail of draft. R. suggested certain changes to improve constitutional status.

Wallace told me last night that he had recommended me to the President and the latter was going to confer with Baruch to ask about me. I told W. again that Baruch was the one man for this job. . . . I told him no one could refuse to accept in this great emergency if President requested and conditions were made possible by the law and administratively.

This evening it was disclosed that benefit payments could not be made except for acreage rental or production removal. Present at this discussion were Wallace, part of the time, Tugwell, Frank, Lee, Davis and myself. . . . [It had been my understanding that] benefit payments could be made along with everything else I had advocated before Senate Finance Committee, the only difference being that the money was to come from processors' tax for acreage rental, etc., instead of import duties as I suggested. I stated that if I understood them correctly now, that the whole bill was based upon raising prices by restricting production; that I should go before the Committees in Congress and to my friends and oppose with all the force I was capable of, and that was final.

Wallace telephoned about 9:30 from White House that he was bringing Y over to see me.

During my discussion with Y Wallace came in, and before Y we [Wallace and I] had a very definite argument. It was clearly disclosed that Wallace favored restriction of production and benefits contingent thereon as distinguished from my view of urging agricultural exports and liquidation of industrial facilities. I told him [Wallace] that if he persisted I should start out immediately to oppose the bill with all the force at my command. Finally he conceded that my view should prevail, and that the bill should be clarified, but warned me that in its administration the bill might be interpreted according to his point of view. I told him I would not throw away the principle for which I had fought, for which this fight has been waged, for 12 years. I said that the President had made certain promises to the country and that he alone must define the principles to be followed, but that the bill must be broad enough to permit administration in accord with the campaign promises; that he had the responsibility for fulfilling those promises and must have adequate authority. This interview demonstrated clearly Wallace's international point of view, as distinguished from my national point of view, and is, perhaps, the most far-reaching discussion of the winter. Y offered to withdraw, but I said "no," unless the Secretary desired it, and the Secretary said it was all right for him to remain. Wallace and I went into another room and he told Lee and the others to change the bill to meet my view.

(April 4, 1933—Tuesday.) B. M. telephoned this morning . . . and suggested to me that I tell the President—

a. That I must know what the bill was to be.
b. That I must be in a position to come directly to him with the Secretary.
c. That I must understand my authority.

These things being clearly understood I would take the matter under advisement. . . .

(April 6, 1933—Thursday.) ———— (tobacco representative) called. . . . He asked how the bill would be administered. I said I did not know, but directed his attention to the War Industries Board regulations. I referred to the fact that Esberg was my tobacco man and he commented that the tobacco trade would not be afraid of any such administration as that. He added, however, that they were fearful of the administration by the young men they had met in the Department, referring especially to Tugwell and Ezekiel.

C. C. D. came over in the evening. We discussed the situation in the Department. He said he was scared about Tugwell, that he was more theoretical than Henry and that he feared Tugwell was slated for Under Secretary. He said T. and W. were too much alike (idealists). He asked if I were going to take the job of administrator, and I said not unless I could agree upon policy.

(Saturday, April 8, 1933). . . . Wallace telephoned about forms Ezekiel wanted to prepare costing 5 to 6 hundred thousand dollars to secure information. I told them to defer action.

(Monday, April 10, 1933). . . . At Wallace's request went to Department to discuss Ezekiel's 500,000,000 forms. Told them to lay off.

(Tuesday, April 11, 1933). . . . Wallace asked me to Department in evening. Still pressing on Ezekiel's forms. I told him if Congress heard about them it would be good night to them—to forget it. . . .

The "economists" and professors knew what they wanted and were determined to get it. I thought I had them checked, but events proved that I was mistaken.

Chapter V

Getting Under Way

The Agricultural Adjustment Act became a law on May 12th, 1933. The original act was fairly simple and, although it gave very broad powers to the Secretary of Agriculture, it was the understanding in the Senate that those powers were going to be exercised only nominally by Messrs. Wallace and Tugwell and that the actual administration would be in the hands of someone with mature experience, guided by an unofficial advisory board of men in whom the public would have confidence.

The Senate did not take the bill at a gulp, as had the House. The Democratic members who had been reelected or newly elected felt that they had come in on a Democratic landslide and not on a Roosevelt landslide. Many of them disliked and distrusted some of the men the President was putting into office. The members of the Senate Committee on Agriculture and Forestry—of which Senator Ellison D. Smith of South Carolina was chairman—were not easily stampeded. It is an open secret that at least Senators Smith, Kendrick of Wyoming, Wheeler of Montana, and Thomas of Oklahoma, on the Democratic side, and Senators Norris of Nebraska, McNary of Oregon, Capper of Kansas and Hatfield of West Virginia, on the Republican side, were considerably less than enthusiastic about some of the various new faces that had come into the farm picture.

The pending bill, it may be recalled, was purely an emergency measure, and only later was it distorted into a production-restricting and farm-regimenting bill. The power to pay men for not producing was in the original bill, and I think it was put there by Mordecai Ezekiel, Economic Adviser to Secretary Wallace. That did not concern me, for the issue had not arisen. The bill had in it all the powers any reasonable administrator could desire, and the extra powers did not matter, for he would not need to use them. That is, as I have learned, a very dangerous attitude to take. Delegated powers should be limited exactly to the work in hand, for an administrator cannot possibly know everything that is undertaken in his name, and a bureau is never content unless it uses its broadest powers. That is the way of government. Had the original powers been more closely circumscribed, the A.A.A. would never have developed away from farm relief and into farm regulation just for the sake of regulation. The lust for power grew, and it will be remembered that later the original act was torn to bits and rewritten by the amendments of August 24th, 1935 put through the 74th Congress. They were mostly real Brain Trust amendments and made possible the use of the original act to make remittance men out of the farmers. The Bankhead Cotton Act and the Kerr Tobacco Act came in 1934 and were both amended in August, 1935 when the Potato Act brought to the attention of the whole public the vicious destructiveness of the system of bureaucratic dictation which had been inflicted on the country.

The original act was, as I have said, drawn by Frederic P. Lee, who had also helped draw the McNary-Haugen bills, and his principal collaborator was Mordecai Ezekiel (representing Secretary Wallace). The extracts that I have previously given from my diary show to what extent others of us were in and out of the drafting. The farm organizations had very little to do with the bill, and it involved some new principles which they knew nothing about. Because of the emergency, they were willing to try anything. Their attitude would have been quite different, had permanent farm legislation been up. It appears, from the hearings before the Senate Committee, that neither Mr. Wallace nor Mr. Tugwell knew much about the bill in detail, but there is no doubt but that they had in their minds the restriction of production. All the more important questions put by the Committee members to either of them had to be answered by Mr. Lee or Dr. Ezekiel. I also appeared before that Committee and the following extracts from the hearings are of particular importance as touching on the restriction of acreage which later became the chief feature of the bill in its administration. The Committee was also very searching concerning the power granted to the Secretary to license processors, dealers and others in the flow from the producer to the consumer:

Mr. PEEK. No, I think the administrative officer must have the broadest power, and personally I disagree with the idea of acreage rental. I think I can go out and rent 50,000,000 acres of farm land and increase production at the same time. . . . So I think the idea of general acreage rental must be handled very carefully, although, owing to the peculiarity of the industry from year to year with the different crops, the authority must be general to deal with it when and where it is.

The CHAIRMAN. If you eliminate any idea of acreage reduction and it becomes generally known that under this plan you are going to raise the price of farm products, aren't you going to have such an increase of products in these crops that come under that protection that the final result will be as disastrous as it is now?

Mr. PEEK. In the first place, Senator, I have tried to make it clear that I would not eliminate that provision from the bill. I would leave it in the bill to be brought up whenever the occasion warranted, and, in the second place, I disagree with the conclusion that prices, higher prices up to a reasonable level, are going to increase production. . . .

Senator NORRIS. There is the very thing that from the very beginning of this farm problem has always bothered me. It seems to me that those figures demonstrate that it isn't a practical way to regulate production by regulating acreage.

Mr. PEEK. Senator, you are entirely correct. The Bureau of Agricultural Economics made a report some years ago to the effect that 75 per cent variation in yield from year to year of all growing crops was due to weather and pest, and not to acreage.

Senator NORRIS. Yes. In other words, God has more to do with this thing than man.

Mr. PEEK. Exactly.

Senator NORRIS. That leads to a conclusion, doesn't it? Fundamentally this bill or any other bill trying to control production by a limitation of acreage is fundamentally unsound, isn't it?

Mr. PEEK. Which one are you speaking of? The House bill?

Senator NORRIS. Yes; or any other bill where the principle involved is trying to limit acreage, curtail production by curtailing acreage of a crop. We never know when we start in how we are coming out on that kind of a proposition.

Mr. PEEK. The bill that passed the House provided for a reduction in the acreage, or reduction in the production, or both.

Senator NORRIS. Well, we agreed a while ago we can't by law enter the province of God Almighty. We can list acreage, but we can't say how much is going to be produced on an acre.

Mr. PEEK. I think that the acreage rental by itself is not sufficient; and, I think, generally applied it would be much more expensive and extravagant than going in and catching the production in the particular place where it was being produced in the particular year. Then, again, any general plan for reduction of acreage throughout the United States, regardless of the deficiency of supply in particular areas, is very unsound. . . .

The CHAIRMAN. I recognize that we have a condition here where the surplus is not the barrier to a rising price, because we have no surplus. It is purely an inability to buy, and I want to understand how if we put a tax on the processor which at once will mark the difference between the farm price and the average of the thing he buys, where are we to get the consumptive power to maintain the enormous rise at once?

Some members of the Committee, notably Senators Thomas and Wheeler, were convinced that nothing in the bill could help farm prices. They wanted monetary measures.

The sentiment in the Senate was so deeply opposed to the grant of such wide powers to the Secretary of Agriculture that it became apparent to those who had the bill in charge that it would not pass as it stood. By some arrangement with which I am not familiar, the authority to devalue the dollar, to issue three billion dollars in greenbacks, to buy silver and otherwise to change our whole monetary system was tacked on to the Agricultural Adjustment Bill. Thus the votes of the inflationists and the silver men were enlisted and the bill was passed. With the monetary sections I am not here concerned. I had nothing to do with putting them into the bill. Of course I had nothing at all to do with the monetary administration. That was in the hands of the Treasury.

The Agricultural Adjustment Act as passed practically put it up to the Administrator to find a method of meeting the emergency, for the bill itself was very general. In the Declaration of Policy, the Act stated a purpose to establish and maintain a balance between production and consumption and to give agricultural commodities a purchasing power with respect to articles that farmers buy equal to the purchasing power of agricultural commodities in the base period. The base period for all commodities except tobacco was August, 1909 to July, 1914 and for tobacco was August, 1919 to July, 1929.

This was a very faulty presentation of the problem in hand, considering the action taken later to restrict production. It is volume multiplied by price that counts. In the 1909-1914 period, comparatively few farmers had automobiles and so the problem posited was in the nature of a statistical yardstick. What we were really concerned with was the exchange of man hours of labor as reflected in annual income. The price alone of an agricultural product no more determines, year in and year out, the total farm income than the hourly rate for labor determines the worker's annual income. The underlying delusion was similar to that of the trades union in taking the price of a unit as an index to total income. For our emergency purposes, the unit price was good enough because we knew, at least roughly, the total quantity of each product that would be consumed and we could calculate total income from unit prices —although, of course, if any prices were too high, food shifts would take place.

To attain a balanced economy, accurate income statistics are needed. Through such statistics, arranged in bookkeeping form, we shall eventually be able to proceed with an accuracy that is impossible if prices instead of income are put into the foreground.

The critical portion of the Act was Part 2 in which it was said: "To provide for reduction in the acreage or reduction in the production for market, or both, of any basic agricultural commodity through agreements with producers or by other voluntary methods and to provide for rental or benefit payments in connection therewith. . . ." As noted in my diary, the words "or benefit payments" had been omitted in the draft and over their insertion we had a hot argument, for without these words the Administrator would have been limited to raising prices by taking acreage out of production—a method that, I cannot too many times repeat, I was completely against.

There were provisions for marketing agreements in which the marketers might combine to raise the prices they would pay to producers—being, in return, granted an immunity from the anti-trust laws—and there was a provision that the Secretary of Agriculture might in effect take over the supervision of any division of marketing through issuing licenses. I had some hopes of being able to effect all the price lifts that we needed through agreements, and I regarded the licensing provision as a club or threat, with a mental reservation that if ever we had to license generally we should be through. I believe that in peace time the control by a government agency of the marketing of farm products is certain to result in chaos.

The provision for a processing tax was about the same as that of the old Rainey Bill. Under Section 12—the appropriating section—I urged writing into the bill: "(b) In addition to the foregoing, the proceeds derived from all taxes imposed under this title are hereby appropriated to be available to the Secretary of Agriculture for expansion of markets and removal of surplus agricultural products. . . ." Under this provision I hoped to be able to dispose of some of the surplus through marketing agreements covering export sales in the manner of the McNary-Haugen and the other bills following the principle of the two-price system. These sentences were stricken out in the wholesale amending of the act which took place in August, 1935 and other amendments substituted.

The original act applied to these commodities: wheat, rye, flax, barley, cotton, field corn, grain sorghums, hogs, cattle, rice, tobacco, sugar beets, sugar cane, peanuts and milk and its products. That was much too broad a list for emergency administration, and by no means all the commodities were basic. It would have been enough to apply the aid to wheat, cotton, hogs, and perhaps rice and tobacco. But with the pressure on Congress to broaden the list of products, there was no time to waste. We had to take whatever bill we could get until something of a more permanent nature could be drafted.

I had no personal axe to grind, for I was active in neither farming nor business and, although I had very decided views, I felt that those views were not merely personal but represented the consensus of farm opinion gathered in a dozen years of fighting for farmers. There was a sense of responsibility to the farmers and to those members of Congress who had voted for the bill against their best judgment and only because they believed I was going to administer it—for word had gone out to this effect. As set out in the first chapter, the President had offered the job to me in April, but I had not accepted pending a complete understanding as to policy. The decision to accept came at a White House gathering on the evening of May 3rd. There were present Secretaries Wallace, Roper, Perkins and Woodin, Attorney General Cummings, Postmaster General Farley, Messrs. Tugwell, Moley, Douglas and Morgenthau, and a large number of other Government officers. It was not a particularly quiet or harmonious meeting, for everyone sensed that if the farm bill went wrong the Administration would be sunk.

Someone in the Department of Agriculture had drawn up an elaborate administrative chart, with the whole administration of the act reporting to the Secretary of Agriculture and through him to the President. The plan as a plan I thought was unworkable. But, in addition, it put the Administrator in a position where he had to go through the Secretary of Agriculture to reach the President. I had already stipulated that if I took the place I must have direct access to the President with the Secretary. Messrs. Baruch and Johnson had drawn up a very simple organization embodying the experience we had gained in the War Industries Board. This I also presented at the meeting. Both plans provoked argument but the Wallace plan met the most favor. I spoke my mind very freely and took no pains to choose gentle words. When the meeting broke up, the President asked Mr. Wallace and me to stay behind. The President took the Wallace chart and from memory transformed it into what amounted to the chart I had submitted and said something to the effect that he thought that was the way it ought to be run. The organization as revised by him met all my objections. Therefore no further reason existed for not becoming Administrator—if he still wanted me after the way I had talked in the meeting. I brought up the subject myself. I asked the President point-blank: "Do you want me to take A.A.A.?"

He indicated he did.

That was nine days before the bill became a law. On the day the bill became a law, and in order that there could be no further misunderstanding, I wrote a letter to Mr. Wallace which said, in part:

Dear Mr. Secretary:

Before undertaking the administration of the agricultural adjustment act, I think it essential to have a clear understanding and agreement of the broad principles of policy that shall prevail. It seems to me that only by this procedure can we be sure that each step taken will tend to accomplish the purposes of the administration as to agriculture.

It seems to me necessary that conferences must be held with industries and trades and with agricultural groups before policy details can be worked out. However, the whole job is one of such nature and difficulty that the authority conferred on the administrator must be as complete as the statute permits and in keeping with the responsibilities assumed.

In other words, it seems necessary that you transfer to the administrator the grant of power conveyed by the legislation, with the understanding that the administrator is serving in your place and that there will be free and continuous collaboration between you and him. In event of differences of opinion there shall be direct access to the President whose decisions shall control.

With reference to bringing in persons from the outside to help, and building up a staff both from within and without the Department, it should be clearly understood that all appointments must be subject to the approval of the administrator, and must be based on ability to do each specific job. The success of this work is so indispensable in the national interest that no other policy is thinkable. Already pressure has been tremendous to obtain promises of positions based upon all kinds of preferences. This cannot be allowed. . . .

It is perhaps impossible at this present juncture to state even broadly the policies that should prevail as to including the Administration's views in negotiations for reciprocal tariff agreements, for making appropriate efforts to regain some of our lost foreign agricultural markets which I esteem not only proper but important, the reduction of acreage or the reduction of production as the case may be, and similar problems. . . .

In a word, it is my view that the great purpose of this legislation is to increase net farm income by raising farm prices and any other means authorized by the law. . . .

On the same day, Mr. Wallace replied with a letter which said, in part:

My dear Mr. Peek:

I think you are quite correct in saying that before undertaking the administration of the Agricultural Adjustment Act there ought to be a complete understanding between us concerning the principles under which the Act ought to be administered and the procedures which are to be pursued. I am quite in agreement that it is necessary to hold conferences with industries and trades and with agricultural groups before details of procedure can be worked out, and that our specific plans ought to be held in abeyance until this has been done. On the broader questions of policy which are involved, it seems to me entirely clear that we ought to undertake acreage reduction in both cotton and corn but the extent to which this ought to go should again depend upon the outcome of our various conferences.

On only one other question is there likely to arise a difference of opinion, it seems to me, and on this question my views are well known to you. It is my feeling that, aside from cotton, we ought not to depend on a foreign market for any considerable outlet of agricultural commodities for some time in the future and that, with this in view, we ought to act for the moment as if we were a self-contained agricultural economy. . . .

There will be no difficulty, I think, about free and continuous collaboration between ourselves, but it is necessarily clear in the terms of the Act that the final responsibility rests upon me and through me upon the President. In any instance in which our opinion concerning general policy differs, we ought, of course, to carry the matter to the President rather than to risk any serious difference between ourselves. Considering his interest in the success of this undertaking, there will be no difficulty about that. Yet, in the very nature of things, since I am the Secretary of Agriculture, the weight of responsibility and decision must rest largely on my shoulders. I have no desire to hamper you in any way in administration, however, and I am sure that we shall be able in practice to collaborate without any grave differences.

As to personnel, I feel that this should be a collaborative matter insofar as the major appointments, at least, are concerned and I should not think of forcing anyone on you to whom you had an objection. At the same time, I should expect that in important decisions you would also consult me when acting. There are a few tentative commitments which have already been made and I should be grateful if you would give special consideration to these.

In undertaking so serious a task as we have before us in the coming months and years, I am grateful to have the prospect of collaborating with so able and energetic an administrator as yourself. I look forward to our association in this enterprise and assure you of my constant support.

This exchange of letters satisfied me that the administration could be conducted along the lines we had planned.

On May 15th I took office and made the following public statement:

In assuming responsibility for the administration of the Agricultural Adjustment Act, it is only fair to agriculture, to so much of industry as is affected by its operation, and to the consuming public, to state the principles of that legislation as I understand them and as it is intended to apply them.

In the first place the sole aim and object of this act is to raise farm prices. Generally speaking, it is to raise them to a point where farm products will purchase as much of industrial products as they did before the War, and to keep farm prices at that level. This is just what farmers through their organizations have been demanding for a dozen years.

To agriculture it should be said that the purpose is not to do something for the farmers. It is to enable farmers to do something for themselves that they have been prevented from doing through many long, painful and distressing years, and that they could not do without this law. It is to enable them to do what all other producing social groups do, and that is (approximately and in the long run) not to produce and send to market more goods than consumers at home and abroad want and have money to pay for.

Unless farmers will work with each other and with government to do that, government cannot maintain fair prices and restore prosperity to them—nobody can. They must help do this particular job. In adopting the law and through the work that will be done under it, the Government goes the limit to help them, but that is the most that it can do or that they in justice and fairness can ask.

To the food and textile industries, I want to make it clear that the spirit and purpose will be to act with as little interference with established institutions and methods—indeed with as little administration of any kind as is consistent with the fixed purpose of the law; namely, to raise farm prices. It is my opinion that much of that purpose can be accomplished by these industries without anything more than the aid that government and agriculture can and will give them.

The first step will be to discuss with industries and trades our purposes, to ask them what they need from farmers and from government, and to call upon them, with the help of those concerned, to work out the difficult task themselves in such manner as will least interfere with their business and established methods, with as little government interference in their affairs as is reasonably possible. But none will be permitted to forget the purpose of the legislation—to raise farm prices in the national interest.

To the consuming public it is unnecessary to say that what is to be done is to bring about economic justice—to right a social wrong—which grew up under our economic system in the false theory that the urban half of our population could enjoy the benefits of an artificial, protective system, leaving the rural half largely outside the benefits of that particular device. It seemed to work all right at first, but lately it has resulted in taking the farmer's crop away from him without paying for it. Nobody wants to do that. I am aware of no objection from labor, or indeed from anybody, to this attempt to do what is right.

Agricultural prices are and for a long time have been unduly depressed and ruinously below their fair relation to other prices. Putting them where they belong has the support of all fair-minded people and will not be a heavy burden on any person or class in our country. Agriculture must be restored to its proper place in the Nation's life, not only for the sake of the farmer but for the general welfare.

Upon the request of Secretary Wallace and myself, the President has requested Mr. Charles J. Brand to act with me as co-administrator. Mr. Brand is recognized throughout the Nation by farmers and the food and textile industries as one of our foremost authorities in the marketing of farm products.

In administering this Act, we shall draw heavily upon the advice and assistance of Frank O. Lowden and B. M. Baruch, who have pledged to the President, Secretary Wallace, and to me their cooperation.

In a month, Texas would begin picking what appeared to be a bumper crop of cotton. Hogs were in a bad way and needed attention at once; so did milk. Only on wheat had we any time left.

We had to get organized before we could do any business. That meant getting the proper people—people who knew their jobs and who we hoped would work together. That we had to organize and do some hiring also occurred to quite a number of other people. They swarmed in on us for jobs. In two weeks from the time I took office, I was told, we had about 25,000 applications, some from deserving Democrats and some from Republicans who felt they were more deserving than the Democrats because they had voted Democratic. I never before fully realized that many office seekers think their voting record is of more moment than their ability to fill any particular position. In any event, this indicates the tremendous number of people seeking employment.

Some of the applicants wrote, and maybe all of them did not follow their letters, but it seems, looking backward, that every applicant must have turned up in person. We paid no attention at all to party lines and Mr. Farley did not interfere with us. Secretary Wallace, Charles J. Brand, who came in as Co-Administrator, and I would not have stood for politics in putting together the service. I do not know to this day how the force was divided politically.

The set-up agreed upon was simple. Under the Administrators were six control or clearing divisions—Office Manager, Analysis Committee, Coordination Office, General Counsel's Office, Comptroller's Office and Office of Consumers' Counsel. The main or operating divisions were four—Production Division, Finance Division, Information and Publicity Division, and Processing and Marketing Division. Under both the Production Division and the Processing and Marketing Division were Wheat, Cotton, and Hogs and Corn Sections. Under the Production Division were additional sections for Replacement Crops and Contract Records. Under Processing and Marketing were additional sections for Food Products, Fisheries, Foreign Trade, and Licensing and Enforcement. Between these two great divisions were the Dairy, Tobacco, Rice and Special Crops Sections.

We had no trouble at all about the principal appointments. Mr. Brand knew government ways thoroughly, for he had spent many years in the Department of Agriculture and had there organized the highly important Bureau of Markets which later became the Bureau of Agricultural Economics. He had been out of the Department since 1925, engaged in private work, so he knew both the public and the private side. I selected Glenn McHugh for my Special Assistant. He was a lawyer whom I had known for years; he had worked in Washington as a legislative counsel in the office of the Legislative Counsel of the Senate, but at the time was Assistant to the President of the Equitable Life Assurance Society. He is now a Vice-President of that Society. As Executive Assistant, I picked Wayne C. Taylor of Chicago; his early experience had been in a bank in Chicago and he had later become a partner in a banking firm and their European manager. At present he is Assistant Secretary of the Treasury.

For the three key divisions, I was lucky enough to get Chester C. Davis for Production, Oscar Johnston for Finance, and General W. I. Westervelt for Processing and Marketing. I had known all these men for a long time. Messrs. Davis and Johnston were old-timers in farm activities and thoroughly experienced. Mr. Johnston was then the manager, at a high salary, of a big British-owned plantation in Mississippi. I arranged to get his release. General Westervelt, as a chief executive of Sears, Roebuck & Co., knew processing and marketing from every angle. He knew government also and had wide experience both here and abroad.

For Publicity, we engaged A. D. Stedman, a Washington correspondent of experience and ability. F. J. Hughes, who was already in the Department, became Office Manager and was very experienced and capable, as were also J. S. Dalton, Chief Economist, and R. H. Barkalow, Legal Adviser, of the Analysis Committee. Mr. Brand secured H. P. Seidemann from the Brookings Institution as Consulting Specialist for the Coordination Office. He proved to be a remarkable man and devised the whole payment machinery—a tremendous job. Mr. Seidemann picked J. B. Payne as Comptroller. C. A. Cobb, a southern newspaper man, was selected for the Cotton Section of the Production Division; and D. S. Murph, a South Carolina lawyer, was suggested by Mr. Brand for the Cotton Section of the Processing Division. Secretary Wallace recommended A. G. Black of Ames, Iowa, as Chief of the Hogs and Corn Section under the Production Division, and we took G. C. Shepard for the same section under the Processing Division. He had been with the Cudahy Packing Company and I had known him in Omaha.

Professor M. L. Wilson was the natural selection of everyone as Chief of the Wheat Section under the Production Division, for he had a thorough knowledge of the subject and had been active in promoting the Domestic Allotment Plan, while for the same section under the Processing Division we took F. A. Theis, a grain man from Kansas City who was recommended by both the grain trade and the cooperatives. For the Food Products Section, we settled on J. D. Dole of California, a member of the famous pineapple family, and from the same State we got J. W. Tapp as Chief of the Special Crops Section. General Westervelt recommended R. C. Miller as Chief of the Foreign Trade Section and G. Carlson as Chief of the Licensing and Enforcement Section—both of these sections being in the General's division. I suggested Professor Clyde L. King of the University of Pennsylvania to head the Dairy Section. We took J. B. Hutson to be Chief of the Tobacco Section, A. J. S. Weaver to be Chief of the Rice Section and R. N. Fiedler to be Chief of the Fisheries Section.

Our two great errors were in accepting Jerome N. Frank from Secretary Wallace as General Counsel and putting in F. C. Howe as Consumers' Counsel. Mr. Brand had previously known Dr. Howe as an earnest worker for consumers' interests, but unfortunately he did not know that Dr. Howe had been seriously bitten by some kind of pink bug and had accumulated a hazy, half radical, half uplifter set of views and attitudes. It turned out that he was against the profit system and was all for abolishing it—without, however, exactly knowing what he wanted to put in its place. That, as subsequently developed, was an attitude that spread through the Legal and Consumers' divisions of the A.A.A. like an epidemic. I later found that no end of intense young men in these divisions were out gunning for the profit system as though it were some kind of rapacious wolf, but not one of them knew what he was going to do if he caught up with and shot the system.

This attitude was illustrated by an experience with Dr.

Tugwell. He thought the powers given to us under the Act were large enough to permit the organizing of a Government corporation to take over the liquor trade when repeal came through. He advanced the thought that the Administration would do well to put all the manufacturers of liquor under license and to have a Government-owned corporation do all the distributing. I told him that possibly Government control would be desirable but a great deal was to be said on both sides of the question and, as far as I was concerned, I would have nothing at all to do with such a scheme unless specifically directed by Congress. We had enough trouble on our hands, I told him, in the job that had been given to us, without sticking out our necks and searching for more trouble. In any event there was not sufficient time to perfect such an organization before repeal would be an actuality. In place of such a procedure we made marketing agreements with the distilling industry under the terms of which the distillers (except one) agreed to pay to the Secretary of Agriculture for the benefit of the farmers the difference between the market price for grains which they bought and parity prices. Through the agreements and codes the industry operated as long as the N.R.A. was in effect and in such a satisfactory manner that new legislation was not enacted to regulate the industry until N.R.A. was declared unconstitutional. The credit for this remarkable result was due to the distillers cooperating with Fred Lee, my private counsel, who prepared the agreements and codes and later as General Counsel of the Federal Alcohol Control Administration had much to do with their administration.

I never personally had any serious differences with Dr. Tugwell—which simply means that he never got clearly in my way. As far as I could discover, he is a bright but not a profound young man. But he is wise enough never to get too far out on any limb or pursue any theory to its ultimate conclusion. He loves words and he loves to make speeches and especially to make speeches which seem to be expositions of some deep and fine social theory. While he often starts and stops with the words, his writings show a deep familiarity with "revolutionary technique." It does not always occur to him perhaps that there is a world where actions must eventually take the place of words.

Dr. Tugwell worked mostly through Secretary Wallace, and the change that came about in Mr. Wallace's viewpoint, I think, was the result of the Tugwell influence. Mr. Wallace is by no means brilliant. I knew both his father and his grandfather. His father was a straightforward, straight-thinking man, always trying to do the right and just thing. This he inherited from his father, whom I remember as a kind of lay preacher and he published one of his sermons in every issue of his farm paper. Secretary Wallace also is deeply religious, but this works out with him in a series of rationalizations, so that his facts always fit his theories. If the theories change, the facts change. For instance, I have heard him deeply and sincerely deplore the arraigning of class against class as the one best way to avoid reaching a sound conclusion on any national subject. And in a few days I have read a speech by him in which he arraigns class against class.

Tugwell and Frank, although very busy, found time for personal office politics. I was very busy, and, having such a broad range of responsibilities and powers, I felt that it was only elementary common sense to have someone on the outside, with no office duties whatsoever and owing allegiance only to me, to advise me on procedure. I explained the situation very plainly to Secretary Wallace and told him that I wanted personal counsel to advise me and would like to retain Frederic P. Lee—who not only knew the bill better than anyone else, but also knew government procedure. I said that I would turn over to Mr. Lee my salary as Administrator. The Secretary agreed. I said I would draft a letter to Mr. Lee and submit it for the Secretary's official approval before despatch. I wrote to Mr. Lee on June 16th, 1933 a letter which, in part, read:

Dear Mr. Lee:

Following our discussion today, I make the following proposal of employment to you:

Commencing today, I desire you to enter my employment as my personal counsel to advise me on matters arising out of the administration of Title I of the Agricultural Adjustment Act. . . .

You will be responsible personally to me and to Mr. McHugh. You are not to serve in any official capacity, but for my convenience I shall designate an office and such assistance as may be necessary for you to function properly. . . .

It is, of course, understood that any matter which I may refer to you for advice under this relationship shall be held in complete confidence, in accordance with the usual relations between attorney and client.

I have consulted with the Secretary of Agriculture with regard to this arrangement, which is not unlike the arrangement under which you were working with him without compensation for several months prior to the enactment of this Act, and he has stated that it meets with his approval.

The proposed arrangement has also been submitted to the Solicitor of the Department of Agriculture, and he advises that it is in no respect contrary to existing law.

They both understand, as of course you do, that this arrangement does not involve the expenditure of any Government funds, but is one which I desire because I know you can be of inestimable assistance to me at this time in the administration of this Act. I therefore want to employ you personally, because I believe that the proper administration at this time is imperative, and unless this job is started right, the result may not be all that we have hoped for. . . .

I advised leading members of both houses of Congress, both Democrats and Republicans, of the arrangement.

To the letter I attached this memorandum, which came back with the approvals as noted:

June 20, 1933

MEMORANDUM FOR THE SECRETARY

Dear Mr. Wallace:

Attached is a letter which I propose to send to Mr. Frederic P. Lee and which I discussed with you yesterday.

Will you advise me whether your Solicitor approves of it and also whether you do?

Very truly yours,

GEORGE N. PEEK

Administrator

Approved by Sec. subject to Solicitor's approval.

P. H. A.

Approved.

SETH THOMAS

Solicitor

That was a very remarkable set-up. It proved to be a very useful one.

Chapter VI

Undercurrents and Cross Currents

Keeping one's feet anywhere near the ground in Washington during the summer of 1933 was not easy. And besides that it was unpopular.

During the War we had a mad rush on Washington but, through the War Industries Board, we gained a degree of order. The jobs that each of us had then to do were somewhat comparable with jobs we had done before and we all had the single objective of winning the War. All the men in charge of important divisions of work had previously had experience in directing men and things and, although their work was new, they had the adaptability that comes with experience.

Compared to the War days, the Washington of 1933 was a madhouse. Many men in high places were wholly without experience in larger affairs and few had ever been in a really big public or private executive position. They often delegated important questions and reserved for themselves affairs that could be handled by a clerk. They were inundated by friends and advisers.

This was especially true of the young lawyers, college professors and social workers to whom the word had somehow gone out that a new dispensation had been given and for the first time the nation was looking to its great, serious, but hitherto unknown army of real thinkers. They came in prepared to brush aside the musty old dodos who had ruined the nation. It was an entirely new species to me. In addition came the normal army of job hunters of whom I have spoken, and finally the regiments of business men and their lawyers, all of them nervous and a good many of them quite excited at the extraordinary rumors that were floating about. The National

Industrial Recovery Act was in the air and its effects were being interpreted in every possible fashion. The confusion was made worse by the squadrons of official and unofficial press agents trying to make the headlines for their principals. The building up by press agents of ordinary, commonplace men into extraordinarily wise and far-seeing statesmen is an interesting process and gives one a fearsome awe of the powers of publicity. The individual who thus gets inflated is never the same again. He comes to believe what is said about him.

I threw myself into my job to accomplish two objectives as quickly as possible. The first was to get rid of the surpluses that had bogged prices, and the second was to push through marketing agreements in which the processors would agree to pay higher prices. In this way I thought we could quickly get money into the hands of the farmers. The processors were mostly willing and anxious to cooperate for the emergency. Their spirit, on the whole, was very fine. The farmers' organizations and the cooperatives were equally anxious to do whatever was in the national interest. We had capable men heading the major divisions of our organization and they were all working hard. But too little got done.

The General Counsel's office appeared to be the neck of the bottle, and it was quickly reported to me that the General Counsel, Jerome Frank, was dealing directly with Messrs. Wallace and Tugwell and that the three of them, together with Dr. Mordecai Ezekiel—whom Mr. Wallace had taken as his economic adviser over the heads of the whole fine and experienced Bureau of Agricultural Economics—were forming something in the nature of a departmental cabal. At first I dismissed the report as ridiculous. Later one of my associates, a level-headed man of standing and experience, arranged to see me alone at the end of the day.

"Do you know what is going on around here?" he asked at once.

"In a general way I hope I do," I answered, "but what have you particularly in mind?"

"Well," he went on, "it seems crazy and maybe it is crazy, or maybe I am crazy, but I have been to several parties now of Tugwell's and Jerome Frank's and they have a very different idea of this Administration from what we have. They are all talking social revolution and they have the idea that it is the mission of the Roosevelt Administration to turn us into some new kind of socialist state. They think the place to start is with the farmers because it is the farmers who in other countries have formed the chief obstacle to socialism.

"What I want to know is this: These fellows are testing me out. They want to see if I am for them or against them. I am not very far in yet. Shall I stop going to these meetings or shall I pretend that I am interested and find out all that I can?"

"By all means go ahead," I answered. "This sort of thing is Greek to me. We never had any of it in the farm country. Find out all you can and maybe then I can understand what it is all about."

It would not be fair to set down all the foolish stuff that came to me as being seriously discussed at these meetings. I was not a student of social revolution and hence I could not appreciate all the high aims or how they were to be realized. It would be more exact to say "chatter" than "discuss," for none of those who talked, I was told, really knew what they were talking about. The common characteristic of all uplifters is an unquenchable thirst for conversation. They were all chain talkers.

Sometimes they were very absurd, as when they had the idea that relief for the unemployed was not to be a temporary expedient but a permanent set-up to care for all those who were "industrially disinherited"—which meant men who had lost their jobs by the moving of industries or by changes in methods.

That a man might be expected to stand on his own feet and do for himself never entered their minds. They blamed all ills on capitalism and were for abolishing it, either by degrees or at once. Since few of them, as far as I could find out, had ever employed anyone, they saw no difficulties in regulating the affairs of millions. They thought charts would do that.

Since they knew neither workers nor farmers, they were very certain that both were well-defined classes very much in need of being educated in the right way and led. They saw no differences between the American workers and farmers and the Russian varieties. They deeply admired everything Russian. Those of them who had been to Russia had worn sovietized glasses all the while and they believed everything they were told. To them Russia was the promised land, and the sooner the United States became like Russia the better for everyone. Just as they could see little wrong in Russia, they could see little good in the United States. For a while the notion was popular among a certain set that relief work should be pushed forward with the intent of driving the whole country on relief and thus making the capitalistic system commit suicide.

They insisted that Harry Hopkins was with them on this and was directing his talents towards forcing relief work to drive out private work and cause an ever greater number of unemployed.

Another group was against relief on the ground that hungry men revolt sooner than fed men. They would have starved the people, on the same theory that the Russians used to force the farmers into collective farming. One, in a position of prominence, was reported to have expressed deep regret over the food distribution as only delaying the great revolution.

Nothing was more certain in their minds than that the revolution was at hand. They differed on what the revolution was to be about and what would be done afterwards. They differed also as to the blood that ought to be shed. Some were for no blood and others for a lot of blood.

These prattlers were for the most part employees of the Government and had taken the oath of allegiance. But they took the position that their high purposes gave them a super-morality that could not be confused with the morality the nation had been using. They were quite above such old-fogy, Tory, reactionary stuff as oaths of office or other religious antiquities. They owed allegiance, not to the United States—patriotism was for the non-thinking. They had a higher allegiance—an allegiance to the Cause. The end justified the means.

None of them, I was informed, when pressed to get down to brass tacks, could explain exactly what the Cause was. They had plenty of words to explain with, but the words did not make sense—they were merely strung together in the patter of a dialectic. That did not bother them. They were self-hypnotists and so by common consent they pretended to know what the Cause was—and let it go at that.

It did not so much concern me at first what the boys and girls did in the evening, so long as they attended to their work during the day, and, on the whole, there seemed to be no harm in their spending their evenings in youthful oratory. But unfortunately they did not do their work during the day and mostly were pretty useless when switched from talking. It took us some time to find out how utterly useless they were, and by then they had dug themselves very firmly into our Administration. Something could have been done about these people, had they been taken firmly in hand at the beginning, the capable ones kept and the others weeded out. But unfortunately the public took these people seriously—and that turned their heads.

None of them ever before had been taken seriously. Most of them were getting salaries which, before entering the Government service, they would have denounced as plutocratic, for many of them, I was told, had previously regarded a hundred dollars as a swollen fortune. They were crazy to get their names in the newspapers and, finding that what is called the radical line attracted attention, they became more and more violently radical—in the hope of getting big reputations as menaces. Being accepted as menaces was just too much for these Lenin baby chicks. They swelled with pride and strutted and there was no way of getting any work out of them—except as it fitted into advancing the Cause.

That had unfortunate consequences for the farmers whom we were supposed to help. Many things were delayed. Therefore it seems worth while in retrospect to set down the principal beliefs which resulted in obstacles to carrying out the Act as it was intended to be administered and which later shaped the whole progress of the Administration away from the original objectives and into a direction exactly contrary to the principles which American life has always followed.

I am unable to trace the exact paternity of any of the beliefs. Practically all of them came from the Collectivist group. They, of course, had gotten them from others. Their philosophies differed, and in that they ran true to form, for I understand that those who call themselves liberals can never agree on what is liberal and what is not. But neither Dr. Tugwell nor Mr. Frank is the kind of man to get into a dispute. They both seem to believe that he who fights and runs away will live to fight another day. They each had schools or groups who paid deferential homage and waited for the words of wisdom to fall. They managed to keep their followers from clashing. Perhaps the payroll had something to do with that, for none of them were anti-capitalistic enough to refuse their pay checks. Under other circumstances the scene would have been funny.

The first principle on which all of them agreed was the essential wickedness and waste of competition. Since few of them had ever been in business and they knew little about competition as the driving force that keeps a man on his toes, they had created a terrifying picture of competition. They implicitly believed the picture in every detail. Probably there was something pathological in their approach to competition, for very few of them had either the experience or the willingness to pull an oar in the national boat—and so they wanted some kind of society in which ability would not be matched against ability. Perhaps the world had been cruel to many of them or perhaps they were merely afraid to meet the world on its own terms.

Anyway they were afraid of competition and concocted a harrowing story of what was called the "tooth and claw" age. They recognized, of course, that competition is the keystone of the American System and that therefore this keystone had to be pulled out. They wanted to replace competition with cooperation, but few of them knew what they meant by cooperation. By dint of constant talking, they succeeded in blotting out of their minds the fact that our country and its people had been raised to a high level of wealth and prosperity by the American competitive system and, had it not been for that system, they would not have had a nice, big Government yard to play in.

These ideas became very harmful when, for example, the lawyers in the marketing agreements and codes that came to us, tried to limit or to eliminate altogether advertising by makers of brands and to transform whole industries into what amounted to cooperative societies under Government supervision. This onslaught on competition worked itself into the subsidizing of farmers for not producing. For they thought that somehow, through Government pressure, the fit and able could be forced down and, through Government money, the unfit could be forced up. And thus everyone, regardless of ability, would be on the same level of mediocrity.

The second important frontal attack was against profits.

Having been in business, I could not fully grasp the horror with which they viewed profits. They seemed to think that profits were inevitable and a part of every commercial transaction. That, I can say with considerable authority, is not true. They had no comprehension at all that ours was a profit and loss system.

The anti-profit line resulted in an insistence on the part of the General Counsel (Mr. Frank) and his fellow lawyers to put into all marketing and code agreements clauses permitting free access by Government officers to business books at all times, price-fixing clauses and finally an effort to force the subscribing concerns to split their profits three ways—one portion going to the Government, another to the stockholders and a third to the consumers in lower prices.

No business concern in its right senses would consent to provisions which amounted to giving up control without getting anything in return, and it was the insistence upon these clauses by the General Counsel's office, against my opposition, that held up many agreements in which the processors were willing to do everything within reason and absolutely to meet our views on bulk purchases from the farmers at figures far above the then market prices.

The drive against profits attracted a good deal of attention, and I took a stand directly opposite to it in my speech before the American Farm Bureau Federation in Chicago in December, 1933. I have quoted a part of that speech in the first chapter.

The third drive was for a planned economy. I cannot better express the ideas which Dr. Tugwell held at that time than he expressed them at a later date—that is, at Los Angeles on October 28, 1935:

It is not so much the getting of profits for the labor of management which causes trouble; it is the unscrupulous use which is made of a system so devised that it may be abused with impunity. Moderate gains cause no difficulties; immoderate ones do. Moderate gains do not form those sterile pools of deflected purchasing power which interrupt the healthy activity of our economy. Immoderate ones are used for speculation, for overexpansion, for the building up of extravagant business structures. There must be such an organization of industry that flows are kept constant, that purchasing power is kept equal to our productive capacity. Only in this way can our complex economic machine be kept going, furnishing services and goods to all.

So long as each industry finds itself in a position in which, through the lack of any general policy of parity, it must fight only for its own existence, and cannot join in policies looking to the general good, we never can conquer the divisive forces which bring us to periodic ruin. Each industry lacking any rules or standards of practice expends a good share of its energy in useless competition for restricted markets, thus raising its costs and making low prices impossible; each industry likewise anticipates the time of disaster which this very policy makes inevitable. It sets aside the surpluses which ought to go to workers in wages or to consumers in lower prices and so dries up the potential market for its own and others' goods. This double process of multiplying costs and hoarding gains can only be cured by cooperative action in industry similar to that which is growing into agriculture. For this whole process to emerge into workable practice I have no doubt that a long time and more patience will be required. I have the feeling also that the compulsion needed for industrial change is more likely to come from the workers than from present owners. So many of the owners stand to gain from disorder and disunity rather than from cooperation that united action for such a purpose seems remote and unlikely. It is the workers who stand to gain most—just as the dirt-farmer stands to gain most in agriculture. These, as I have said, are our natural progressive allies in the days of change which are now upon us. And so, we come back to the question of strategy. The farmers and the workers must not permit themselves to be separated. Theirs is a common cause. And hope and confidence ought to flow from the obvious gains to be got from its forthright recognition.

My preliminary drive, and I shall get to that shortly, was to dispose of depressing surpluses and, if possible, to raise domestic prices by agreement. Those were emergency measures and defensible as such. The objective of the Collectivist group was to use the Act to bring about a planned agriculture and to keep the farmers from finding out what was going on by deluging them with money. The plan, which seems to show up in the amendments to the Act, was first to undermine the independence of the farmer through putting him on a dole and, when that had been done, to regulate agriculture exactly as the Departmental bureaucrats saw fit. If the Government holds his mortgage and can decide his income by saying how much he may plant and what he will get for his crops, a farmer can assert his independence only by giving up all that he has worked for through the years.

This is the sort of thing which the A.A.A. eventually was diverted into. There is no use in mincing words. The A.A.A. became a means of buying the farmer's birthright as a preliminary to breaking down the whole individualistic system of the country.

The fourth great idea did not give me any trouble because it was so fantastic. It is set out in the above extract from Dr. Tugwell's Los Angeles address—that is, the uniting of the farmers and the workmen against something or other known as the plutocracy. The idea was to convince the farmers that they were slaves of the wealthy and, if only they asserted their independence and joined with the workmen, they could run the country. This is the old I.W.W. appeal which was imported from Europe in the days before the Russian Revolution. It neglects the outstanding fact that most farmers are capitalists and that labor generally has a real stake in the capitalistic system. Under no circumstances will they listen to such stuff. But if the A.A.A. had worked out according to the plans, farmers would have had no more than nominal ownership of their land. If the use of land is entirely directed by the Government, being on the books as the owner does not amount to much. Ownership then becomes a hollow distinction.

We had other troubles. Secretary Wallace suddenly started a drive to add to our divisions a Director of Public Interests. He was to work with a Committee on the Protection of the Public Interests, consisting of representatives from the Departments of Agriculture, Labor, and Commerce and from the Federal Trade Commission.

I never exactly found out how the public interest was to be defined or what the director was to do. I doubt if anyone knew. Maybe the inner circle thought the title was too fine not to be used or maybe they had someone of academic distinction who needed a job. Anyhow the project was killed.

In the meantime the National Industrial Recovery Act had been passed and General Hugh S. Johnson had set up the Recovery Administration. I was very much in favor of the Act as it was passed and I believed that the stabilization of a few key industries would help the general picture—a few codes in industry would supplement what we were hoping to do with our marketing agreements.

All at once, out of a clear sky, General Johnson sprang "The President's Reemployment Program." The General is always impatient of delay. He had planned and executed the registration for the draft in 1917 and he knew that a quick drive could cover the nation in a few days. The N.R.A. was moving slowly and it seemed that winter would be half over before any important number of codes would be ready. The business groups were dickering, and inside each group certain cliques were maneuvering for position. The General got the idea that with one big push he could raise wages, shorten hours enough to mop up several millions of the unemployed and get the country moving before higher prices blocked the way.

He thought that he could carry out something very like the

draft and on the same kind of wave of emotion. He sold the idea to the President—I imagine that it appealed to his sense of the dramatic. General Johnson believed in the plan as nation-saving; he had his whole soul in it and he could not see the extent of the difficulties either in forcing it through or in gauging its economic effects.

It had previously been arranged that codes in the food industries would come under the A.A.A. It was not the effect on our code-making that bothered me. It was the fact that under the Johnson plan the prices of everything that the farmer had to buy would be raised and he would be just as far away from getting an exchange value for his products as though the A.A.A. had never been invented.

Some nights later General Johnson, Glenn McHugh and I had a meeting for several hours. The general was determined to force through his scheme and he said he had the President behind him. I was just as determined to block the plan. I could not see it as other than a monkey-wrench thrown into the machinery of recovery. He was highly nervous and irritable. He talked without reservations. So did I. That was not unusual for us when we disagreed. The net result was zero. We had many other meetings—with the same result.

Even if it had been possible to put a rational farm program into effect, the N.R.A. shift of policy would probably have negatived the desired results. However, as it turned out, those in the highest authority did not want a rational farm program. Their ends were better served by confusion.

Chapter VII

The Plow-Up and the Kill

Washington in 1933 was trying to do too many things at once. And so, instead of a few things being done well, a great many things were done badly and many other things were done which should not have been done at all.

It is a prime fault of our system of Government that the President must pass upon more matters than he can possibly know about. President Roosevelt took over in his enthusiasm far more than any one man could handle. He had to depend on those around him. But, partly because the President did not avail himself of the most capable advisers and partly because no one exactly knew the policies of the Administration, most matters that needed decision went straight to the President's desk.

Before we had even opened the A.A.A. offices, cotton took over our door-step. We were in the middle of the whole complex cotton problem before we even had time to think. Cotton was ripening in the southern fields of the Cotton Belt. Cotton had been bringing from 5.5 to 6.1 cents a pound on the farm, and the weather was fighting to register a bumper crop. Another 17,000,000 bale crop such as had rolled in during 1931 seemed to be in prospect. We had to do something at once—that is, we thought we had to.

There is no space here to go into the story of cotton. American cotton ruled the world for a longer period than any other international raw material. Its history illustrates all the advantages and disadvantages of depending upon a crop, half of which must be sold abroad and whose value depends less upon domestic costs or consumption than upon the foreign conditions. Because of cotton, the South has never had the opportunity to take advantage of the American standard of living. It has had to regulate its standards by the international standards. If buying power abroad were low and the mills of England and Germany were slack, cotton prices fell and the Southern grower had to tighten his belt.

The only people in the South consistently to make any money out of cotton have been the handlers and the shippers. To them, volume means more than price and hence their interests are mostly adverse to the growers'. The most prominent advocates of low tariffs and un-American standards of living are to be found among the international cotton brokers. Of course there are exceptions. Thus it comes about that those who speak most loudly for cotton represent, as a rule, not the cotton farmers but the bankers, the brokers, the shipping men and the great army that lives on handling cotton for export. These interests need not be denounced. They diligently mind what they think are their best interests. But, if they were somewhat more intelligently selfish, they would know that breaking down the tariff structure of the United States would smash our domestic economy and they would go down in the smash.

Cotton is the ideal crop for the application of the two-price system—an American price for the American market and foreign prices for the foreign markets. It might as well be recognized that American cotton is at the beginning of the end of its world monopoly. Our country had 29,000,000 acres in cotton in 1921 and the rest of the world had 28,000,000 acres. By 1926 our acreage had increased to 45,000,000 and the world's to 42,000,000. Our big increases came in Texas and Oklahoma which are now the low-cost cotton-producing areas. In many of the older cotton states, the land has been allowed to run down and could now be put to better uses than cotton growing. It is certain, in the long look forward, that the world is going to use less of our cotton and not more. It is an economic absurdity for England to buy our cotton, turn it into cloth and ship the cloth to India and China, when both India and China can raise and manufacture cotton at home. That they are now doing. The Japanese are large takers of our cotton, but if they get a foothold in China, as undoubtedly they will, they will raise cotton and supply China, for it is only a question of time before both the British and the Japanese are shut out of the Indian market. It is an economic absurdity—which unfortunately we encourage—for the Japanese to buy our raw cotton and send it back to us as finished goods.

Our newest and strongest cotton competitor in the Western Hemisphere is Brazil. American cotton handlers are pretty well into the export trade in Brazilian cotton and for some years to come Brazilian cotton will be largely an export crop. Inevitably Brazil will manufacture its cotton and sell it to Latin-America as cloth. Coffee has taught the Brazilians the great lesson that a nation which depends upon the export of raw materials can never be free.

During the War, when I was Commissioner of Finished Products of the War Industries Board, I had a good deal to do with the textiles and I learned enough to know that no man who is not born and brought up in cotton textiles can ever really know the divisions and ramifications of the business. An enormous number of people that one ordinarily never hears about are in the chain between the producer and the consumer. Between the farmer and the manufacturer are ginners, buyers, warehousers, compressors, transportation agencies, brokers, cotton exchanges and I do not know how many other principals and agents. Between the manufacturer and the consumer are mill agents, brokers, jobbers, converters and many others. A very great number of people ride—or try to ride—on each bale of cotton. The cotton business is very old, and each of these agencies arose at some time to meet a need and to perform a useful function—many of them came in to help finance in the days when the country was short of capital. But it is gravely to be doubted that the cotton business today is of a nature to require more middlemen than any other business. Indeed cotton is an outstanding example to those who imagine that the primary function of production is to support people rather than to supply goods. Finished cottons are not nearly as cheap as they ought to be, considering what the cotton grower gets. The reason is that too many people have to be supported, and naturally not all of these people make really good livings.

It was not our job in the A.A.A. to rearrange the cotton industry. We were working against the sun. In some sections of southern Texas, cotton was almost ready to pick. The previous year, 1931-1932, had yielded a crop of 13,000,000 bales. Statistics of the Department of Agriculture indicated a carry-over in the United States at the end of the 1932-1933 season of 8,081,000 bales, as compared with an average of 3,842,000 bales (1926-31 inclusive). The carry-over in foreign countries of American cotton was 6,385,000 bales, as compared with an average carry-over of 3,768,000 bales.

Under ordinary circumstances, I should have advocated raising the domestic price and somehow getting rid of the surplus abroad, but circumstances were far from ordinary because our foreign customers had neither the means to buy and store more cotton nor the markets to justify buying in what had been considered normal amounts. The foreign markets for American textiles were practically blocked off through tariffs, administrative regulations, quota systems, exchange controls and various special agreements, and at the same time the Japanese, by reason of the state of their exchange and the low cost of their labor, were putting cotton textiles into all markets at prices which no competitors could touch. The Japanese were simply playing hob with world trade. With a big carry-over, both at home and abroad, and with a bumper crop in sight, it seemed necessary to arrest the production of the crop that was maturing. I had held it justifiable to remove a surplus as and when it appeared and that the apparent economic loss in doing this would be less than the eventual economic loss of permitting the surplus to swamp the market. The method is one to be used charily and only in an emergency, for at any time there is great difficulty in distinguishing between a real glut and a healthy surplus which ought to be conserved against a short crop. But surplus removal can be justified only as a part of a program. It cannot be the whole program. The philosophy underlying such action is very different from the philosophy of a planned agriculture brought about through acreage limitation. There is, at the best, a deal of guessing when taking out part of a growing crop—for a lot of things may happen before harvest time. But taking out acreage before the crop is planted is simply a shot in the dark.

We decided that the emergency demanded the arresting of the crop and that it was our duty to take out 3,000,000 potential bales in order to reduce what appeared to be a bumper crop in the making to the 1928-32 average of 14,000,000 bales. We held that, with the very great carry-overs, such action was fully warranted. We did not reach this decision in any bureaucratic way but only after consultation with the representatives of the producers, dealers and manufacturers. We began consideration of the project on May 23rd, and by the middle of June we had decided on the rental of 10,000,000 acres as offered by the farmers of their own free will. Since a flat acreage payment would have given us only the poorest land and thus not materially have cut down the crop, the cotton experts worked out a sliding scale of payments ranging from $7 up to $20 an acre according to the estimated yield of the land. We arranged to raise the money to pay this rental by a processing tax of 4.2 cents a pound on the cotton going into domestic production. We hoped thus to push cotton up to a fair price

—at least 15 cents a pound. That was a figure high enough under the circumstances to give a reasonable return to the producers and at the same time not burden the consumers. On cotton going into export, there would of course be no processing tax and we hoped that cutting down the American crop would give a lift to world prices.

There was a provision in the Agricultural Adjustment Act by which farmers, by taking slightly lower benefit payments, might have an option at 6 cents a pound on the cotton already in the hands of Government agencies as a legacy from the Farm Board. Each farmer was entitled to take options on an amount of cotton approximately equal to the amount that he gave up by renting acreage.

We got our program under way in July, using local committees, a vast amount of publicity and all the effort we could to have the contracts signed quickly. We actually took out of production 10,400,000 acres. The crop harvested turned out to be slightly in excess of 13,000,000 bales, and it was estimated by our cotton people that, had it not been for the acreage surrendered in exchange for benefit payments, the crop would have been larger by more than 4,000,000 bales. The payments amounted to $110,000,000.

It is unfortunately impossible exactly to appraise the effects of our actions. The President cut the dollar loose from gold, and this of itself had some effect in making domestic paper money prices higher than world gold prices. That induced some cotton speculation, as did also the belief among cotton manufacturers that our efforts in the A.A.A. would raise prices. Manufacturers anticipated their requirements. But also the N.R.A. came into being and the cotton code was in the making. Cotton prices in July went to 10.6 cents a pound—before the A.A.A. had really done anything. The advance must be put down to a speculative attempt to beat the gun—that is, to get as much cotton as possible manufactured before the code wages went in.

Once the cotton code went into effect, cotton demand and cotton prices began to decline. The N.R.A. worked directly against us. In order to save our program, we found it necessary to organize the Commodity Credit Corporation which made loans on cotton at 10 cents a pound with funds furnished by the Reconstruction Finance Corporation. I urged this action. I felt that foreign demand would come. The effect of these loans, coupled with the later failure to sell abroad, was practically to revert to the practices of the Farm Board, for naturally if a cotton grower could get 10 cents at home, even if the transaction were called a loan, he would not sell abroad or at home at a lower price without having the difference made up to him in some way. These loans were made only to growers who would agree to reduce their acreage in 1934 according to a formula to be drawn by the A.A.A. Thus, quite innocently and on the plea that not otherwise could the loans be made good, was the A.A.A. led into proposing the reduction of cotton plantings in 1934 by about 15,000,000 acres. This reduction was presumably to be voluntary. But the fact that a man in 1933 could get a loan of 10 cents on his cotton only by agreeing to make a contract in the future made the voluntary feature specious.

Those who wanted a controlled and regimented farm production based on acreage limitations won out by the very force of circumstances. The loans dammed up the surplus, made the cotton problem more complex than ever, and shifted any attempt at its solution over into 1934.

The quantity of unmanufactured cotton exported in 1933 was 5.8 per cent less than in 1932 but 10.2 per cent greater than the 1928-32 average. The price realized ranged from 7 to 9 cents a pound and the total sum received for the cotton exported was 15.4 per cent greater than in 1932 but 30.3 per cent below the average. The exports of cotton duck and tire fabric declined in quantity 19.6 per cent below 1932 and 33.5 per cent below the five-year average. Thus, although the farmers gained something on the price of the export sales, they lost in the cotton going into domestic production for the export trade.

Since then we have steadily lost our position in cotton in world trade without greatly helping domestic prices.

Certainly the present policy is destroying the foreign markets for American cotton. These markets over the years might have dwindled, but it also might be expected that American consumption would gradually rise, and, with proper attention to new land uses, our dependence upon export markets for cotton might have been minimized naturally and with a moderate amount of Governmental aid. But the preoccupation of Messrs. Wallace, Tugwell et al. with establishing a planned agriculture has hastened foreign cotton growing. It has started something of a boom. A former member of my staff in the A.A.A. wrote to me recently:

> I have just returned from Peru and Chile. Believe me, they are plowing up sugar land and they are also cultivating every possible bit of land they can and are putting it into cotton. In nearly every South American city there is a statue of Simon Bolivar, the Great Liberator, but after another year or two of this, I think they will replace them with statues of Henry Wallace, the Great Santa Claus.

The world cotton figures show that foreign cotton production is increasing at about the rate we decrease. Thus the limiting of our own acreage does not affect world prices. It only limits our cotton production and our share in the world's markets.

The pig-killing adventures of the A.A.A., together with the subsequent corn-hog program of production control, achieved more notoriety than any other acts of the A.A.A.

It might as well be said right at the beginning that this program was not without its political implications, for, whereas the cotton control was in regions that commonly voted the Democratic ticket, the corn and hog experiments were in regions which were either normally Republican or which had a way of being on the fence. All the chief corn and hog states voted for Roosevelt, and a problem which concerned many party men was how to keep their votes in line.

I have not the least desire to dodge any of the responsibility for the killing of the pigs or any part of the corn-hog program which took effect while I was Administrator. I had no part in shaping the program. It was presented to me by the Hogs and Corn Sections of the A.A.A. as the consensus of opinion among both producers and processors, and as such there seemed nothing to do but go along with it in view of the existing emergency. I did not know until later that the steam roller had been used to get producer agreements. I did know that a marketing agreement with the processors—an essential to any real plan—had been prevented by the group in the A.A.A. which was trying to get control of the big packers apparently as a prelude to controlling other private business.

The hogs and corn program distributed a large sum of money to producers. As a program to put the corn-hog producers on an exchange level in farm income, it failed utterly. And it failed because the chief under-cover attention was given to diverting the Agricultural Adjustment Act into a farm and food business regimenting device. What these people called "reform"—that is, the destruction of the American System—was made an issue paramount to putting the corn-hog farmers on their feet. The money was poured out, not alone to help the farmers but to keep them quiet while their future liberty to earn in the American fashion was being taken away from them.

In the summer of 1933, the packers were loaded with both

pork and lard. We found that about 13 per cent more hogs were bred to farrow in the fall than in 1932. Ordinarily a small corn crop means a low hog supply a year later, and in July the corn crop was estimated at only 2,200,000,000 bushels. The Department economists predicted that we would have a big hog production anyway in the winter of 1933-34. Prices were very low and the farmers everywhere were in distress. Many were bankrupt and few could see anything but bankruptcy ahead. I have spent most of my life in the Corn Belt and I know the corn-hog farmers and their problem better than I know any other problems of agriculture. It was the one on which we had principally worked through the many years of fighting for the McNary-Haugen and other bills. I knew absolutely that these farmers and their real leaders had always been absolutely against any farm measure which involved the limitation of production or which put them in the position of being charity wards of the Government. The average corn-hog farmer is a substantial citizen with a very considerable investment. It takes money to breed and finish hogs for market.

The situation was a difficult but not an impossible one, for it seemed entirely possible to arrange a marketing agreement with the packers by which, if properly protected and assisted, the price paid for hogs could be raised. They could eliminate some of the factors which caused the farmer often to get less than the full market price for his hogs and then, through the aid of Government agencies, dispose of the surplus hogs in foreign trade, if necessary, at a price lower than the domestic. The two-price system was particularly easy to put into effect with hogs because of the comparatively small number of big buyers, and these buyers had it in their power, with Government help, to influence the market price. All this I had talked over with the packers and with representative hog producers, such as Earl Smith, long before the Agricultural Adjustment Act was passed, and it was with the intention of following this program that I took the position of Administrator of the Act.

It was therefore somewhat of a surprise to find Secretary Wallace, with Roswell Garst of Iowa, his partner in the seed-corn business, out in the hog country suggesting hog-producer associations while we were still organizing the A.A.A. There came into being an informal "Producers' Committee", which, while not officially selected by Secretary Wallace, had on it Roswell Garst, Chairman of the Iowa Corn-Hog Committee; Edward A. O'Neal, President of the American Farm Bureau Federation; and Ralph H. Moyer, Secretary of the Iowa Corn-Hog Committee. These three men were in complete sympathy with (not to say dominated by) the Secretary and Dr. A. G. Black, Chief of the Hogs and Corn Section of the Production Division and a Wallace appointee from Iowa. The other members of the committee, Earl C. Smith, President of the Illinois Agricultural Association, and Clifford V. Gregory, Editor of the Prairie Farmer, belonged to the two-price school, had been active through the years in the McNary-Haugen legislation and had always been opposed to crop production control as a method of adjusting farm prices and values. This committee was later expanded and put on a formal basis as a result of state producer meetings in Iowa, Kansas, Nebraska, South Dakota, Minnesota, Ohio, Illinois, Wisconsin, Indiana and Missouri encouraged by Secretary Wallace and Dr. Black. At each of these meetings, state committees were appointed, and it was arranged to have a national meeting at Des Moines on July 18th to select a national committee. The Des Moines meeting went through according to plans and created what was called the "National Corn-Hog Producers Committee of Twenty-five". Earl C. Smith became its chairman and Ralph H. Moyer its secretary. The meeting named a sub-committee of five to carry on negotiations with the packers and to formulate a plan. This committee turned out to have exactly the same personnel as the original committee of five recognized by Secretary Wallace and Dr. Black.

The full committee met at Chicago on July 20th to confer with the representatives of the packers and to adopt a definite program. The first discussion had to do with the killing of pregnant sows. During the course of this, a committeeman from Ohio suggested buying and killing pigs weighing 100 pounds or less. This proposition was immediately pushed forward and was so well received by certain of the members as to raise a doubt that it was entirely unexpected. Dan Hildebrand of Nebraska and Joe Mercer of Kansas fought the plan, and the meeting decidedly leaned away from the restriction of production and toward a marketing plan. It adopted this seven-point program, and only the first point had anything to do with limitation:

1. Development of a production reductien plan.
2. Investigation of possibilities for enlarging the outlet for hog products at home and abroad.
3. Removal of such restrictions upon processors imposed by antitrust laws, as is shown to be essential for the effectuation of economies in operation, provided the results of such economies will be reflected in high hog prices.
4. Prevention of pyramiding processing taxes so that retail prices are not excessively increased.
5. Utilization of revenue from processing taxes and compensating taxes to keep hogs, cattle, sheep, and corn in proper relationship at parity price levels.
6. Gradual application of the processing tax, commencing with a moderate initial level, so as to hold down the floor stock taxes and to minimize any effect that the tax might have upon immediate price of hogs.
7. Avoidance of provisions in the agreement or relaxation of the Antitrust Act which would permit discrimination in favor of direct buying.

On July 26th, the producers' committee of five signed an agreement with Thomas E. Wilson, W. Whitfield Woods, and

John W. Rath, representing the Institute of American Meat Packers. The agreement set out that the producers' committee favored the development of a program for production control and the processors agreed to cooperate.

They further agreed to work to secure the approval of a marketing agreement to effect economies in distributing and selling, to urge the Government to negotiate reciprocal trade agreements to increase the export of hog products, to inaugurate a domestic sales campaign to push hog products, and to cooperate to keep expenses at a reasonable figure. The program was finally boiled down to four points, as follows:

1. Restoration of foreign markets for hog products through international agreements based on reciprocity.
2. Diversion of 2,000,000,000 pounds out of the regular consumer market by (a) subsidizing exports, (b) diversion to non-competitive consumption, as through the Red Cross and Emergency Relief, and (c) diversion to nonfood uses, such as tankage, whole hogs, or inferior cuts of hog products.
3. Develop marketing agreements which will effect economies in buying, processing, selling, and distribution, a percentage of which can be passed back to the farmer.
4. Control of production of both corn and hogs, either directly or indirectly.

The force within the Department which found its expression in apparently bona fide resolutions of the producers was for pig-killing and production control. There was little interest in extending either the foreign or the domestic markets. On August 10th, in Washington, the National Corn-Hog Producers' Committee brought in a report as for the producers which exactly expressed what Secretary Wallace, Dr. Black and Mr. Garst had been contending for and which ignored all the marketing points that had been presented by some of the producers and the processors.

The Department had on hand for immediate issue what was called "an economic appraisal" of the plan. Of course, this economic appraisal not only endorsed the proposal but also tied it into a permanent reduction program later to be formulated. Since this economic appraisal is something of a curiosity, it seems worth presenting in conjunction with the resolutions. In part it read as follows:

An immediate need from the standpoint of national recovery is to increase farm purchasing power as well as to increase pay rolls generally. Higher hog prices would add materially to farmers' buying power. The purchase of light pigs and sows at a price well above the prevailing market will add to the farmers' income during the next 6 weeks. . . .

The diversion of this quantity of hog products, 4,000,000 pigs and 1,000,000 brood sows, into nonedible uses and for relief purposes in noncompeting channels of consumption actually removes between 600,000,000 and 700,000,000 pounds of hogs, live weight, from fall and winter supplies. Furthermore, the 4,000,000 pigs will weigh about 500,000,000 pounds less than if they were marketed at weights that might be expected in a year of short feed crops. If the plan actually succeeds in taking 400,000 brood sows out that might otherwise have farrowed this fall, the marketings next spring and summer will be reduced by perhaps 500,000,000 more pounds. The total reduction in tonnage for the 1933-34 marketing season, as a result of this emergency program, is estimated to be between 1,400,000,000 and 1,800,000,000 pounds of hogs, live weight, or between 12 and 16 per cent.

This reduction can be expected to increase hog prices for the season by 25 to 35 per cent, possibly 40 per cent above what they otherwise would be without the plan.

It should be recognized that this is only an emergency and temporary program; if repeated in the future, it would be much less effective than when first tried.

Unless this program to reduce hog tonnage during the 1933-34 season is followed immediately by a definite program that calls for a substantial reduction in corn acreage and production in 1934, as well as a material decrease in sows farrowing in the spring of 1934, the after effects of this temporary program will be disastrous to hog prices during the 1934-35 season and thereafter. This artificial increase of hog prices unless accompanied by a substantial advance in corn prices is likely to result in a hog-corn ratio favorable to the maintenance or an expansion in the 1934 spring pig crop. The long-time aspects of the program cannot be overlooked during the period when a short-time program is being put into operation.

At Chicago, on August 18th, Secretary Wallace announced the sow- and pig-killing program. The plan was to buy a maximum of 1,000,000 sows, weighing not less than 275 pounds and due to farrow in the fall, and to buy a maximum of 4,000,000 pigs and light-weight hogs between 25 and 100 pounds, at premium prices.

On August 23rd the buying began and on September 29th it stopped. A good deal of trouble arose in getting the pigs to the marketing points, and speculators intervened in many situations, but on the whole the slaughter was carried through with reasonable efficiency considering the nature of the undertaking. The offerings did not run according to schedule and the purchases did not take off the market the surplus that was crushing prices. Instead of the farmers selling a million sows ready to farrow in the fall, they sold only 222,149. They held back their sows in the expectation that pigs would be worth more money. Of the pigs weighing from 70 to 100 pounds, there were bought 1,083,650. For these sows and pigs comprising the only portion that was or could be turned into food under the existing conditions, the A.A.A. paid $9,283,359.90. The big offerings were of little pigs which could not be handled by the packers for food purposes and which therefore had to be turned into inedible products, such as grease and fertilizer. These little pigs were bought to the number of 5,105,067 at a cost of $21,359,742.05. The program thus put something over thirty millions in cash into the hands of the hog producers. As an emergency measure it had its merits, but it did not meet the long range problem.

The packing interests proposed something different. They wanted a processing tax starting at 10 cents per hundredweight on November 1, 1933 and rising by stages to 60 cents for the August-October, 1934 period. Supplementing this, they wanted a marketing agreement and an undertaking by the A.A.A. to buy, on or before November 1, 1933, 150,000,000 pounds of surplus meats and lard from the stocks in the hands of the processors and remove it from competitive channels, either to be shipped abroad or to be added to the home relief allotments. They believed that the heavy stocks in their hands, together with the heavy processing tax that the trade feared, were the chief weight holding down prices. The marketing agreement was never made. I declined to make an issue of it, as with tobacco, because the packers would not agree to pay certain minimum prices. They did express the opinion that these minimum prices would be reached. But an expression of opinion did not satisfy me. The processing tax was finally fixed by Secretary Wallace at 50 cents per hundredweight. This led to an unfortunate situation. The processors' committee said they had agreed with the producers' committee on July 26th on an initial processing tax of 10 cents per hundredweight—or about 25 cents a head. With this understanding, General Westervelt, as head of the Processing and Marketing Division, had made certain commitments for the A.A.A. The Secretary during the latter part of October wavered between a 25-cent and a 50-cent tax. Chester Davis and General Westervelt later got the Secretary to agree to a 10-cent per hundredweight tax, and he started for Chicago with such a tax in mind. I was told that on the way Jerome Frank buttonholed him and dissuaded him from signing. Why the General Counsel should have mixed into a purely administrative matter of the kind, I do not know. The breach of faith with the processors was too much for General Westervelt, and he insisted on resigning. I persuaded him to stay on.

Chapter VIII

Recovery or Reform?

Earl Smith never agreed with the economists' views as to procedure. He advocated paying a premium on the lighter weight hogs or penalizing through price the very heavy hogs. This he thought could be accomplished by an agreement between the buyers and the representatives of the producers. He was unable, however, to make the economists see it.

We had a few bright spots. Wheat was one of them. Professor Wilson was at the head of our Wheat Section and, with due regard for the drought which swept so much of the wheat country, put his plan effectively into operation.

But much of our time was taken in simply trying to find out why agreements and codes did not get through and in avoiding an open clash with the Tugwell-Frank group. We had to fight for recovery as against reform. The cabal tried to carry matters directly to the Secretary instead of routing them through the A.A.A. This was in the face of the fact that it was understood as early as July, 1933, that the A.A.A. was only temporary and the permanent work would be transferred to the Department as rapidly as possible. They pushed their own people into key positions. The employment of lawyers caused endless trouble. At one time, Mr. Frank had 130 men on his staff at salaries far above those generally paid in Government service. I remember especially one man whom Frank took on at $4200 a year, although he had graduated from law school only that spring. Lee Pressman was another picked out as a favorite. He was either a friend of Jerome Frank and Dr. Tugwell or became one, and, when Dr. Tugwell organized his Resettlement Service, he took Mr. Pressman with him.

Mr. Brand was more intimately concerned with personnel

than I was, and he wrote me a long memorandum on September 12th. At that time the Inner Circle was making a drive against James E. Jones whom Mr. Brand had placed in charge of selecting personnel. He stood in the way of some of the appointments suggested by the Frank group and also he would not consent to the salaries demanded. Mr. Brand is a substantial, balanced man and his presentation of conditions came from the heart of one trying to do a big job in the midst of pettiness. Here are some extracts:

The proposal that Agricultural Adjustment Administration positions whether classified or un-classified, be approved by the Secretary's immediate office under restrictions a, b, c, and d, is in my judgment violative of the understanding with the President under which the responsibility of organizing and conducting the Agricultural Adjustment Administration was accepted. Therefore, I cannot agree to the proposition as stated. To illustrate my reasons, I need only remind you that our general counsel was selected by the Secretary under precisely the program outlined. . . .

Increasingly for many weeks members of the staff, contrary to the formal written rules of procedure of the Administration, have carried many matters direct to the Secretary and his office. This is thoroughly bad administration. In some cases decisions on important matters appear to have been made, of which my first knowledge was obtained from the press on the following day.

The Secretary's instructions to you that henceforth all intercourse with the Bureau of the Budget shall be through his office is likewise in contradiction with the agreement with the President as to how the work under the Agricultural Adjustment Administration was to be administered. It seems to me that we should ask the President to state whether our understanding or the Secretary's on these matters is correct. I know that you have not relied on your memory on this point, but have kept the pencilled sheet showing the President's idea as to our administrative relations to the office of the Secretary.

If we are to do our job the staff must be responsible to us

in appropriate degree. The Secretary's requested course of procedure would further undermine the sense of responsibility and loyalty so essential to getting a big and difficult task done. The acceptance of his various proposals concerning personnel relations, would, in my opinion, quickly destroy our leadership in the Administration.

There has been a "jam" in the personnel situation, but it has not been due to negligence or incompetence on the part of anyone. Since May 12 when the Agricultural Adjustment Act was signed, we have made approximately 3,500 appointments. I estimate that our present staff numbers more than 2,800. . . . Delays inside the Department have generally been due to one or more of the following:

1. Failure on the part of the officer making the appointment to supply adequate information on which to base action, or to submit appropriate endorsements. Up to a few weeks ago lack of adequate information has characterized particularly the requests emanating from the office of the general counsel.

2. Recommendations of salaries in excess of rates justifiable for the work to be done, for the experience of the person to be employed, or in relation to the compensation paid elsewhere in the government for like service. The F——— and M——— cases are in point. It is my understanding that Mr. F.'s appointment has been approved at $4,200. This was done as of August 15 without your approval or mine. He graduated from law school this spring. Under the salaries' classification act, the scale of which has been recommended by the special committee appointed by direction of the Executive Council, a new graduate would rate an entrance salary of $2,400. Under the act the maximum for the grade is $2,600. . . .

The 51 attorneys in the law division receive an average yearly compensation of slightly more than $5,300. The average salary of the approximately 30 lawyers in the Solicitor's office is $4,250. The average yearly salary of all the lawyers in the Department of Justice, I was told today by the Assistant Attorney General, is approximately $4,200. We shall not be able to justify this situation before the Committee on Expenditures of the Department of Agriculture in the House of Representatives when our expenditures are subjected to investigation. . . .

Mr. M. was offered a position in the Administration at a time when he was receiving a salary of $1,320 per annum in the Crop Production Loan Division. Mr. Frank recommended a salary of $5,000 per annum. This seemed to me grossly excessive for the job of a docket clerk. Originally the only objection to his appointment related to the salary rate. Subsequently many other questions with which you are familiar arose. Subsequently also he consented to a rate of $3,800 per annum. I have no doubt that with proper negotiation he would have consented readily to accept a salary of $2,400, a rate likewise more in keeping with the duties that should be performed by a hearing clerk.

No man with experience in the selection of personnel, after an examination of the cloud of endorsements furnished by Mr. M. and after reading his claims to excellence, would in my judgment have dreamed of appointing him. Dr. Y. told me on the telephone, after I explained that he was to be made chief hearing clerk, that he regarded him as "unqualified." May I add he is not only unqualified but disqualified and incompetent. I need recite only a single instance. . . .

3. Proposals to pay salaries in excess of the minimum set forth in the applicant's own personnel memorandum data. An example of this situation is the case of T. F., also recommended by the general counsel. Mr. F. had one year of law, had never occupied a permanent job before, was not yet 21 years of age, in his application expressed willingness to accept $1,440 per annum, and was recommended by Mr. Frank as a junior attorney at $2,000. . . .

4. Recommendations for appointment to legal positions in a few cases of persons that were not to perform legal duties. The K——— case falls in this category. Mr. K.'s duties were purely clerical, but Mr. Frank recommended his appointment as an attorney. . . .

Inadvertently the Secretary himself has, I fear, contributed very greatly to our difficulties. For instance, on August 11 he joined in recommending the appointment of Lee Pressman as chief attorney at $6,000 per annum. I had taken this matter up with Mr. Frank and the recommendation was made after he had obtained Pressman's consent to this figure, although Pressman wanted $7,000. Within a few days I learned that the Secretary himself changed our $6,000 to $7,000 on the appointment paper, and under date of September 11 the Bureau of the Budget approved $7,000, undoubtedly under the misapprehension that it was done with our approval. . . .

5. . . . The dastardly whispering campaign . . . has gone so far that I am told that Dr. A. G. Black has stated, in the presence of other employees that not only . . . but even I myself "are going to be fired."

It is impossible for me to imagine a greater impropriety. It warrants giving consideration to the necessity of asking Dr. Black to make proper apologies or to resign. I am sure you will agree with me that such statements are highly improper and should be rebuked. It is unthinkable that such conduct should be permitted to go on. If continued it can only result in the complete destruction of the esprit de corps of the Administration.

The relations between the Administrator's office and the General Counsel were not helped by the visit which Secretary Wallace, Mr. Brand and I had made to the President and his suggestion, at our instance, that Mr. Frank be transferred from the A.A.A. to some other branch of the Government. That I have told about in the first chapter. The inner ring was evidently out to "get" Mr. Brand; they also wanted to be rid of me. They wanted to purge the A.A.A. of all business men or any others who did not welcome the coming of the new day of revolution.

Mr. Brand was a marketing expert and he knew what could be done by the cooperative effort of the big food processors. It may be recalled that Mr. Brand had, years before, organized the highly important Bureau of Markets of the Department of Agriculture—which became the Bureau of Agricultural Economics. He organized for the A.A.A. a Food Industries Advisory Board made up of the leading food men of the country. Among its members were: Earl D. Babst, Chairman of the Board of the American Sugar Refining Company; James F. Bell, President, General Mills, Inc.; Colby M. Chester, President, General Foods Corporation; Gordon C. Corbaley, President, The American Institute of Food Distribution, Inc.; J. S. Crutchfield, President, American Fruit Growers, Inc.; R. R. Deupree, President (Chairman of the FIA Board), The Procter & Gamble Company; Arthur C. Dorrance, President, Campbell Soup Company; S. M. Flickinger, President, S. M. Flickinger Co., Inc.; A. F. Goodwin, Chairman of the Board, First National Stores, Inc.; John A. Hartford, President, Great Atlantic & Pacific Tea Co.; William F. Heide, President, Henry Heide, Incorporated; Howard Heinz, President, H. J. Heinz Company; A. T. Johnston, President, The Borden Company; Joseph H. Kline, Housum-Kline Company; M. Lee Marshall, Chairman of the Board, Continental Baking Corporation; William M. D. Miller, President, Pennsylvania Grocers Association; G. M. Moffett, President, Corn Products Refining Company; John W. Morey, President, Morey Mercantile Company; Francis E. Kamper, President, C. J. Kamper Grocery Co.; Albert H. Morrill, President, The Kroger Grocery & Baking Company; Walworth Pierce, President, S. S. Pierce Company; Frederic S. Snyder, Former Chairman of the Board, Institute of American Meat Packers; Sylvan L. Stix, Vice President, Seeman Brothers, Inc.; John Stuart, President, Quaker Oats Company; G. F. Swift, President, Swift & Company; Charles C. Teague, President, California Fruit Growers Company; Roy E. Tomlinson, President, National Biscuit Company; Karl Triest, President, Haas Baruch & Company; Fred Wolferman, President, Fred Wolferman, Inc.; S. Clay Williams, President, R. J. Reynolds Tobacco Company; Leonard E. Wood, President, California Packing Corporation; and Samuel Zemurray, Managing Director, United Fruit Company.

These men represented the ownership and experience of many of the food manufacturing and distributing industries. They were eager to do anything in their power to help out our work. Arthur Dorrance of the Campbell Soup Company volunteered to raise the buying price of tomatoes by five dollars a ton. John A. Hartford of the A & P, Albert Morrill of the Kroger stores and A. F. Goodwin, speaking for Charles Francis Adams of the First National Stores, agreed to distribute all relief foods at cost. The manufacturers with but one or two exceptions had agreed to supply them similarly. The men were anxious to do anything within reason and some things beyond reason. In effect they volunteered for the duration of the war. Mr. Brand had something really big in hand—something which might have gone very far in a wholly American spirit. Dr. Tugwell addressed the gathering. His speech unfortunately was not reported.

In effect he told the men who had come to help that they were not straight—that they would have to go into some new kind of school and learn business all over again in a new way. He was contemptuous of their offers and their efforts. The men had come to help frame a plan. Tugwell suggested no plan. He simply rambled on. No one knew just what he was talking about. As he proceeded, no one cared. After later discussions the committee disbanded.

It may be that Dr. Tugwell made his speech in order to force Mr. Brand out. It may be that he made it to prevent men of business experience and broad knowledge from getting a foothold in the A.A.A. It may be that he made his speech for both these reasons. Or it just may be that he did not know any better. I do not know.

The collectivist group within the Department became bolder. In the tobacco agreements they made a drive to take over control of the industry.

The meetings between the tobacco representatives and the

attorneys from our General Counsel's office grew bitter. The tobacco companies in the flue-cured markets had agreed, after several meetings and some persuasion, to set a buying price about 40 per cent above the market. The farmers desperately needed the money. The A.A.A. attorneys, instead of getting the agreement through and helping the farmers, held out for a supervisory control and an incessant inspection of the books. They frequently threatened, I was told, to take over the industry. The tobacco men appealed to me. I found they had right and justice on their side. I decided to take the matter directly to the President as a major issue—for unless the drive to control business were halted in the Department, we were going to get just nowhere in helping the farmer through marketing agreements. On October 5th, I wrote a full memorandum and on the next Sunday night I presented the whole question to the President in the presence of Secretaries Roper, Ickes, and Wallace and General Johnson. Here are some extracts from that memorandum:

The flue-cured markets opened in eastern North Carolina late in August. The large supply of tobacco and the low prices offered for it created a situation so critical that on September 1 the Governors of North and South Carolina closed all markets until September 25, and appealed to the Secretary and our Administration for aid. The markets re-opened on September 25, and prices have risen somewhat in anticipation of assistance from us. . . . This agreement is proposed to meet the situation.

(*a*) Parties—The agreement is a limited marketing agreement between the Secretary of Agriculture and 8 of the leading domestic manufacturers. This domestic group of 8 customarily purchases 90 per cent of the flue-cured tobacco used for domestic manufacture. The buyers of export grades (about 60 per cent of the total crop) were unwilling to enter into this marketing agreement.

(*b*) Terms—This domestic group agrees to purchase between September 25, 1933, and March 31, 1934, at an average price of 17 cents per pound, a minimum of 250,000,000 pounds of the present crop of this tobacco. This represents about 50 per cent of the unsold market supply, and the rest of the crop will, as usual, be bought for export. . . .

(*c*) Objectives—Parity price is estimated to be 17 cents, and increases by 50 per cent last year's price and the market price early this season. Therefore, the farmer should receive an increase in price on the domestic portion amounting to between $12,000,000 and $15,000,000 if the agreement is effective. It is also expected that the price of the tobacco sold for export may be increased proportionately because of buying by the domestic group, so the total increase to the farmer may aggregate between $20,000,000 and $25,000,000. . . .

This agreement has raised certain issues with respect to the basic policy of our Administration. At the public hearing and in many conferences since, not only between the domestic group and our officers, but also in our Administration Council, the following issues have been discussed and are here stated because of their fundamental importance:

. . . The manufacturers feel, because of licensing and other provisions inserted by our group in the first draft of the present agreement and because of charts, specific comments on excessive profits, advertising, and other matters, there is a disposition by some members of our Administration to assume control of the industry as soon as possible. Therefore, they have attempted to determine by definition in the agreement the extent of control intended, because they state the possibility of their undertaking this agreement depends on the extent of the control to be exercised. . . . Some of our representatives have suggested, because of the apparent impasse with respect to these issues, that in lieu of this agreement—

(1) We take direct control of the markets by licensing all buyers at once.

(2) We enter the markets immediately to stabilize prices at or near parity by purchasing flue-cured tobacco; . . .

I feel, and I have the concurrence of the majority of our Administration Council in this feeling, that this agreement should be approved. . . .

I recommend the agreement because I conceive our primary job is to get a fair price to the farmer, and in so doing we should also protect the consumer. I do not conceive that the Government should take over or control, by license or otherwise, any industry which appears to be willing to cooperate with us in attaining these objectives.

The President approved my stand and suggested that the agreement be signed. That overruled Secretary Wallace and Jerome Frank. They did not like it. Secretary Wallace called a meeting in the evening a couple of days later and invited Clay Williams, chairman of the group representing the tobacco companies. For four hours the Collectivists talked their philosophy. Mr. Williams took them on one at a time. A day or two afterwards the agreement was signed. The net result to the farmers was that whereas they had received from their 1932 crop of flue-cured tobacco $43,000,000—from the 1933 crop, due to a better and higher grade crop and higher prices as the result of the agreement, they received more than $122,000,000, only $9,000,000 of which came from benefit payments. Shortly before I left A.A.A., a committee from North Carolina, headed by Governor Ehringhaus and Senator Bailey, called on me to extend formal thanks for what had been done for the people of North Carolina. Among other things, Governor Ehringhaus said, "Not only has the economic position of our people changed, but their hearts and souls have changed"—so the fight was worth while.

The show-down on tobacco made the cabal even more determined. It became out of the question to get anything done against a group working for objectives other than those which the A.A.A. had been set up to achieve. Messrs. Lee, McHugh, Taylor and Westervelt impressed this upon me unmistakably. I determined to make another drive to get rid of Jerome Frank, and on November 15th I sent this note to Secretary Wallace:

Dear Henry:

The situation with Mr. Frank as General Counsel has become almost impossible to a number of our most valuable assistants and to me. I therefore urge his removal and the selection by us of a new General Counsel. If you do not agree, may we not discuss the subject with the President?

Not receiving an answer, I sent, on November 25th, this further note:

Dear Henry:

May I remind you of my note of November 15 about the General Counsel. I suggested in that note his removal and the selection of a new General Counsel, and urged that if you did not agree, we discuss the matter with the President. Since that time in our discussions I have indicated to you that I have lost all confidence in Mr. Frank. You, of course, understand it is my desire to do whatever the President asks me to, but if this matter is to be presented to him for determination, I should like to be present at the discussion.

I received no reply to the second note. Many disturbing things were happening. I learned that milk agreements were being held up for the same reasons that had blocked the tobacco agreements. What was going on may be gathered from this letter which I received from a responsible attorney:

However, there is one condition which I think should be eliminated from the department. Bear in mind that producers of milk have to deal with distributors in the disposal of their product and, I believe the great majority of the people of this country still adhere to the theory that continuance of private business is a national policy.

On the 17th instant, in a conversation with Mr. Lee Pressman, of the legal division of the A.A.A., he asked me what I thought of the Government taking over the control of milk.

I said that municipal operation of milk plants was not feasible, nor was a monopoly to one company feasible. Mr. Pressman said he meant the Government of the United States to take over such operation and when I countered by saying then why not grocery stores and department stores, etc., he said "Why not?"

When I said that is "State Socialism" or "Communism," he said "Call it what you may, this plan is failing, and government operation has to come."

Other agreements and codes were held up. I complained to the President and at his request supplied him with a detailed list of them.

Dr. Tugwell evidently thought it high time to throw out an anchor to windward—as evidenced by this memorandum from General Westervelt dated November 29th:

Dear Mr. Peek:

Dr. Tugwell, the Assistant Secretary of Agriculture, was in my office this afternoon and expressed himself as being interested in getting codes and agreements through as rapidly as possible. Dr. Tugwell stated that under no circumstances did he wish to be placed in the position of delaying action on any codes and agreements. . . .

With reference to the question of access to books of industry, the Assistant Secretary would naturally like to get complete access, but was of the opinion that if this could not be had, some satisfactory middle ground might be reached. . . .

It had been our original intention, as I have previously set out, to provide in the A.A.A. the needed machinery to run the two-price system—an American price for American consumption and competitive foreign prices for export. We had used the device, after a fashion, with the wheat of the Pacific Northwest, but later the drought solved the wheat export problem for the time being. The issue came squarely up with butter at the very time the Government was supporting the market through loans. Secretary Wallace about-faced and repudiated what most of us had regarded as a fundamental of the Act.

We had arranged for the opening up in Europe of a considerable market for American butter, provided we could put the butter in at a competitive price. That price was lower than our domestic price—it is not necessary here to go into all the intricate details of translating a foreign price in managed currency into an American paper money price. I requested an advance of $500,000 out of the moneys to be raised by processing taxes, in order to equalize the difference between the domestic and the foreign price.

The order for the advance of funds had to be signed by the Secretary of Agriculture. Mr. Wallace was at Warm Springs with the President, leaving Professor Tugwell in charge as Acting Secretary. The question was squarely one of bringing into play the two-price system and making the tariff effective on agricultural products. That had been the objective of the farm fight over the years. That had been the specific remedy promised by Governor Roosevelt in his Topeka speech to carry out the pledges of the Democratic Platform. That, and not the socialization of agriculture, had been the ostensible purpose of the Agricultural Adjustment Act. A good deal more than butter was involved in the question. The decision had to be between the American tariff system and the socialization of agriculture so as to cut production to the requirements of a planned economy.

Professor Tugwell telephoned Secretary Wallace and, as a result, sent a memorandum to Major Robert M. Littlejohn, in direct charge of the matter for the A.A.A., refusing the authorization on the ground that the Secretary, as a matter of general policy, did not look with favor upon the subsidizing of exports and would not authorize dumping. It so happened that dumping was not involved in this case, for the importing nation had no objection to receiving the butter. The "subsidizing of exports" was involved and had to be involved, for "subsidizing" or "assisting" is a part of the two-price system. On December 1st, I wrote to the Secretary a memorandum in which I said, in part:

We are now engaged in shipping wheat from the Pacific coast to foreign countries and are meeting the competition of other foreign countries. Recently we made up the difference to the War Department on butter for shipment to the Philippines between the price quoted by a foreign country and the price prevailing in the domestic market. In both of these cases the money to make up the difference between foreign and domestic prices will come from the avails of processing taxes. These activities and similar ones are contemplated and authorized under Section 12 (b) of our Act.

On the next day, Professor Tugwell wrote a memorandum to the Secretary, sending a copy to me. In this he said:

My decision not to consent was my own, but I assumed that you would agree that our agricultural trade cannot possibly be improved by selling abroad at a price lower than the market at home. This practice has been condemned in every international conference; it was the subject of special treatment in our recent tariff truce agreement; it is recognized as provocative of retaliation. I also assumed from your recent statements that a sound foreign trade must be based on equal exchange between countries. The practice of subsidization is only a method of escaping from the acceptance of imports, it amounts to a bonus to customers to take goods off our hands regardless of willingness to accept goods from them.

The Tugwell memorandum thus set out a position absolutely contrary to the pledged agricultural policy of the Administration and declared in favor of the internationalist position advocated by Secretaries Hull and Wallace but which had been scotched by the President's message to the London Conference. This memorandum definitely settled the point. The Agricultural Adjustment Act would not be used for the purposes for which it was drawn, and the President's campaign pledges became a scrap of paper. Professor Tugwell was not acting on his own but with the consent of Secretary Wallace, who was at Warm Springs with the President. Perhaps the Secretary discussed the pledge-scrapping with the President. I do not know. On December 4th, I sent this memorandum to the Secretary:

I have noted Dr. Tugwell's memorandum to you concerning the export of butter.

There is an apparent difference of opinion between us as to the policy involved. His statement—"I also assumed from your recent statements that a sound foreign trade must be based on equal exchange between countries"—is interpreted by me to be a free trade policy, as opposed to the barter policy, which I favor and which I thought the Committee on Foreign Trade Policy was set up to effectuate.

On the bottom of the memorandum, the Secretary wrote: "This interpretation does not seem warranted to me," and returned it. That is the only explanation which has ever been made of why the Agricultural Adjustment Act was turned from a device to help the farmer into a power to regiment him. In effect the Secretary declared that public funds raised by processing taxes must not be used to promote plenty. He had no objection—the record shows—to using such funds with wanton lavishness to promote scarcity.

That was the beginning of the end. If the marketing agreement and the foreign trade features of the Act were to be dropped and the whole attention centered upon limiting and regimenting production—if the Act were going to be used against the farmer and the nation instead of for them, I did not want to administer it. I wanted to be on the outside fighting it.

I had no personal quarrel with Secretary Wallace, but I told him that, according to my original stipulation with the President, I should have to discover from the President in person exactly how he wanted the Act administered. If he wanted it the Wallace way, I should have to leave. If he wanted it my way, then Mr. Wallace's course was to cooperate.

The show-down on interpretation never came. The President, as I set out in the first chapter, sent for me and discussed a new job. He said he wanted to keep both Mr. Wallace and me in his Administration and thought that I was especially fitted to work out a foreign trade program. All these facts I have already related.

I resigned on December 11th, 1933. General Westervelt resigned at about the same time, as did numerous others. Messrs. McHugh, Taylor, Miller and a number of others went with me in the new work. Fred Lee went to the Federal Alcohol Control Administration as general counsel.

The unanswered question is whether or not Mr. Brand and I were ever anything more than window dressing to give confidence to Congress and the farmers until the secret plans could be matured. It will be remembered that Congress—and especially the Senate—was against the Act if it were to be administered by Wallace and Tugwell. Had the Wallace-Tugwell plans been known in the beginning, most certainly neither the farmers nor Congress would have accepted the Act.

It would seem that Mr. Brand and I were kept in front only until public funds could be used to organize a machine and purchase the acquiescence of enough of the farmers to establish the system of regimented production.

Everything I have since learned confirms me. For instance, take this letter from one of my former assistants:

> I went down there at your request, and only at your request. Rex Tugwell years ago wrote his doctor's thesis under me. I called on him. He introduced me to Jerome Frank as his friend. This led to many conferences among the three of us that might not otherwise have been held. I was not in every conference but I was, I believe, in enough to know what was going on. . . .
>
> In the early days before my appointment and just before you took office, you and I talked over the price situation. You believed that to raise prices on milk, affecting every consumer and most farmers in the United States, would be one good means of letting the people of the United States learn that the administration was in earnest. I pointed out that prices should be increased by September 1st to be effective.
>
> In one of my early talks with Secretary Wallace he told

me that he wanted milk prices put up. He pointed out that this we could do at once, whereas his checks would not reach the farmers until August. Just as soon as his checks were out he went out to Wisconsin and said that the Cooperative leaders were "milk distributors in overalls." I shall always feel that he wanted the Coops killed just as soon as he could get his own plan of regimenting farmers sufficiently before the public. . . .

The Chief of the "—— Bureau" was a Socialist. The efforts of that world-famous Socialist were directed at killing milk distributors and advancing the cause of public ownership of the milk supply. His comments as to the agreements were always petty, and never revealed any understanding of the matter.

Jerome Frank was "counsel." Time after time he told me that he "had been the paid servant of these big plutocrats," always referring to big business men, that he had "made $80,000 a year working for them," that he "was through working for them," and that he "was going to destroy them if he could." This was not an occasional remark. This was his usual approach. As to milk licenses, he rewrote them often in words that meant nothing to me. I often said to him that if any interpretation as to their meaning arose, I would have to refer such to him because I did not know what his language meant. . . . He had outside conversations with people looking toward changing policies, so as to place on the distributors a competitive situation they could not live under. I do not believe that a single one of the agreements put up to you had price differentials not justified by the facts. I was trying to meet the demand of the farmers for a better price on milk. The results of his efforts were to "kill the distributors." Then came the time when he became so personal in his drive at you that his remarks could not be taken seriously.

From all of these folks came such remarks frequently as the following: "The capital system is all done for anyhow. We might just as well kick in its slats now as later. Why wait for the next Depression?" Most of that crowd, in their effects, were Communists. Indeed one day one of the Coop leaders told me that he could get tips from the Communists' headquarters in New York City as to what was going on before I knew what was in the wind.

CHAPTER IX

THE MUDDLE OF FOREIGN POLICY

THE new job which the President asked me to undertake in December, 1933—that of preparing a report and making recommendations on foreign trade policy—was a real job and exactly in line with the Five Points that I originally gave to the President as a condition precedent to taking office in his Administration. I recommended something in the nature of a foreign trade authority as a way of managing the two-price system—that is, of getting an American price for domestic consumption and a world price for export. The Administration had been trying to settle on a foreign trade policy but without any results whatsoever. The Democratic platform had been explicit enough to give a guide. But the emergency in which the Administration found itself was taken as an excuse by everyone in authority to advance whatever pet theory he had been nursing. It seemed that the emergency was an excuse for anything. For instance, those who had previously advocated joining the League of Nations as a peace gesture found all at once that World Cooperation was essential to domestic recovery and reemployment. Likewise the free traders discovered that our tariffs—the Hawley-Smoot Act in particular—had caused the depression and that the only cure was free trade. No one that I can recall mentioned the party platform. The doctrinaires were in the saddle and would have nothing less than a perfect world. The perfect world was one remade according to their doctrines. The President stood in the center of what might be described more elegantly but what to me was just a mental mess. Everyone had opinions and theories in abundance, but few had any facts.

There could be no policy until one school of thought definitely triumphed. The collectivists who wanted a planned economy with a great increase of government could not advocate any movement in favor of lower tariffs because an inrush of lower-priced foreign goods would knock out all their schemes for fitting domestic supply to domestic demand. The A.A.A. was developing as a method of planning the economy of farming and there was no point that I could see in reducing domestic acreage if foreign acreage were going to take its place. I had planned to dispose of the domestic farm surplus abroad in whatever manner seemed most expedient and to keep an American price through the tariff and if necessary through licensing imports under Section 8 of the A.A.A. The N.R.A. with its price and wage provisions was trying to sustain American industrial prices, wages and purchasing power on an American scale, and N.I.R.A. contained provisions that could be used to prevent raids by foreign goods. The two great recovery measures thus were founded on the idea of effective tariff and other protection.

The internationalists had exactly the opposite thought. They held that international trade was the fountain of domestic prosperity and that the United States and all the other nations of the world were in the economic doldrums because they did not trade enough, and that, if only tariff and other barriers throughout the world were lowered, trade would start up and domestic prosperity would follow. They had the opinion, or rather conviction, that international trade was a cause of prosperity and somehow differed from domestic trade which is a result of prosperity. This school had temporarily triumphed after the inauguration, and Secretary Hull went to the World Economic Conference at London, confident that he would be able to enter into agreements putting the United States on an internationalist basis. However, the internationalist approach seemed to be demolished by the President in his message of July 3rd to the Conference in which he said:

. . . I do not relish the thought that insistence on such action (stabilization) should be made the excuse for continuance of the basic economic errors that underlie so much of the present worldwide depression. . . . The sound internal economic system of a nation is a greater factor in its well-being than the price of its currency in changing terms of currencies of other nations. . . . We must rather mitigate existing embargoes to make easier the exchange of products of which one nation has and the other has not. . . .

In this message the President put his foot down on any attempt to commit the United States to any kind of international stabilization agreement or trade policy designed primarily to further international free trade. He stood up for foreign trade, not as a thing of and for itself, but as an adjunct to domestic prosperity. That was exactly my view, but I had nothing to do with his message, and I do not know who inspired it.

I cannot see that foreign trade differs in any important respect from ordinary domestic trade or that it is necessary to bring into its discussion any principles of ethics or of philosophy that do not equally hold with domestic trade. The United States within its continental boundaries normally does about one-half the business of the whole world. We have an immense free trade area of our own, and our primary problem is to see that within our own borders the returns for productive effort by various groups are maintained upon levels which will permit the free exchange of products between these groups. Our problem is to maintain free trade at home within a balanced economy.

This means that an American price must everywhere in our country be maintained for American effort. That is the object of the tariff and the protective system. The whole farm struggle for what we called "equality" has been to get an American price for that part of our farm products which was sold in the American market. If we have within our borders any considerable group which has not the American standards of living, then we must raise the standards of that group to the American level or the American level will sink to the level of the lower group. If the whole world had the same level of living standards, free trade might be possible and even desirable, but in that event it still would be limited by the obvious advantages derived from the growing and making of most things near to the point of consumption. For instance, if only 5 per cent of a population wears shoes, there is no consumption to warrant the establishing of a shoe factory big enough to take advantage of the economies of modern shoe machinery, and it will be cheaper to bring in shoes from some remote point that has enough shoe wearers to support a modern factory. But if 80 per cent of a large population wears shoes, it will pay better to establish a shoe factory at home and to train local labor to run the machinery—for nowadays the art of making shoes does not belong to any guild, and shoe machinery may be set up anywhere and workers trained within a few weeks or months. That is exactly what has been going on in the United States and what must go on in the rest of the world if it is to progress. In America we have been steadily cutting out the wastes of transportation. Instead of a single steel center at Pittsburgh, we now have centers at Chicago, Birmingham and on the Pacific Coast, with others in the making. Almost every big corporation has branch plants in every big consumptive area. It is just as illogical to try to found a foreign trade program on restoring old trade routes as it would be to found a domestic trade program on restoring all of the shoe and textile industries to New England.

Foreign trade, like domestic trade, is fleeting. The goods that go into trade are constantly changing and so are the buyers and the sellers. Every man in business knows that it is very dangerous to depend on a single customer or to have only a few big customers and no little ones coming along to take their places. Everyone in or out of business knows that a sale for which one does not get paid is not so much a sale as an involuntary donation.

Exports have been of particular significance to American agriculture. During the twenty-three years from 1909 to 1932, of our agricultural income, 18 per cent came from exports while only an average of 5 per cent of our industrial income came from export sales during the same period. Just because these proportions held through a period (which included a great war) does not mean that in the future any possible arrangement, Governmental or otherwise, can freeze those proportions and that, even if they were frozen, everyone would be happy. Circumstances throughout the world may be such that in any year the proportion of exports may be higher or lower. For instance, during the years 1925-29 we sold abroad 56 per cent of our cotton, 21 per cent of our wheat, 40 per cent of our tobacco and 10 per cent of our pork production. That was an unusually high proportion, but that export trade was artificially stimulated by loans, most of which have since proved worthless. As far as the nation was concerned, the figures represent only agriculture's share in a vast foreign volume of selling which turned out to be a stupendous donation. It did not seem to me to require any philosophical erudition to appraise the value of a foreign trade in which we gave away our goods. Everyone in the Administration agreed on that point. They all agreed that whatever had been done in the past was wrong. That is about all that the factions in the Administration ever agreed on.

The internationalists seemed to believe that the big "export" period—in which we merely gave away our goods—was the period to take as normal for export trade. While denouncing the policies which had brought about the trade, they saw no inconsistency in taking the dollar volume of that trade as a standard. For instance, on May 2nd, 1933, when in the ascendant and before going to London, Mr. Hull said: "The United States was the workshop of the world during the war and should have maintained that relative position since that time. . . . The obsolete, pre-war economic theory that prevailed here and elsewhere ignored our transformation from a debtor and a young undeveloped country to the greatest creditor and surplus-producing nation in history." He further spoke of our "suicidal theory" which had continued "to build our tariff and commercial policy around the sole idea of safeguarding the home market."

Secretary Wallace, on May 13th, 1934, said: "We must wake up the Eastern industrialist to the conviction that now he has to act differently. It may be necessary to make shifts in the tariff which may be very unpopular. It may be necessary to make changes that will be very unpopular in certain industrial neighborhoods."

These quotations fairly represent the internationalist or slightly disguised free trade element which dominated the Administration up until the President's message to the London Conference. The assertions by Secretaries Hull and Wallace and others of the free trade group were important, if true. In effect they said:

(1) The country had lost a valuable share of trade because of its tariff policy.

(2) Changes in the tariff policy would bring back the trade.

(3) The chief change required was a lowering of our tariff duties.

(4) The lowering of our tariff duties was a necessary part of our change from a debtor to a creditor nation.

(5) Lowering duties would increase imports and automatically increase exports and also provide the wherewithal for our debtors to pay us their debts.

These propositions were put forth as revelations of the laws of nature. To me they did not make sense. It seemed to me that a very plain business proposition was being complicated by general statements not backed up by any facts and that our principal need in settling upon a policy was a few facts. It was taken for granted that lowering our tariffs would increase our imports and also increase our exports. But no one knew exactly how that would come about. It was taken for granted that an increase in general exports would mean an increase in agricultural exports. But no one knew how that was going to come about. It was taken for granted that an increase in imports would mean a general pay-up by all our debtors. But no one knew how that was going to come about.

Certainly an increase in imports of such products as we could make or grow at home would decrease the number of available American jobs. The decrease in those jobs would add to the number of those already unemployed. It was taken for granted or passed over that all these discharged people and more would find employment in the increased export trade. But no one knew exactly how this would come about. The great need was for facts—to discover the course and nature of our trade in the past and thus to learn something for the future. It seemed approaching the reckless to change the commercial policy of a great nation and affect the lives of one hundred and twenty millions of people without making an examination of the accounts. An executive who changed the policy of a private corporation without even bothering to discover what that corporation had been doing in the past would not stand much of a chance in a stockholders' suit for mismanagement. I discovered, to my astonishment, that the internationalists in the Administration not only had no facts, but also did not want any facts. They simply knew what they knew and they did not want to know why they knew it or what it was they knew. They worshipped their convictions in much the same way as a Chinaman worships his ancestors, and they regarded any questioning of their creed as sacrilegious and hence not debatable. They rather acted as though facts were useful only to the lower orders of intelligence. That was the settled attitude of the internationalists in the Administration. Those of us who had commercial records were just too dumb to understand.

No one in the group clamoring for the reduction of tariffs and blaming all our woes upon tariff policy had any comprehension of what the American tariff policy actually had been or the reasons behind it. Listening to the talk, one would get the impression that the United States was and always had been a failure. It appeared that the nation through its history had only been building a Tower of Babel which had finally toppled. That, of course, was unfortunate, but it was fortunate, they seemed to think, that the inevitable collapse had come at a time when real brains were in the national service.

They further obscured the picture by talking of exports and imports in terms of dollars instead of in terms of volume. They blamed all the trade troubles on the Hawley-Smoot Tariff Act of 1930 and they talked a great deal about the need for "scientific tariff-making by experts." Later, when Secretary Hull and his professors secured full control of the making of reciprocal trade agreements, I learned that the word "scientific" as applied to tariffs had a special technical definition and did not necessarily mean the application of special scientific knowledge to the subject.

The American tariff system, as it had gradually been worked out over the years by the only truly scientific method —that is, the method of trial and error—had put on the free list most raw materials which could not be easily produced in America. Thus under the Dingley Act of 1897, 44.9 per cent of our imports came in free of duty, under the Underwood Act of 1913, 66.3 per cent came in free of duty, and under the Hawley-Smoot Act of 1930, 66.7 per cent came in free of duty. The Hawley-Smoot Act started out to be a revision upwards of duties on agricultural products, but the Congress considerably extended their revisions. However, it was primarily an agricultural tariff, for in it the average rate on dutiable agricultural raw materials was increased from 38.1 per cent to 48.9 per cent, while the average rate on dutiable non-agricultural products was increased only from 31 per cent to 34.3 per cent. Under this Act, for the fiscal year ending in 1932, all American imports paid an average of 17.9 per cent. During the same period, the duties collected by Great Britain, spread over the entirety of her imports, amounted to 17.4 per cent. I could not understand then and I cannot understand now the type of mind which permits British lecturers to denounce our American tariff institutions and advocate a species of free trade for the United States while ignoring the fact that the British average duty is within five-tenths of 1 per cent of that of the United States. I have never in any of the internationalist programs seen any objection to the British tariff scales. It is only the American tariff that is really objectionable. Since the American home market is of more importance to exporting nations than the markets of all of the rest of the world combined, I can easily see why a great deal of foreign energy can well be devoted to getting into it. But why our own officials should gulp those arguments whole is quite beyond my comprehension.

During the calendar year 1932, of all our imports for consumption, 66.9 per cent came in free of duty. This is a very important point to remember, for later on in the reciprocal tariff negotiations the Administration took it upon itself to freeze our free list. It thereby not only bound the United States against acting in certain directions, but also took from us our greatest bargaining power in disposing of goods.

As I said above, a favorite device of those advocating a species of free trade was the use of dollar rather than quantity figures to show the tremendous drop in world trade. According to the estimates of the League of Nations, world trade in 1932 had dropped about 62 per cent in dollar value from 1929. But in volume the drop had been only about 25 per cent. Taking the value figures, it would seem that a catastrophe had overtaken world trade. That indeed had happened, but it was more a price than a volume catastrophe. An inspection of our own trade figures showed much the same condition. The value of our exports declined from an average of $4,397,000,000 for the years 1921-25 to $2,424,000,000 for the calendar year 1931. But this tremendous drop in price was accompanied by a quantity drop of only about 11 per cent. On a quantity basis, our exports of agricultural products in 1932 stood at 84 on the index which takes 1923-25 as 100, and it is notable that in the five-year pre-war period the quantity index of agricultural exports was only 89. The exports of cotton in 1932 amounted to 9,060,000 bales, which was an increase of about 31 per cent over 1931 and was 40 per cent higher than the 1921-25 average. Indeed 71 per cent of the year's crop was exported. The trouble was price. The quantity of cotton exported in 1932 was 21 per cent above that exported in 1929, but the value was less by $426,000,000.

I have given all these figures in order to show how greatly our real foreign trade problem was misrepresented by showing it in terms of value. Our primary problem was not to increase our imports, in the illusion that thus we might increase our exports, but so to direct our exports of agricultural commodities that the prices received for the portions going into export would not govern the prices at home. The figures showed that our exports of foodstuffs were gradually declining as compared with our total production of foodstuffs. We shall be in a splendid condition when our country consumes practically all that our farms can raise—then the problem of giving to the farmer the full advantages of the tariff will be more simple. However, that is a condition which will have to come about naturally. Artificially limiting the production of the farms to an amount equal to domestic consumption is far from being the same thing as consuming everything that the farmer can raise.

The point is that in 1933 it was plainly evident that we could dispose of many agricultural surpluses abroad—if we did not care about prices. Certainly no one could quarrel with the volume of cotton exported in 1932, but only the handlers and shipping men had benefited from that trade. The cotton farmer had not received enough to cover his expenses.

World trade, it is true, had changed, but the great change had been brought about, not by our tariff, but by England going over to the protective system—in an exceedingly skilled way. It is from England that most of our economists took what they know about foreign trade. But our economists are now teaching the lessons that England has stopped following.

After the Napoleonic Wars, England gradually became the world center, both of finance and of manufacturing, and just before the middle of the last century she repealed her so-called Corn Laws which imposed duties on certain foodstuffs. England had built up her commercial power under an elaborate system of tariffs and embargoes starting back in the time of Queen Elizabeth. Through taking advantage of the invention of the steam engine and the application of steam power to production, she had reached a point where no duties on manufactured products were necessary because no country in the world was industrially advanced enough to compete in the British home market. The industrialists wanted to pay low wages, and this they could do only if food were cheap. The agitation to repeal the Corn Laws, led by Cobden, was not merely a battle of philosophies. It was a fight to the finish between the industrialists and the agriculturalists. The agriculturalists lost because their interests were not great enough to combat the combined forces of the industrialists and the financiers. It is well to bear in mind that the industrialists had a supreme world position. They had the same kind of tariff as our automobile people have today—that is, they had no competitors. The British agriculturalists had competitors everywhere—they had to meet the products of virgin lands. So British free trade was not really free trade at all but only a deliberate sacrifice of the purchasing power of the British agricultural communities in order to get cheap food to compensate for low industrial wages. British "free trade" also promoted the establishing of a world-wide banking system built upon gold, and it is difficult to decide whether the real force of the British has lain in industry or in banking.

Long before the war, the rising power of German industrialism shook the foundations of the British industrial-banking structure, and in the years just before the war England was more a banking than an industrial nation. One of the several results of the war and the treaties was to remove the menace of German competition. But, if only to show the futility of believing that competition can be removed by the destruction of the competitor, Japan after the war rapidly began to take the place left vacant by Germany and to cut into British markets that Germany had never been able successfully to penetrate.

Thereupon England set about revising her housekeeping. She did not rout the professors out of their studies and turn the problem over to them. In November, 1929 she appointed a distinguished committee of business men, financiers and economists, with Lord Macmillan as chairman, to find the facts and to make recommendations on the facts. In view of what has happened to us by permitting a single group of theorists to formulate American trade policy, it is interesting to note how the British Committee met the problem.

When we turn to the experts for enlightenment we find that they fall into two classes. On the one hand we have those who are engaged in the practical business of banking and finance and daily operate the elaborate system of adjustments of which the financial mechanism is composed. On the other hand we have the theoretical economists who as observers and critics endeavour to expound the rationale of that system. Between these two classes of experts—the practical financiers and the theoretical political economists—a certain antagonism is inevitable. The theorist seeks to rationalise the processes which he observes and to construct a scientific edifice of principles. The practical man finds in his office that he has to deal with a world ruled not by principles but by compromises and is impatient of the formulas of the study which he generally fails to comprehend. Indeed the epithets "academic", "theoretical", "doctrinaire", commonly applied to the philosophic thinker, have acquired a derogatory innuendo in the parlance of a nation which prides itself on its practical common sense and has an innate distrust of intellectual cleverness. The truth, as usual, lies midway. It is as foolish to disregard the analyses and generalisations of the scientific observer as it would be to believe that the world of finance could be successfully conducted by university professors. Each class has its contribution to make and it has been our endeavour to extract from the contributions of both such guidance as we could.

The Macmillan Committee brought in the most thorough report on foreign trade and finance that has ever been made. The Committee found that England did not know its actual position in foreign trade and finance because it had no definite bookkeeping figures on the financial factors as apart from the goods factors entering into foreign trade. Great Britain for many years imported a larger volume of goods than she exported, and all the economists said that the difference was made up by the sums which England received as interest on her foreign investments and for shipping, insurance and other services. The Committee found that the figures that had been used to justify this conclusion were merely guesses and recommended that exact books be kept so that the international position of the country would not rest on guesswork. This conclusion is of peculiar interest because of the propaganda that the United States as a creditor nation would have to reduce its duties and take goods in payment of its interest charges. This whole propaganda, as advanced particularly by Secretaries Hull and Wallace, was founded on the supposedly British practice. But, while our people were with profound admiration pointing out the British course as the proper one to follow, the British were repudiating that course. In the same manner, while our internationalists were pointing to the necessity of lowering our duties in order to promote employment, the British were raising their duties to promote domestic employment. The Macmillan Committee on this point said:

The fundamental argument for unrestricted Free Trade does not apply without qualification to an economic system which is neither in equilibrium nor in sight of equilibrium. For if a country's productive resources are normally fully employed, a tariff cannot increase output, but can only divert production from one direction into another, whilst there is a general presumption that the natural direction for the employment of resources, which they can reach on their merits and without being given special advantages at the expense of others, will yield a superior national dividend. But if this condition of full employment is neither fulfilled nor likely to be fulfilled for some time, then the position is totally different, since a tariff may bring about a net increase of production and not merely a diversion.

It appears to us, therefore, that, if imports were to be controlled, whether by a tariff with compensation for exports, or by Import Boards, or in some other way and home-produced goods substituted for them, there is a presumption, so long as present circumstances last, that this would mean a net increase of employment and of national productivity. . . .

Since many of the arguments in favour of a restriction of imports apply equally in favour of schemes of assistance to exports, some system of restricting imports, accompanied by a policy of giving advantages to the export industries, would seem to be the most practical plan of action.

Finally the immediate effect of such measures in reviving business confidence and a spirit of enterprise scarcely needs to be emphasised.

The Committee presented its report to Parliament in June, 1931 and thereupon began a new era in the commerce of the world.

The great, definite shift in British policy had to do with building up the home market and especially home agriculture. They had the acumen to see that a healthy foreign trade could not exist without a healthy and balanced domestic economy. And of course a balanced domestic economy means that those engaged in agriculture must be able to exchange their products for those of industry. Specifically, these are the policies which Great Britain adopted:

(1) She instituted protective duties of various kinds, both for industry and for agriculture.

(2) In September, 1931 she went off the gold standard and adopted a managed currency. She did this with surpassing skill. The Macmillan Report had raised the question of the country's international balance and further, but unpublished, research disclosed that the receipts of interest, service and other money items were not making up the large difference between the amount of goods imported and the amount exported—in short, that the country was not meeting its bills. England went off gold as a method of effecting a composition with creditors and she did it so well that the creditors have never known they were being composed with. More than that, the British bankers created an opportunity out of disaster by taking the colonies and most of the nations accustomed to trade with Britain off the gold standard at the same time and tying them to managed sterling.

When the full facts are known, the British departure from gold will be recognized as one of the great economic maneuvers in all history. As will be later brought out when considering the effect of our trade agreement program upon our economy, the British, by substituting a managed paper sterling standard for their old managed gold standard, created a favorable position for themselves which we failed to recognize or to meet.

(3) Following the recommendations of the Macmillan Report, Britain returned to the practice of keeping detailed books upon her foreign commercial and financial transactions, country by country. I say "returned" because there is ample evidence that up until about 1850, Great Britain kept accurate books upon her foreign transactions. Since the readoption of the practice, every movement of Great Britain has been based upon bookkeeping data. The British in their foreign affairs are now being governed by the accepted accounting precepts of business.

(4) She proceeded to strengthen and build up her economic relations with her various dominions upon a basis of mutual interest through the Ottawa Agreements and other arrangements.

(5) She further adopted a policy of making similar special commercial and financial arrangements with other nations upon the basis of mutual interest—"Buy from those who buy from us."

(6) Along with free trade and the gold standard, she moved away from the unconditional most-favored-nation policy which she had been instrumental in advancing in previous decades and declared for a *conditional* most-favored-nation policy.

Between the conditional and unconditional most-favored-nation policies is an important distinction which is not always recognized or understood. Our State Department has adopted exactly the policy which England scrapped.

Most-favored-nation treatment means that we promise to nations with whom we make commercial agreements that we will extend to them as favorable treatment with respect to tariff duties and the like as we do to any other country, and they in turn promise to give corresponding treatment to our goods. Sometimes, however, two nations make tariff bargains whereby they extend special tariff and other concessions to each other on a quid pro quo basis.

Under the conditional most-favored-nation policy we

should stand prepared to give concessions to any third nation, provided that nation makes corresponding concessions to us. But under the unconditional most-favored-nation policy, we automatically extend the concessions without demanding specific equivalent concessions from the third nation.

In theory the unconditional most-favored-nation principle is designed to reduce tariff and other barriers to trade. In practice, however, it is noteworthy that the attempt of many nations to make it the basis of their foreign trade policies has been accompanied by the increasing use of devices such as quota systems, exchange controls, trick classification of commodities, and so forth, which, in effect, defeat the purpose of the unconditional most-favored-nation theory, and lead to a multiplication of the very trade barriers which were to be reduced.

The most-favored-nation clause has been taken, by most Americans, as a not very important specimen of diplomatic phraseology. Since the adoption of the Hull policies, this innocent and apparently innocuous clause, has unfortunately entered into the life of every American. For through these clauses a general reduction is being brought about in the American tariff without the main question of lowering the tariff having been presented either to the people or to the Congress. The clause is being used by the Administration to thwart the will of the people as expressed in every national election in which the tariff has been the issue.

The British program has changed the trade face of the world. Acting upon exact bookkeeping information, Great Britain has built up her home market and extended her foreign markets upon a discriminating, factual basis. Other nations have followed the same course and have placed their foreign trade on the basis of national interest. England, by her exchange and other agreements, is collecting a large part of the interest due upon her foreign loans. Other nations are doing likewise. Some nations have gone in frankly for state trading, and international trade has tended more and more to become a matter of agreement between nations. Where finance stands in the way, actual barter has been resorted to. Everywhere home markets are protected by tariffs, quotas, controls or special agreements. I have record or knowledge of more than four hundred trade agreements of one sort or another between various nations of the world, from the benefits of which we are excluded. These agreements are not based on theories but squarely on considerations of mutual advantage. Germany, as everyone knows, has been very short of foreign exchange with which to buy needed goods, and so Germany during 1934 and 1935 went into barter in such a big way that the record of her barter transactions fills a good-sized book. For instance, she traded machinery, goods and chemicals with Brazil for coffee, cotton, tobacco and cocoa, and she made much the same kind of bargain with Colombia. She traded coal and barbed wire with Cuba for molasses and honey. Almost every nation has tried some barter. Belgium traded glass with Australia for frozen meat. Denmark traded steamships and machines with Russia for lumber and fertilizer. And so on and so on.

In the A.A.A. during 1933, we tried to do what the world was doing. We had the authority to do that under the Agricultural Adjustment Act, particularly Section 12—and that section did not get there by accident. It was put there at my request. As I have already mentioned, we organized the North Pacific Emergency Export Association and disposed of more than 28,000,000 bushels of wheat to more than 40 countries, both as wheat and as flour, and relieved a difficult surplus situation in the Pacific Northwest. In October, 1933 we took up the possibilities of establishing quotas for the importation of liquors, on the repeal of the 18th Amendment, and laid the ground to exchange surplus farm products for liquors on practically a goods-for-goods basis. We found a great willingness to trade. For instance, Italy had instituted a policy of importing only a minimum amount of American tobacco, for Premier Mussolini had decided to hold down Italy's importations of other than industrial necessities. But, in spite of this, Italy readily agreed to trade wines for more than a million pounds of tobacco and we made good deals with France and Spain. These barter arrangements for wines and liquors, not directly competitive with American products, had gone pretty far before the policy of the Administration stopped all of these activities and removed the possibilities of disposing of our agricultural surplus in the fashion that all the world was following. Our internationalists have steadily objected to disposing of agricultural surpluses either by barter or by any subsidized method which might possibly be referred to as "dumping"—even though the foreign nation on the other end of the deal was perfectly willing to take the goods. Apparently it was all right for American taxpayers to stand the expense of foreign dumping and destruction at home but very wrong for us to salvage any of the loss by selling abroad at competitive prices. That, however, is getting ahead of the story.

The Administration, through various Cabinet members, the Tariff Commission and the A.A.A., had been investigating the possibilities inherent in reciprocal trade agreements. Dr. John Lee Coulter, who had formerly been on the Tariff Commission and also knew agriculture from a practical viewpoint, prepared for me in September, 1933 a comprehensive memorandum on trade agreements. Some parts are pertinent—especially his views on tariff reductions. He wrote:

A flat reduction in tariffs on all articles from all countries to all countries would result in many disturbing repercussions. . . . My theory is that the more effective method of approach is through direct negotiations, which would take into account specific articles of trade (whether protected by an ad valorem or a specific rate of duty). Even in these cases, however, the question is not one of merely raising or lowering the rate of duty. It is a matter of writing reciprocal trade agreements and modifying the rules which apply to the particular article from the particular country or countries. In order to make this clear, I cite below several approaches and illustrations.

By subclassification of products a reduction in the duty may exceed the specified amount for classes of important products not like or similar to domestic products. Thus, countable cotton cloth above yarn counts of say 120 might be set aside with a very substantial reduction in the rate of duty thus permitting the importation of very fine and expensive types of cloth which are not produced in this country, and at the same time maintain the present general tariff arrangement for the great mass of domestic production. Several European countries, if given an opportunity to compete in this market with very fine and expensive types of cloth with a low duty, would in turn open a market for larger quantities of our agricultural products. . . .

In negotiating trade agreements, it should be possible to transfer either a specific article or a specific grade or class of that article from the free list to the dutiable list, or vice versa. This would have in mind the opening of a window, or door, or gateway for the development of import and export trade. . . .

In negotiating trade agreements, it should be possible to use other bases of value than those specified in Section 402 of the Tariff Act, which defines foreign invoice values. In the case of chinaware, unit values from England may average $5 to $10 per dozen pieces, whereas from Japan they may average 25 to 50 cents per dozen pieces. Under the present method of assessing the tariff, the actual duty paid per dozen pieces on imports from Japan is absurdly low, while the same rate of duty applied to fine chinaware from England and France has practically served as an embargo. In other words, the present duty operates to let the Japanese mass production of chinaware into the American market practically duty free, while it serves almost as an embargo against the British and French and other European very fine wares. The American market should be protected against the mass production from Japan, which would give employment in this country to great numbers of laborers, while on the other hand, the rate should be relatively low on the fancy high priced ware from Europe, since we produce very little of that sort of goods in this country and it gives very little domestic employment. Because of the present arrangement the Japanese receive a very small amount for their chinaware and it is very little aid to our export business. Development of the fancy chinaware trade with Europe would make it possible for these European countries to buy large quantities of low value farm products from us. . . .

Without getting too much into detail, a gateway might very well be built to let in manganese ore, tungsten, and other similar products, practically not produced in this country, thus making possible an opportunity for large exports. There are other basic products, such as cork products from Portugal and Spain, also the olive oil products from the Mediterranean countries of Europe. The same thing might be said of the real sardine industry of the Mediterranean as distinct from the "so-called" sardines from the Scandinavian areas.

The way I look at the subject is that a thousand gateways could be opened which would lead to the building up of the export market of the United States, since hundreds of thousands of foreign workers, diverted from agricultural production or from unemployment, would immediately become a valuable market for the products of American farms, fisheries, forests, and factories.

In the above, I have really not attempted to list large numbers of specific articles. What I have tried to do more is to point out that the problem is one of subclassification or changing from specific to ad valorem rates, or vice versa; or changing the bases of value in some cases; or specifying maximum and minimum specific rates to ad valorem general rates, or vice versa; or shifting in some cases from free to dutiable, and others from dutiable to free. Of course, the simple thing to do would be merely to change all world rates a flat 10 per cent, for instance, but my detailed study of tariff problems leads me to the conclusion that this would accomplish very little and might do a very great deal of harm.

I made an opportunity to discuss Dr. Coulter's memorandum with Secretary Hull, and in consequence, on September 20th, 1933, I wrote this letter to Mr. Hull, enclosing the memorandum:

Dear Mr. Secretary:

Following our brief discussion after the Executive Council meeting last week, I am attaching hereto a statement discussing certain tariff matters and our foreign trade, which I think you will find of considerable interest. I shall be glad to disclose to you the name of the author of this statement.

I am also attaching a report on "World Trade Barriers in Relation to American Agriculture," prepared by the Bureau of Agricultural Economics in response to Senate Resolution No. 280. This report stresses the dependence of American agriculture on foreign markets and shows how barriers of various kinds have interfered with our agricultural exports to those markets. . . .

I believe that a strong, persistent and well-planned policy looking toward the revival of international trade is of the utmost importance. There are, of course, two major approaches to this problem. Under an emergency short-time approach every effort should be made to effect trade "deals" between this and other countries that are mutually advantageous. We should explore, for example, the possibilities of selling wheat to China, pork to Russia, and the like. Direct barter, to obviate exchange difficulties, in some cases may be possible.

The longer-time approach would contemplate a reorientation of national policy and laying the groundwork for more permanent development of international trade. This would require the exploration of economic, political, and other considerations affecting the trade between this and other countries and the negotiation of tariff and other concessions to remove the barriers to trade. In my judgment the time is especially opportune to redirect the Nation's thought in this direction.

A certain amount of special machinery has already been created to expand our foreign markets. An interdepartmental board on reciprocity treaties has been active for several months past and undoubtedly has been doing good work. The Agricultural Adjustment Administration has a small unit, the purpose of which is to negotiate wherever possible the sale of agricultural commodities. Other institutions of the Government have been doing a certain amount of basic research work that will be very helpful in laying the groundwork for a longer time approach to the solution of the problem. While all of these efforts are worth while, I believe that more vigorous and better coordinated effort with reference to the development of our foreign trade is imperatively needed.

It has occurred to me that the designation by the President of a special committee to deal with this problem, and through which the activities of all Government departments and institutions would be coordinated, would be most helpful. I would suggest that this committee have no other duties. I suggest further that any statistical data utilized should be set forth on two bases—(1) measured by the volume of the commodities, and (2) measured by value expressed in dollars.

My letter and the memorandum served to bring matters to a head, and the President on November 11th wrote to me this letter setting up the Executive Committee on Commercial Policy:

My dear Mr. Peek:

It appears to me that the growing complexity of American commercial relations with foreign countries requires a new step in the systematization of the handling of these relations. This new step in systematization is dictated by two sets of circumstances:

(1) Under the Administration's program of recovery, numerous departments are assigned powers or duties which directly touch upon trade relations with other countries. It is plain that the acts of each of the separate branches of the Government must be brought into a coherent policy system with the acts of all the rest.

(2) The changing policies of other Governments and the changing methods of regulating international trade greatly complicate the Government's task of proper direction of American trade.

I therefore have decided to designate one officer in the Department of State to carry the primary responsibility of supervising the international commercial policy of this Government into a coherent whole. Hereafter may I ask that you give the necessary instructions in your Department that before any acts are taken under legislation or otherwise which directly affect the export and import trade in this country, this official should be consulted concerning the action and his approval secured.

It is my idea that this official should be the chairman of an Executive Committee for the coordination of commercial policy and the negotiation of commercial treaties and trade agreements, and that in his decisions he would be very largely carrying out the judgment of the Committee. Upon this Committee your Department will be represented.

It is my further expectation that as this Committee develops its work, all subordinate interdepartmental committees engaged in the work of negotiating commercial treaties, the elaboration of trade agreements, et cetera, will report to the responsible official and through him to the governing committee.

I also request that you instruct your Department that this official, as chairman of the coordinating Committee, should be the regular channel of communication with all foreign Governments on all policy matters affecting American export and import trade.

The arrangements contemplated in this order will be elaborated in further directions which will be transmitted later.

I have asked Mr. Phillips, Under Secretary of State, to undertake these duties as chairman of the coordinating Committee until such time as a permanent selection is made. Therefore, pending further notice, he will be chairman pro tem.

The original committee was headed pro tem by William Phillips, Under Secretary of State. He was shortly replaced by Professor Francis B. Sayre, Assistant Secretary of State, who became permanent chairman of the committee. Walter J. Cummings at first represented the Treasury. He was succeeded by Marriner S. Eccles of the Federal Reserve Board and

Professor Jacob Viner of the University of Chicago. Professor Viner was born and had received his academic training in Canada. The Department of Commerce was represented by Professor John Dickinson, a lawyer and Assistant Secretary of Commerce, and Professor Willard L. Thorp, an economist and Acting Chief of the Bureau of Foreign and Domestic Commerce. The latter was succeeded by Professor Claudius T. Murchison, Chief of the Bureau of Foreign and Domestic Commerce in 1934-35. The Department of Agriculture was represented by Professor Tugwell and the N.R.A. by Oscar B. Ryder, who had previously been with the Tariff Commission. General Westervelt at first attended for the A.A.A., but when he left that Administration with me he was succeeded by Professors L. R. Edminster and H. R. Tolley. The Tariff Commission was represented by Chairman Robert L. O'Brien and Thomas Walker Page. Later when I became Special Adviser to the President on Foreign Trade I was also a member of the committee. The committee throughout its existence, I may say in passing, was dominated by Professor Sayre and his associates in the State Department. It will be noted that, unlike the Macmillan Committee, the committee was almost entirely made up of professors and bureau officials and that practical business or financial experience of any sort was only slightly represented.

The committee spent a deal of time in discussing how to draw a bill permitting reciprocal trade agreements. That I shall take up in the next chapter. My own job, when in December I was asked out of the office of Administrator of the A.A.A., was to find what facts I could and draw a report for the President on what might best be done with our foreign trade. I submitted it on December 30th, 1933. That report was fairly long and detailed. I recommended to the President setting up a Foreign Trade Administration thus:

Immediately under and responsible to you there should be a Foreign Trade Administrator. The duties of the Administrator would be in the nature of those of a coordinator, except as they become administrative in connection with the activities of the United States Foreign Trade Corporation, hereinafter referred to. His primary function should be to translate into action the non-political and non-diplomatic phases of our foreign trade policy, and he should also serve as chairman of an Advisory Commercial Policy Board and as a member of the existing Interdepartmental Advisory Board on Reciprocity Treaties.

The Advisory Commercial Policy Board would continue the advisory functions of the existing Executive Committee on Commercial Policy, and would make recommendations on commercial policy to the President and to the Foreign Trade Administration. Since the executive and coordinating functions of the Committee are included in the proposed Foreign Trade Administration, it is recommended that the existing Committee be discontinued and a new Advisory Board be established as herein outlined. The representation on the Board recommended has been broadened to include representatives of the Federal Reserve Board and of the Reconstruction Finance Corporation. Our foreign commercial policy is so closely linked with our domestic and foreign credit and monetary policies that I believe it essential to emphasize this connection and to coordinate credit and trade activities. . . .

It is proposed to establish a corporation to be known as the United States Foreign Trade Corporation, through which industry, agricultural and commercial, may be guided with respect to its foreign trade. The primary function of this corporation should be to see that our domestic industries are assisted in developing foreign trade, guided in their related credit activities, and advised of the effect upon our agriculture and industry—indeed upon our national welfare—of export and import trade.

More particularly, I recommended an audit of all our foreign trade and the inauguration of a system of bookkeeping for our international accounts, thus:

1. The coordination of all fact-finding machinery in this field in the structure of the Government of the United States;

2. The comprehensive recordation for such a period as would be deemed adequate to form a mature judgment, of the actual trade movement by volume and value particularly in and out of the United States, in the world as a whole;

3. The analysis of the non-commercial movements affecting the balances of payments of the United States and the other principal agricultural, commercial and industrial countries;

4. The ascertainment of the credit structure of the United States and of the different nations of the world having trade relations with the United States;

5. The correlation of all the factors which in the last ten years have materially affected the course of trade and the trend of the elements which enter into international balances of payments;

6. The systematic and searching review and classification of our trade, both of importation and exportation, with particular reference to recent significant developments;

7. The careful investigation of the background of international engagements upon which our government has built up what is known as its commercial policy in the past;

8. Equally careful analysis of the commercial policies, and their precedents and justifications, of other countries in the world;

9. The sympathetic consideration of the best interests to be served in connection with the application of a particular policy to the situation of any given branch of agriculture, industry or commerce;

10. The development of a national system of bookkeeping of all the "in" and "out" items, thoroughly dependable and authoritative in all respects, so that the President of the United States may be at all times in full possession of all the facts requisite to the employment, in the best interests of the nation as a whole, of such further necessary powers for bargaining on tariff rates, or otherwise protecting the agricultural and industrial interests of this country, as may be conferred upon him.

My report was completely disregarded. The internationalists did not want any inconvenient facts. They wanted to destroy the American protective system.

Chapter X

Founding an Un-American Policy

The year 1934 was a critical one in shaping American foreign trade policies. The internationalist group headed by Secretary Hull was temporarily in eclipse after the comedy of the London Economic Conference, which had been conceived as a drive to take the United States into active collaboration with the League of Nations and to cancel the war debts. Both the League and the Bank for International Settlements were heavily represented at the conference—which was indeed in charge of the League. The British and French delegates who dominated the Conference were, I am told, greatly worried over the rising power of the Japanese in the Orient and the drift to dictatorships on the Continent. Someone got the bright notion that if only the American tariff were lowered, the unemployed of Europe could find jobs in making goods for the American market and this would not incline toward either Fascism or Communism. I do not know who first got the idea. It may or may not have been Secretary Hull. At any rate, he either then or later accepted it. For it later appeared, in disguised form, as the ruling passion of our State Department.

This whole program was tied up with world peace. The connection is not entirely obvious. One can very well see why having foreign nations make for us goods that we could better make for ourselves might help to keep them peaceful and happy. But should that be our first consideration? I do know that the American people have always been opposed to low tariffs and international alliances, and also I know that under the American System any program making a fundamental change in our national mode ought to be simply framed and then submitted to the people. A public servant, in my opinion, is bound to stay within the limits of his mandate. If he does not like the mandate, he should not accept it. But if he does accept it, the mandate is binding.

That did not seem to be the view of those most actively urging our complete cooperation with the League of Nations. Oddly enough, those who most ardently desire our membership in the League also advocate the lowering of tariffs and the cancellation of the war debts. The League partisans, together with the other internationalists, began a great and heavily financed campaign which seemed to have as its end the shaping of public opinion to favor some action disguised under the cloak of a reciprocal trade treaty act that would amount to a general lowering of tariffs and an increasing of America's dependence upon world (i.e., League of Nations) economy.

Someone convinced Secretary Wallace that the nation immediately had to settle upon a definite course with respect to world peace and foreign trade, and, taking advantage of his deeply religious, emotional character, had him write a small book which tied world peace, the tariffs and agriculture all together. This book was published jointly by the World Peace Foundation and the Foreign Policy Association—both League of Nations propaganda organizations and both partial dependents of the Carnegie Peace Foundation.

The book was given an immense publicity and was made the subject of lecture courses and forums all over the country. The President had once run for the Vice-Presidency on a League of Nations ticket. Perhaps the drive through Secretary Wallace was aimed to get the farm vote—which had always been against the League.

The book was a very curious document. It was based on the notion that the world capacity to produce had outrun the capacity to consume and that a new economy was needed. That was the Tugwell philosophy of scarcity. Here are some extracts that show the general trend of the book:

It should be recognized that our surplus problems here in the United States, and the resulting necessity of keeping parts of our factories idle and withdrawing acreage, or of widening foreign markets, or of doing these things in combination, is really part of a world surplus problem. This country has more industrial as well as more agricultural capacity than it needs for home consumption. Surplus capacity in industry shows up mainly in unemployment, rather than in a persistent accumulation of commodities; but in all branches of our economic life there is an identical tendency for production to outrun consumption. Other nations have just the same trouble, as we know from the prevalence of unemployment and dole systems throughout the world. . . .

The planned middle course I propose as a basis for present discussion is one precisely halfway between these two extremes: a line of march along which we would lower tariffs enough to bring in another half-billion dollars worth of goods annually, and permanently retract of our good agricultural land some 25 million acres. . . .

To depict the pain this course would cause industry on the one hand, and agriculture on the other, would be but to restate in less demanding terms, facts and speculations developed in previous sections of this pamphlet, in respect to the price of unmodified isolation, on the one hand, and of an unmodified drive for world markets, on the other. The fact that agriculture would suffer far the more under isolation, and that industry would bear the brunt of changes necessary to widespread renewal of world trade, may here, however, be briefly reiterated; for here is a fact suggesting that a planned middle course is the fairest and wisest for all concerned. . . .

If we are going to increase foreign purchasing power enough to sell abroad our normal surpluses of cotton, wheat and tobacco at a decent price, we shall have to accept nearly a billion dollars more goods from abroad than we did in 1929. We shall have to get that much more in order to service the debts that are coming to us from abroad and have enough left over to pay us a fair price for what we send abroad.

The Wallace theory of picking a middle course between what he called free trade and nationalism was wholly acceptable to the internationalists. They are always careful to deny that they want free trade and instead try for low duties—which in practice mean no duties at all. They are after free trade wearing a low-tariff hat. Afterwards in his book "New Frontiers," Mr. Wallace tried further to go in two directions at once. In that book he said:

> . . . We must invent, build and put to work new social machinery. This machinery will carry out the Sermon on the Mount as well as the present social machinery carries out and intensifies the law of the jungle. . . .
>
> The 10 million unemployed plus the 5 million living on land which can never be farmed are a continuing menace to the established industry and agriculture of the United States. . . .
>
> Personally, I have long favored a combination of the national and the international approach, but I recognize that this also has its peculiar difficulties. Such a course is hard to define with the necessary precision. In practice it means that the Agricultural Adjustment Administration would have to go ahead for a good many years keeping out of use perhaps 20 or 30 million acres of plow land, while the Presidential tariff powers of 1934 are being exercised as rapidly as is just and possible to restore a foreign demand for our surplus farm products. . . .
>
> Politically, the middle course is somewhat difficult. On the one hand it exposes the Administration to the criticism of those who do not like acreage control, and on the other hand to the criticism of those who do not like low tariffs. Logically, of course, a defender of high tariffs cannot object to acreage control under the post-war situation. But actually, the high tariff people, for hell-raising purposes, often disregard the logic of their position, defending high tariffs with one breath, attacking all efforts to adjust the international economy to the fact of high tariffs with the next. . . .
>
> As the tariffs are gradually reduced, may it not be wise to work out a plan for liquidating, definitely, yet slowly, these inefficient industries?

The delusion that, if only we imported more goods, we should also export more goods, was widespread. The members of the Executive Committee on Commercial Policy were so gripped with the prospect that some of them drew up an elaborate plan in which the industries they considered inefficient were to be snuffed out by lowering tariffs. On that point they were quite specific but they did not know at all what goods the foreigners would elect to buy from us!

They just took for granted that the goods we most wanted to sell would be the ones the foreigners would most want to buy. That is one of several places where their lack of business training showed up. Everyone knows that price has a lot to do with selling and that, if through the N.R.A. and the A.A.A. the Administration raised prices, the foreigners, after they had sold to us, might take their funds and buy elsewhere. The fact that the proceeds of an import sale provide American exchange which is good in any market of the world never occurred to any of those who imagined that imports had to breed exports. The plan to draw a reciprocal trade agreement bill giving power to some Government body to write death sentences for certain branches of our industries never got very far. I suggested that Congress might be less than enthusiastic about it.

The full program of the internationalists had not then been put down on paper. It was set out later in the year 1934 in a report by a committee imposingly entitled "The Commission of Inquiry into National Policy in International Economic Relations." The idea of such a report was brought up by the Social Science Research Council in 1933 and, having been endorsed by President Roosevelt, the funds were provided by the Rockefeller Foundation. The Commission was headed by President Hutchins of the University of Chicago and included a number of excellent professors who were long on theory and short on basic facts.

The recommendations of the report are important as showing how far the internationalist spirit can go, and, although the volume was not issued until late in 1934, some extracts can be given here to clarify what the low-tariff people had in their minds, for they have been able to bring about much that is recommended in the program. The Commission, whether by design or not, was academic scenery for Secretary Hull. Here are some extracts:

International economic relations cannot be greatly improved until the distrust and tension now prevailing in the world are relieved. Therefore we recommend that our government adopt the following measures:

1. Continued participation in the Disarmament Conference, cooperation with the League of Nations in such of its activities as cannot involve us in European conflicts, and adherence to the World Court. We commend the recent action of Congress in adhering to the Arms Convention and in joining the International Labor Organization. We urge it to make the necessary appropriations for the latter without delay.

2. Continuance of present policy in South America and the Caribbean as exemplified by the Montevideo Conference, the repeal of the Platt Amendment, and the withdrawal of troops from Haiti.

3. Immediate withdrawal from the Philippines on terms that will protect their economic life from injury by American tariffs.

4. Placing of Oriental immigration on a nondiscriminatory basis.

5. Repeal of the Johnson Act forbidding loans to countries in default.

6. Immediate settlement of the war debts. We do not believe that the interests of the United States require any payment. Since, however, some countries desire to pay something, we recommend the appointment of a commission with full power to effect settlements. We suggest a lump-sum payment, possibly to be effected through the transfer of securities to be obtained by foreign governments through the exchange of their

bonds for American issues held by their nationals or by any other method that minimizes transfer difficulties. The proposed commission should have discretion to accept in part settlement defaulted obligations of political units of the United States.

7. We recommend that our government make it clear that future investments abroad are at the investor's risk. We point out the possibilities of friction involved in even the customary diplomatic representations as to foreign investments. The investor should be remitted for assistance or redress to the authorities of the country where the investment is made.

To achieve a more wholesome balance in the international accounts of the United States we recommend that our government take the following measures:

1. The Tariff

a. The removal of tariffs in all cases in which no serious addition to unemployment would result. . . .

b. If these measures do not prove adequate to increase imports to the necessary degree, rates on other commodities would be lowered, with the proviso that the increases in the volume of goods admitted be subject to control in order to minimize the danger of unemployment. . . .

c. We recommend that the government consider the payment, under proper safeguards, of a dismissal wage to labor thrown out of employment as a direct consequence of sudden changes in the tariff.

d. We favor the speedy negotiation of reciprocal trade agreements pending downward revision of the tariff. We do not regard reciprocal trade agreements as a substitute for tariff revision because the Trade Agreements Act limits reductions to only 50 per cent of existing rates and only to cases where other countries reciprocate. We recommend the conclusion of such agreements only on condition that they be used to enlarge rather than divert world trade. We suggest an arrangement under which most-favored-nation treatment would be accorded all countries that make such agreements with us.

The Hutchins Report was largely the work of Professor Alvin H. Hansen. This Professor Hutchins freely acknowledged in the report itself. He said: "The report rests on the work of Mr. Hansen . . . without Mr. Hansen the Commission would have committed many grievous errors."

The real significance of the report is that Professor Hansen became an economic adviser (with the title of Chief Economic Analyst) to Secretary Hull in July, 1934—only a few weeks after the Reciprocal Trade Agreements Act became a law. This does not mean that Mr. Hull endorsed the Hutchins Report in the form of which it finally appeared, but it is scarcely possible that he would have asked Professor Hansen to join him in an intimate capacity, had he not known his views and been sympathetic with them. Mr. Hull does not like people who differ with him and does not willingly have them around. For instance, Raymond Moley.

Professor Hansen was an excellent example of the kind of man to whom the actual working out of great national foreign policies was entrusted. Essentially he was a classroom statesman. Born in the Northwest, he became an instructor and then a professor of economics, travelled for a year in Europe on a fellowship—that is, he had the standard academic background. He is, I believe, an excellent professor of economics, with more initiative than is usual among professors, but, as is also unfortunately so usual among professors, he relied mainly upon that which had already been written in books. That was not his fault. And, like many other professors, he was intolerant or suspicious of practical knowledge and common sense. That is the doctrinaire attitude which was usual among the economists and lawyers brought into the Administration. I have commented on Professor Hansen not as an individual but as a type and also to bring out that the report of the Hutchins Commission was not a considered and balanced document like the Macmillan Report, but a piece of endowed propaganda.

The program that I have listed above as presented by the Commission is the program that Secretary Hull and his professors have been following—although, for political reasons, they have unfolded it slowly.

Nothing of this attitude, however, was being disclosed in the early part of 1934. Every action of the President evidenced a desire to promote a trade policy in which the material interests of the country would be the essential consideration. He had his mind fixed on unemployment at home. He was talking of Yankee trading and seemed by his message to the London Economic Conference, definitely to have withdrawn even the possibility of authorizing excursions into internationalism. I believe he was acting in accordance with the report I had submitted to him as chairman of the temporary committee. He encouraged me to go ahead. I do not know how he managed with Secretary Hull. The President encouraged me with apparent whole-heartedness. He asked me to become president of the Export-Import Bank (which was created by an Executive Order on February 2nd, 1934) and on March 23rd he designated me as Special Adviser to the President on Foreign Trade. Both these appointments were under the authority of the National Industrial Recovery Act and were exactly in line with my recommendations in my report of December 30th, 1933. As Special Adviser, I had the authority to set up the machinery for a comprehensive audit for the foreign trade of our country over a period of years, in order that we might shape our foreign trade policy on the facts—just as the British had been doing after the Macmillan Report. I shall take up this audit in the next chapter.

Now I shall dispose of the banks—even though it gets me ahead of my story. The banks were not important so much for what they did as for what they showed it was not necessary to do. Ambassador Bullitt, who had been appointed to Russia, thought there were great possibilities in Russian trade —if only financing could be arranged. I did not share his enthusiasm. He asked me to take the presidency of the bank which he had discussed with the President for the purpose of financing trade with the Soviets. I told him that I did not like banking and had no interest at all in being president of any bank, much less of a Government bank dealing with the hazards of foreign trade. He had Jesse Jones in for luncheon with me further to urge my acceptance. I held out. Then the President telephoned. I told him that I was not interested in the bank and that I wanted to go on with my foreign trade studies.

He asked me to continue the studies and take the bank also.

That left me no alternative. I took the presidency as a job without salary. The bank had an imposing board of trustees and an elaborate official set-up, but, before it had a chance to consider anything, the Russian debt settlement came up. It will be remembered that a most decided difference developed between Litvinoff and the President as to exactly what Litvinoff had agreed his government would do about the debts. On March 16th the trustees of the bank resolved to do nothing until the diplomatic differences were settled, and, since they never were settled, the bank never functioned.

On March 9th, the Second Export-Import Bank was set up by an Executive Order and created into a banking corporation under the Code of the District of Columbia. This bank was at first limited to financing transactions with Cuba, but later its field was made general. There seemed to be a need for the bank, for, with foreign trade throughout the world coming increasingly into the hands of governments, the American trader was at a decided disadvantage—at least so it seemed—in not having behind him a non-diplomatic, business arm of the Government. We financed a few transactions, notably several sales of minted silver coinage to Cuba and a million-dollar sale of tobacco to Spain. But I had no intention of playing Santa Claus and putting the Government credit behind I.O.U.'s that would have to be renewed and renewed until they died of old age. That cramped our activities.

The need for Government credit aid in foreign trade, it developed, was not nearly so great as I had been led to suppose. During that time, commercial banks were not lending freely—or at least that was the complaint. I had been told that millions and millions of dollars' worth of goods could not be exported because of the refusal of the banks to finance. I found that generally speaking this was not true and that most legitimate transactions went through the banks without trouble. A not inconsiderable proportion of the applications that came to us were for foreign trade promotions in which the Government was expected to put up all the money, take all the risk and stay away from the profits.

Most of the people legitimately in foreign trade believed that a Government bank could aid—provided it stood behind the commercial banks instead of competing with them. That also was my idea. But our foreign trade people themselves could not agree on exactly what form our help should take. One group wanted us to solve the exchange problem. Some thirty-five nations had put on exchange restrictions. An exchange restriction is a type of government action against which individuals are helpless. To illustrate: suppose Smith in New York makes a shipment to his old customer Jonsky in Blankland. Let us say that Jonsky's bank is ready to honor the draft. But then the Blankland government steps in and says that it has decided, in order to protect its central bank reserve, to prohibit any gold or exchange leaving the country. The Blankland treasury thereupon sequesters Jonsky's money and Smith finds that, instead of an ordinary private debt owing to him by

Jonsky, he has a claim against Blankland which will pay him only as and when it gets ready and on the terms it chooses. That is "blocked exchange." We were diligently urged to have the Bank pay off all the American creditors, take their blocked exchange and deal with the countries as we could. That, it seemed to me, was not a business for the Bank to undertake without full cooperation of the State Department. This was not forthcoming. I did suggest then—and insisted throughout all my term of office—that in making any reciprocal trade agreement with a country that was withholding payment justly due to Americans, we should incorporate provisions covering those payments. Every country in the world was doing that. But when the trade agreements came to be made, our professors lightly passed over the subject of American debts and left American creditors high and dry. I shall come back to this point when I consider the agreements.

Another division of the export people thought that the Government might help in intermediate and long-term financing. The field for action here was attractive at first glance but, as we went into the subject, it appeared that the need was not so much for money as to find ways and means through a Government agency for getting paid in goods or services. This was largely a question of proper accounting between the countries involved, so that our traders would not play—as they have been forced to play—against loaded dice. These are very practical considerations which the British and other nations now accept as of course in their foreign trade. They should have been taken up in each of our trade agreements. They were effectively touched upon in none.

A third class of exporters wanted the Bank to go into credit insurance in the manner of certain of the foreign governments—notably the British. But this was so clearly beyond the charter of the Bank that I could only recommend that the men most interested get together to obtain the needed authority from Congress. I promised to help in whatever way I could, but nothing at all came of the credit insurance proposal. Among the smaller exporters arose some demand for short time financing of the character which the commercial banks could easily handle. It turned out that good credit risks could be managed privately and that about our only field would be in bad credit risks or risks extending over a very long period.

The bank investigations convinced me, along with the work in accounting that I was doing as Special Trade Adviser, that the word "credit" had taken on a new meaning in foreign trade and that many exporters and importers either did not realize the change or did not want to realize it. I could not be a party to making loans which would simply shift the losses to the public. Some exporters fully realize that sales abroad must be real sales and be paid for by the foreign purchasers, but others do not care how the bills are eventually paid, so long as they get their money. Some of the professional foreign trade boomers are in this second class, including some of the paid officials of the foreign trade associations. With the world as it now is, goods cannot be legitimately exported unless a means of payment is arranged for in advance. Credit in the money sense may be out of the question and the transaction may get around to actual barter. Some loans may legitimately be made, but government loans to promote foreign trade are more often doles rather than loans. Our foreign trade has never had the benefit of sound and considered credit information, for such information depends upon an exact knowledge of international balances as well as the credit standing of the foreign buyer. With exact credit information, finance becomes a reasonable proposition. Without such information, there can be no financing; there can be only gambling.

Since the creation of the Executive Committee on Commercial Policy in the latter months of 1933, it had been working on a bill to permit the making of reciprocal trade agreements. This I have noted in a previous chapter. During that period, it was the fashion among the New Dealers to take as a starting point for any bill the precept that Congress was incapable of wise legislation and that a good bill was one in which the Congress delegated its powers to the President and passed out of the picture. That would clear the way for the professors and New Dealers to administer the bill more or less as they saw fit, for, of course, the President could not actually perform more than a mere fraction of the duties delegated to him.

I believed that in all matters of policy the Congress should retain its complete power, but I also believed that in making foreign trade agreements it might be proper and necessary to delegate power within specific limits to some responsible body like a Foreign Trade Board, under the President, to meet some of the quick shifts so common in this bargaining world. I have already mentioned that the professors, following the lines later brought out by the Hutchins Commission, drafted a kind of bill naming the inefficient American industries which were to be killed by withdrawal of tariff protection. In that way, it was proposed to get more imports and, it was taken for granted, more exports. That suggestion got out in a newspaper story and it did not take much effort to kill it. That was the only serious outbreak of internationalism during the framing of the bill.

The Executive Committee on Commercial Policy for a while considered writing a whole new tariff bill. Its members were for the most part inexperienced in getting legislation in Congress, and it had to be explained to them that not even a Congress with an enormous Democratic majority would take a tariff bill in whatever shape handed to them—in the way they had taken the "must" bills. With the aid of Frederic P.

Lee and Glenn McHugh, I drafted an amendment to the Hawley-Smoot Act of 1930. It was as follows:

Notwithstanding any other provisions of existing law, whenever the President finds that our foreign trade may be promoted or stimulated and/or that our foreign markets may be expanded and/or that our surplus commodities, agricultural or otherwise, may be advantageously moved into the export market by arrangements, contractual or otherwise, with any foreign country or the nationals thereof, he is authorized (as a part of or as applicable to any such arrangement) to specify, with respect to any products of or articles imported from any foreign country, by proclamation or Executive order such new and/or revised rates of duty, not to exceed 50 per centum ad valorem or its equivalent, and/or to make such changes either in classification and/or in the basis of value as he considers desirable to effectuate the purposes of the arrangement. On and after the date specified in such proclamation or Executive order there shall be levied, collected and paid upon the products or articles so specified such new and/or revised rates of duty *if such products or articles are imported into the United States in accordance with such arrangement.*

This I sent to Professor Sayre on January 16th, 1934 with a letter which said, in part:

This draft is intended to be suggestive only and obviously has to be expanded somewhat to fit in properly with other related sections of the Tariff Act, but I feel that the Legislative Counsel of the Senate or House could easily whip something of this kind into shape in a very short time. Their service, as you know, is available primarily to Committees of Congress, but I feel certain that Senator Harrison or Chairman Doughton would cooperate with you and make available to you the help of the draftsmen most familiar with tariff problems in the Legislative Counsels' office.

My feeling is that an amendment of this limited nature would stand a much better chance of passing Congress than a comprehensive tariff bill such as your committee has been working upon.

He replied on the next day:

> Thank you greatly for your letter of January sixteenth enclosing your copy of the rough draft of a proposed amendment to the Tariff Act which you read at the last meeting of the Executive Committee on Commercial Policy. I am glad to have this and it may be that we will decide to move in this direction. That, however, is a matter which will have to be considered further and I am not sure but that the President should be the one to determine it.

That draft was the foundation of the bill which was finally drafted in the State Department and sent to the House. It was provided that the President could, as in my draft, raise or lower duties by 50 per cent, supplemented by the proviso that no article could be transferred to or from the free list.

There was never so much as a suggestion in the Executive Committee on Commercial Policy that the bill would be used to lower tariffs in general or for any purposes other than promoting trade. The purpose of the bill was clearly set out in the preamble to which we all agreed. This is worth quoting, in the light of what has happened:

> For the purpose of expanding foreign markets for the products of the United States (as a means of assisting in the present emergency in restoring the American standard of living, in overcoming domestic unemployment and the present economic depression, in increasing the purchasing power of the American public, and in establishing and maintaining a better relationship among various branches of American agriculture, industry, mining, and commerce) by regulating the admission of foreign goods into the United States in accordance with the characteristics and needs of various branches of American production so that foreign markets will be made available to those branches of American production which require and are capable of developing such outlets by affording

corresponding market opportunities for foreign products in the United States, the President, whenever he finds as a fact that any existing duties or other import restrictions of the United States or any foreign country are unduly burdening and restricting the foreign trade of the United States and that the purpose above declared will be promoted by the means hereinafter specified, is authorized from time to time . . .

Before the House and Senate Committees, no official suggested a general lowering of tariffs. Some of the testimony before the Committees is not only interesting but pertinent. The bill was advanced as an aid to domestic prosperity and, although the possibility of generalization of rates through the most-favored-nation clause was brought up incidentally, generalization was not presented as a way of making a general tariff reduction. In fact it was carefully explained that any tendency in this direction would be sharply limited by including in any specific trade agreement only those commodities of which the country in question was the principal source of supply. The practical impossibility of giving effect to such a counsel of perfection was not discussed. Secretary Hull, before the Ways and Means Committee testified:

> It should be kept in mind that American labor at good wages produces the billions of commodities we export, while our imports chiefly comprise commodities we do not produce in this country at all or in sufficient quantities, with the result that American labor is helped rather than hurt by most of our imports.
>
> Unfortunately, too few persons stop to study and understand the mechanism of international finance and commerce. The entire policy as proposed by the pending House bill, would rest upon trade relationships that would be mutually and equally profitable, both to our own and other countries. While naturally no detailed plans and methods relative to the proposed negotiations have been formulated, it can be stated with emphasis that each trade agreement undertaken would be considered with care and caution, and only after the fullest con-

sideration of all pertinent information. Nothing would be done blindly or hastily. . . .

The primary object of this new proposal is both to reopen the old and seek new outlets for our surplus production, through the gradual moderation of the excessive and more extreme impediments to the admission of American products into foreign markets. At the same time by force of example we would be encouraging the advance of a world-wide movement for the readjustment downward of excessive trade barriers.

The favored-nation doctrine in its unconditional form, or the principle of equality of treatment, would be continued as a policy of our Government. There would be no occasion therefore, for the denouncement of existing treaties before our Government could proceed with negotiations. . . .

Secretary Hull was specifically questioned on the matter of generalization:

Mr. Hill. What would be the effect of the operation of a trade agreement under the authority of this proposed legislation on nations with whom we have agreements for favored-nation treatment? For instance, suppose under this legislation the President should negotiate a trade agreement with Great Britain wherein certain adjustments were made of tariff duties to that country charged to imports from that country—what would be the effect as to those rates upon the duties to be charged to other countries with whom we have agreements as to favored-nation treatment?

Mr. Hull. Our Government during recent years, I think, beginning with a statement by President Harding in 1923, adopted the policy of favored-nation treatment in its unconditional form.

Some people construe that policy of equality of treatment to extend only to those nations with which we have favored-nation relations. Others construe it to relate to all countries; that is, when you enter into a treaty with one country involving mutual concessions and proceed to generalize them, the favors would extend to all countries.

Under this bill that matter is left open so that it can be administered with unlimited application to all countries, or as applying only to those countries with which this country has favored-nation relations.

Naturally, in entering upon negotiations under such authority as is proposed here, our Government would be very careful and very particular to see what would be the result of including a main item or items in any particular arrangement.

Its disposition naturally would be to contact primarily with those countries which are the chief suppliers of one or more commodities, and I think there are 25 or 30 of them, so that we would see what would be the effect of generalizing the advantages we might extend to a country in return for certain advantages it would extend to us, both as between us and between other countries, and that would include the wider opportunity to us to bargain with other countries and it would encourage other countries to want to bargain with us.

Mr. Hill. Now, I want to get as clearly as I can the effect on the countries with whom we have favored-nation treaty agreements. We will enter into a trade agreement under this proposed legislation with Germany whereby we may reduce the tariff duties on certain specific commodities coming into this country from Germany. Now, would the effect of such an agreement automatically give the same modified rate under the trade agreement with Germany to Great Britain or any other government with which we have a favored-nation treaty?

Mr. Hull. Yes; and if I may illustrate, take, for instance, France. We know France is the chief supplier to this country of champagne. We would not hesitate to enter into mutually agreeable relations with France and generalize whatever advantage we should grant. France would always be the chief beneficiary, because we would know there would be no danger of injuring anybody else.

Mr. Hill. Any other country that might be a producer of champagne or wines would have the same rate of duty into this country as France might have under those circumstances—that is, I mean any country with whom we have a favored-nation agreement?

Mr. Hull. Yes. The whole tendency of this would be to encourage other countries from the standpoint of self-interest to want to negotiate and come in with us on definite things where it would be mutually agreeable and profitable, and as a general policy to cease all of the tendencies to obstruct more and more the process of international finance and commerce.

MR. HILL. It would have a tendency to bring all countries to a point where they would be willing to negotiate for favored-nation agreements?

MR. HULL. It would develop that spirit.

The bill was advocated by Secretary Hull as a recovery measure desired by the President. He did not ask authority to revise the whole tariff system—to write a new tariff bill. Thus:

MR. MCCORMACK. I understand the President deems this as absolutely necessary as a part of the recovery program?

MR. HULL. Absolutely; otherwise I do not think there would have been the slightest disposition to propose such a measure. . . .

MR. COOPER. Mr. Secretary, is this a fair statement of the purpose to be accomplished by the pending bill now under consideration by this committee. During the last year we have enacted legislation recommended by the Administration conferring upon the President broad discretionary authority affecting business affairs of this country, and this bill simply carries forward and confers upon the executive branch of the Government the same type of broad discretionary authority with reference to international trade?

MR. HULL. Yes, and it confers it in a way that I think the Supreme Court will hold is a valid transfer of authority.

MR. COOPER. And as suggested by a former question, it is a very vital and essential part of the present recovery program of the Administration?

MR. HULL. Absolutely.

Secretary Wallace, before the same committee, was led into admitting that he favored snuffing out some industries. But, being pressed, he became hazy and could think of only lace. Here are some extracts—the question of Chairman Doughton, a Democrat, shows what was in the minds of the Committee.

The Chairman. Mr. Secretary, you of course have given full study to this bill. In your judgment, if enacted into law, will it be beneficial to agriculture without working any injurious effects upon industry?

Mr. Wallace. . . . As producers, those who produce for the export market would be beneficially affected by this bill; those which are so inefficient that they cannot meet foreign competition would, in case the powers of this bill were exercised to lower the tariff, be perhaps unfavorably affected. . . . Well, sir, it would seem to me to be altogether out of place to go into any great details . . .

Mr. Treadway. No; it is not. We want details; at least, I do. I tried to get them from the Secretary of State this morning without success; but I did do what I could to make the effort, at least.

Mr. Wallace. I think there are certain grades of lace that Massachusetts does not make.

Mr. Treadway. I realize there is a little lace; that is true; but that is not a textile, is it? Would you define fine imported laces as corresponding to cloth?

Mr. Wallace. Laces carry all the way from 100 to 120 per cent; I suppose they must have intended . . .

Mr. Treadway. Yes, but New Jersey produces laces; they can be produced in New Jersey. We went all through that in the tariff act.

Mr. Wallace. If you cannot produce them, why did you put on the tariff?

Mr. Treadway. Suppose you put every lace and curtain factory of the States of New Jersey and Pennsylvania out of business by this reciprocal method, how big an impression on the exportation of our goods will that make, by bringing those few lace curtains into this country? Now if that is the reciprocal trade you men want to get, let us understand it.

Mr. Wallace. On the other hand, sir, a domestic expansion in these inefficient industries will cause unemployment in the efficient industries and in our export agriculture. Now because of the fact there have been these groups, representing in total a very small percentage of our population, but highly organized groups for impact on Congress, it is because of that we have got in this terrible muddle, creating tremendous injustice to our more efficient—and most of our people are efficient—our more efficient exporting industries and reacting through them on this great eastern section of the population. I feel if you had responded less to these small groups, inefficient from the world point of view, that your own cities would be enormously more prosperous than they are today.

Mr. Treadway. Now, Mr. Secretary, you speak of inefficient small industries. Take a community, say, of 50 thousand people with a factory in it employing three or four thousand hands, how would you class that? Where are you going to draw the line of distinction both as to inefficiency and smallness?

Mr. Wallace. May I refer you to the statement I made earlier in response to a question of the chairman, that of our total gainfully employed population of, say, 48 million, about 5 million are employed by the factories of the type that might be affected to some extent by lower tariffs. I would say that is a relatively small group; considering the gains that would accrue to the rest of the population.

Mr. Treadway. I think, Mr. Secretary, when you refer to small industries, if that is the type of industry it is proposed to put out of business by these reciprocal agreements and treaties, you are vitally hitting perhaps not a center of population but a very vital part of the population of this country—when you are centering your efforts to destroy industry in New England. Now let us be fair and frank about it. We have a great many small industries—under the definition you are giving us, they are small—but are not the men and women employed in those industries entitled to a livelihood and not to be obliged to move out from their homes, which they have inherited from generation to generation, and to go to some big center, in order to let in some of this type of goods you are talking about—lace curtains from abroad?

Mr. Wallace. Are they inefficient, sir?

Mr. Treadway. No, sir; they are not. I claim and always shall—and our friend Crowther would back me up if he were not ill today—I have claimed always that aside from satisfying the whims of people, you can get everything that any man or woman ought to wear or own made here at home, under our jurisdiction. . . .

MR. WALLACE. I would just like to say this, sir, that if the Congress and the people of the United States all agree with you, I trust you will cooperate to the fullest possible extent to enable us to retire the agriculture which we formerly were able to sell abroad when we were a debtor Nation, and which we are no longer able to sell abroad as a creditor Nation.

MR. TREADWAY. I represent an agricultural district, Mr. Secretary, as well as an industrial one.

MR. WALLACE. I am speaking to the national problem, sir.

MR. TREADWAY. Well, I am here as the representative of a certain area and you, as the Secretary of Agriculture, of course, are the representative of the whole country; but you ought to look at the picture from the viewpoint of a congressional member a little bit. And indeed we must, Mr. Secretary. We cannot outvote our friends on this other side here, but we can at least protest in behalf of the people we represent, if you are endeavoring to put them out of business in industry or agriculture, either one.

MR. WALLACE. It seems to me, sir, that the essence of the New Deal, if I may be permitted to say it, is to take account of human rights. It would seem to me, also, that a man of the character of the President, in administering powers of this sort, would not be so inhuman as to retire in any barbarous way, such as you seem to contemplate, inefficient industries. . . .

MR. REED. Mr. Secretary, I am very much interested in your remarks in regard to the tariff. I am just wondering, in view of the philosophy which you have advanced here that it is essential to have a low tariff since we are a creditor nation, would you, if you had the power now, as Secretary of Agriculture, lower the tariffs all along the line that we now have on the books for the benefit of agriculture? Would you lower the tariffs, for instance, on butter, milk, eggs, wheat, and all these farm products? Do you think that would benefit the situation now?

MR. WALLACE. Why, obviously lower tariffs on agricultural products would not benefit agriculture in those cases where they are effective. . . .

MR. REED. Then, do you believe, if that tariff were lowered now, it would help agriculture?

MR. WALLACE. Well, I am to some extent a partisan of agriculture and I would hold on to all the agricultural tariffs I could get; from the national point of view, it seems to me that agriculture is entitled to exactly the same kind of tariff benefit as industry—to that, and no more.

MR. REED. All right. Now, let us carry that just a step further: Do you believe it would benefit the United States, benefit it agriculturally and industrially, to wipe out all tariffs? Do you think that would solve our problem now?

MR. WALLACE. This bill has nothing to do with that.

MR. REED. No; but I am asking if you would care to reduce them all along the line, for both industry and agriculture? Do you think it would help at all?

MR. WALLACE. I think it is a mistake to make changes rapidly. From that point of view, I personally am inclined to agree with Secretary Hull that the proper approach is to make gradual reductions, and I am inclined to look on the Tariff Act of 1833, 100 years ago, as a very good type of tariff act. At that time, all tariffs above 20 per cent were agreed to be reduced by 10 per cent a year and that reduction was made until 1843. That was a sensible approach in those days. At the present time, the world situation is such that that approach does not seem to be practicable and this seems to be the only practicable approach which men of long experience have been able to work out.

MR. REED. Then do I infer from your remarks, as carrying out your philosophy, that in order to bring more business to this country you would gradually wipe out all tariffs?

MR. WALLACE. No, sir; you do not understand me correctly.

MR. REED. I just wanted to make sure. You said the Tariff Act of 1833, and I wanted to make sure. . . .

In view of the fact that Germany ultimately was shut out of the trade agreement scheme, these remarks are of interest:

MR. WALLACE. . . . . An increase in any kind of imports strengthens the demand for our exports, no matter where the imports come from. Markets can be created that way that do not appear to exist today. I think it would be quite possible to increase Germany's purchasing power for our lard. Germany, in the old days, was the leading consumer of American lard. Germany today has a tariff of 16 cents a pound on lard, which is nearly three times the present price of lard in this country. Lard is an important product to your State and to my State. I think we should increase Germany's purchasing power for lard very materially in case we import a normal quantity of German goods.

MR. KNUTSON. What would we bring in from Germany?

MR. WALLACE. Germany has a large number of small industries.

MR. KNUTSON. Are they efficient?

MR. WALLACE. They seem to be more efficient than our own; they are willing to sell at lower prices. The Germans are undoubtedly able to sell toys for less than our people are able to sell toys.

MR. KNUTSON. They pay less for labor, do they not, Mr. Secretary? Their living conditions are not comparable with the living conditions of our labor; the German laboring man does not ride back and forth in an automobile from home to work.

MR. WALLACE. The United States has the highest wages of any country in the world, and it has come, not as a result of the tariff, but as a result of the American laboring man being more productive, and his wages have been based on productivity and efficiency; productivity and efficiency are the criteria, and not the tariff.

Professor Dickinson, of the Department of Commerce, had quite a different view. He testified:

Coming down to the specific purpose of this bill, and the specific way in which it will operate, the question has properly been asked how this bill will operate to increase American exports beyond their present low level.

I would suggest that that is not its only purpose. Its purpose is at least to maintain them where they may be, so far as possible at their present level, without subjecting them to a further decrease from continually mounting tariff barriers abroad.

How will the bill operate toward those ends? I can conceive of at least three ways.

In the first place its operation may not require any decrease in duties at all. The President may make an agreement with a particular foreign country whereby this country will agree not to raise duties on one or more types of articles imported from that particular country, if the country in question will, in return, agree either to lower, or not to increase duties on American goods, or to take some specified quantity of American goods which will represent a larger total than it has been taking from us recently, or a larger total than it might otherwise take from us.

That is the first way in which this bill will make it possible to increase, or at least to protect our exports, without in any way lowering the duties supposed to exist for the protection of American industry.

I can conceive of another and a second way in which the powers proposed to be conferred by this bill may be used to protect and increase our export trade.

There are many articles in our tariff schedule on which a very high rate of duty is charged, although the articles are not produced in the United States at all. The duty is imposed on them because they might conceivably in some sort of way be used as substitutes for something that is produced in the United States, and out of an excess of caution the American producers of these latter articles have reached out and closed the door to their admission.

When the bill reached the House, debate was limited by agreement and was perfunctory. The opposition knew that the bill had to pass and nothing could be done about it. In the Senate the discussion was more vigorous. Senator Fletcher tried to get an amendment prohibiting the lowering of duties on agricultural products—in accordance with the President's pre-election pledge. He was voted down. The Senate did put in a clause preventing the use of the powers to cancel war debts.

Some of the Senators distrusted generalizing the benefits

—Senators Vandenberg, Austin and Long were very much to the point. But Senator Pat Harrison explained it as a help toward bargaining and in effect disclaimed any thought of a general tariff reduction. He said:

Under the provisions of the bill the proclaimed duties and other import restrictions shall not be confined alone to articles coming from those foreign countries which are parties to such trade agreements. The United States has already entered into treaties and agreements with the great majority of nations under which the parties agree to grant to each other the treatment accorded to the most favored nation. It would, therefore, be impossible, without violation of these treaties, to restrict the privileges of a trade agreement to the single nation with which the agreement is made. It would also be unwise; for the effort to give special favors to individual nations is the pathway to keen competition, discrimination, and eventual trade warfare. If concessions made under the agreements are withheld from countries with which agreements have not been concluded, we cannot expect such countries to extend to us concessions which they have made under similar agreements with other countries. Since foreign countries have concluded many more such agreements than we have, American commerce would lose heavily from the withdrawal of most-favored-nation treatment from us. Advantages obtained by reciprocity with some countries might thus be nullified by discrimination in others. The sound pathway to follow in international trade lies through a generalization of rates and an equality of treatment to all. For this reason the privileges granted to each nation are to be applied under the terms of the bill to all countries alike. To this general policy, however, the proposed legislation makes certain exceptions. The President may withdraw the enjoyment of such rates from any country "because of its discriminatory treatment of American commerce" or because of "other acts or policies which in his opinion tend to defeat the purposes" of the measure.

The bill became a law on June 12th, 1934. Its main provisions were the grant to the President, over a period of three years, of the right to make reciprocal trade agreements and, in the course of doing so, to lower or to raise tariffs by 50 per cent. In conclusion the Act read:

Before any foreign trade agreement is concluded with any foreign government or instrumentality thereof under the provisions of this Act, reasonable public notice of the intention to negotiate an agreement with such government or instrumentality shall be given in order that any interested person may have an opportunity to present his views to the President, or to such agency as the President may designate, under such rules and regulations as the President may prescribe; and before concluding such agreement the President shall seek information and advice with respect thereto from the United States Tariff Commission, the Departments of State, Agriculture, and Commerce and from such other sources as he may deem appropriate.

This provision was inserted at the insistence of Congress to afford interests and industries which might be affected by tariff changes a fair chance to present their views. It soon became apparent that the hearings were of a pro forma character and that the vital decisions were made by star chamber procedure in the State Department and White House.

The bill was announced as a means to make Yankee trading possible. We were to be real Yankees. Lloyds Bank, in its bulletin for June, 1934, said mournfully:

Great Britain, it is true, has entered into a few more bilateral agreements, but the scope for agreements of this sort proves to be much less extensive than was hoped. . . . Bilateral agreements tend to divert trade rather than to increase it, and if President Roosevelt obtains the powers from Congress for which he is asking, the outlook for further successful bargains by Great Britain will be black indeed. The President is most likely to use his powers, if he gets them, to make tariff agreements not with Great Britain, but in competition with her.

The British need not have been apprehensive. They did not then know what Secretary Hull and his professors could do with and to a trade agreement. They know now!

Chapter XI

Simple Arithmetic

Under the very broad powers given to me by the President in his Executive Order of March 23rd, 1934, establishing the office of Special Adviser on Foreign Trade, I was, among other things, "authorized to obtain, review, and coordinate the information, statistics, and data with reference to the foreign trade of the United States. . . ." This was in accord with the recommendation which I had officially made to the President in December, 1933 and gave the opportunity, for the first time, to set up the foreign trade books of the country in simple accounting fashion and to envisage the results of our trade just as though the nation were a corporation.

I made three reports. The first, on May 23rd, 1934, was an income account showing the results of our foreign transactions from July 1st, 1896 to December 31st, 1933. The second, on August 30th, 1934, covered the same period but was more in the nature of a balance sheet showing our position with the world. Both accounts were in the form of letters to the President and were printed as public documents. The results were startling. They clearly showed that our foreign trade and lending had been steadily draining away the liquid assets of the nation. The President was impressed. To neither letter did the internationalists in the Administration pay the slightest attention. They went on with their policies without regard to the arithmetic of the facts.

My third letter was submitted on April 30th, 1935 and brought the accounts up to December 31st, 1934. It showed what had been happening to us as a result of neglecting the accounts—how, while we were struggling to get out of the depression and to increase employment, the internationalists were permitting our resources to be drained and were actually promoting unemployment. Since this third letter has to do with a condition which has continued to date and which is daily transferring the control of an ever-increasing portion of our resources to foreign hands, I shall reserve it for a subsequent chapter summing up the results of our foreign trade policies to date. Here it is enough to discuss the basic work of the first two accounts and to give the information which was given to the President and to the others in charge of our foreign trade policies before they went forward with their theories. Since the facts of the accounts and the implications to be drawn from them are very clear, I am not indulging in hindsight when I say that what has happened in the way of selling out the United States at a discount would not have happened, had the precepts of ordinary accounting prudence been followed.

The need for accounting in our foreign trade requires some little explanation—largely because it is so simple that its neglect is to most people incomprehensible. Most of the more devastating errors in our foreign trade policy come from neglecting business practices of such an elementary nature that not even a peanut stand could carry on without them. It is hard for the average man to believe that our national foreign trade policies have been formulated on a shockingly incomplete set of facts and that the abstruse, ex cathedra pronouncements of our Secretary of State, his professors and the internationalists generally are results, not of current research but merely of wishful thinking in terms of a dead and gone economic and financial era.

Let us start with these propositions:

(1) It is the duty of our Government not to take any action which will diminish the opportunities for the profitable employment of the citizens of the United States. With that everyone will agree. Therefore, it is acting against the interests of the United States for any Administration to advance a

policy which takes away jobs from American workers or farmers and gives them to foreign workers or farmers.

(2) It is not in the interest of the nation to adopt any policy which makes the United States, in peace or in war, needlessly dependent upon the will of any foreign nation for any essential supply. We were crippled in the Revolutionary War because the British had not permitted the Colonies to develop the iron industry much beyond the casting of pigs for shipment to England. We were crippled in the Great War because Germany, using the two-price system, had kept our chemical industry out of the more important fields, and also we were dependent on Chile for nitrates.

(3) It is not in the national interest to permit ourselves to become dependent when we can remain independent. We can control our own economy only to the extent that we are independent. This applies to exports with the same force that it applies to imports.

Foreign trade is simply trade and has no especial virtues which make it preferable to domestic trade. Trade does not of itself add to our wealth. We grow wealthy only as we produce more than we consume, and trade, whether foreign or domestic, is of value only if it enables us to exchange what we can make and do not need for what we cannot make and do need.

Applying these principles to foreign trade and considering the nation as a unit, we do a useful thing if we exchange one hour of labor for one hour of foreign labor, only if the one hour of foreign labor could not have been performed by an American. We do not, as is sometimes imagined, increase our wealth if we exchange one hour of American labor for two or more hours of foreign labor. That looks like a bargain, but it is a bad bargain, for not only do we deprive the American of his opportunity to work, but also we withdraw from the workman affected a purchasing power which reacts to the benefit of other sections of industry and of agriculture generally. Also we may weaken our self-reliance. For instance, one hour's work by an automobile mechanic will exchange for several days' work of a Japanese textile worker, but no one would seriously advocate letting the Japanese take over our textile business, on the ground that thereby our own nation would become wealthier

These principles are so elementary that it would seem unnecessary to state them, were it not that our national policy has been framed in complete disregard of them. That is where the accounting comes in.

Our country, in its trade with the world, can be considered as one big corporation in the business of buying (that is, importing) and selling (that is, exporting) to a great many other corporations (that is, nations) scattered all over the world. Of course most of the business is actually done between individuals resident in these nations, but, just as the transactions of the subsidiaries of a great corporation all get into the accounts of the parent corporation, so do the accounts of the individuals in foreign trade eventually merge into the national income account. For instance, if the individuals in the A country buy a great deal more from the individuals in the B country than those in the B country buy from them, the merchants of the A country will have to dig into their resources—which are a part of the national resources—to pay the bills. That is why, from time immemorial, nations have kept careful account of the export and import of goods in order to prevent the draining off of resources through buying more than could be paid for. If a nation exported more than it imported, the trade balance was said to be "favorable." But if it imported more than it exported, then the balance was said to be "unfavorable." These terms are somewhat misleading, for an excess of exports over imports is not favorable if the excess is not paid for, while an excess of imports over exports may not be unfavorable if the excess goes to paying debts. Particularly is this true if the imports are non-competitive.

It is at once apparent that the records of the exchange of

goods cannot tell the whole story and that, if we are to know where we are at any time as a nation, we must know all the transactions and not simply the transactions in goods. In short, we must know as a nation the entirety of our foreign trade and not simply that portion of it represented by goods. We must know what we have sold and to whom, and what we got in return. Further than that we must analyze our customers (that is, the nations) to see how we stand with each. The British had found, as is shown by the Macmillan Report, to which I have before referred—and which is the best report on the actualities of foreign trade ever written—that the British Empire had been following a false policy because it had not been following the facts. It was quite apparent from the discussion which we had in the Administration that, although many thought they knew all about our foreign trade, little of the knowledge was based on complete facts. For instance, everyone assumed:

(1) That the United States was a great creditor nation because it had made some heavy loans. Secretary Wallace had evolved a whole farm limitation theory on the assumption that before the war we had been a debtor nation and since had become a great creditor nation. Whether one is a creditor or a debtor is a matter of fact to be determined only by the accounts.

(2) That imports breed exports as of course. That is a question of fact.

(3) That triangular trade is important. For instance, Brazil sells us more than we buy from her. This results in an indebtedness to Brazil on the books in New York. But Brazil owes England, and the British take our debt to Brazil in payment of Brazil's debt to her and presumably buy goods in the American market. That is not triangular trade. It is triangular payment. Its extent and importance in the foreign trade of the United States is not definitely known. As Special Adviser I started a series of individual country studies which when finished would have afforded a basis for determining this and other questions. They were not completed at the time I left

office. However, from the data available I suspect that the importance of so-called triangular trade to the United States has been greatly over-rated. League of Nations studies suggest that in international trade in general it is relatively small and that it is tending to decrease as a result of increasing direct trade between nations. However this may be, the record discloses that the purchasing power in dollars of a foreign country, whether created by direct trade or indirectly by triangular payments, is frequently used, not to buy American goods or to make payments on debts due us, but for the purchase of securities in our markets. In other words, increased merchandise imports do not necessarily mean increased agricultural and industrial exports, either directly or indirectly, which fact should not be obscured by grandiose references to "the need for more imports" or to "the demands of triangular trade."

An international account in these days consists of many items in addition to goods. The shipping charges and insurance that we pay to foreign nations are equivalent to imports—that is, they are debit items. So is interest paid by us abroad. When our tourists go abroad and spend money, they transfer American wealth to foreigners, and so their expenditures are debits. The sums which immigrants send home from here are, in the same fashion, debits. There is a whole class of money and credit transactions which has nothing at all to do with the payment of goods. Gold and silver are goods and, although formerly the movement of gold and silver was usually in payment for goods, that is no longer true and they may be considered as goods that can also be used as money. In addition to all these transactions are the purely money transactions which have to do with the transfer of credits or capital in the form of credit. These need have no relation at all to the buying and selling of goods. Thus the record of trade balances in goods may or may not give a true picture of a country's condition.

The almost incredible fact is that our country, although it had kept exact records of the exchanges of goods, had no corresponding records of the money transactions—that is, we had never had a complete picture of our international position. Our whole foreign trade picture changed when we went off gold in the spring of 1933. While we did not begin raising the price of gold until the autumn of 1933 and did not devalue until January, 1934, it was the fact of going off gold that made the preparation and examination of our accounts imperative. In spite of our experience of 1931 when the nation was almost wrecked by gold withdrawals and in spite of Great Britain's departure from gold and resumption of bookkeeping, the hope was still strong in 1933 that the old gold standard would be restored in some manner and would be able to fulfil its previous function of automatically serving as the balancing item of trade. Hence the pressure for stabilization, in which Secretary Hull shared, at the London Economic Conference. The President's message definitely relegated gold to the status of a commodity. With the example of Great Britain before us, we should at once have gone after our accounts. As a matter of fact, Great Britain was cagey enough to get going on her accounts as a result of the Macmillan recommendations before abandoning gold. However, the wisdom of our quick action in April, 1933, is beside the point—the real point is that having taken it, we were constrained by every consideration of prudence and common sense to find out where we stood on our accounts, what the trend was, and to base our policy on the fact of having gone off gold, rather than on the nebulous hope of restoring the United States and the whole world to the automatic or semi-automatic gold standard which had gone.

The utterly incredible fact is that the internationalists in charge of making our trade policies could not see that a complete account was essential to a sound policy, if we were to hold a place in the changing world.

The President, in an address to the N.R.A. code authorities on March 5th, 1934, had said: "Economic balance is our objective. . . . We seek also balance—that our trade with other nations be increased on both sides of the ledger."

We had never had an international ledger. At the best, we had some journal and cash entries. I set up a division of international accounts within my office and appointed Raymond H. Weins Comptroller of International Accounts. He was formerly assistant to Hon. John Barton Payne, Chairman of the U. S. Shipping Board. Associated with him were Charles Darlington, Jr., formerly of the Bank for International Settlements and now of the State Department; Dr. August Maffry, now of the Department of Commerce; and Herman King of the Federal Reserve Board. They collaborated with Dr. Amos Taylor and Dr. Paul Dickens of the Department of Commerce. These men and their assistants worked with the many departments of the Government where figures had been assembled. Where no figures existed and estimates had to be made, they used all the available data to keep down the inevitable margins of error. I took my first report to the President in person and he read it over as I sat by his desk. He took a pencil and started to do some editing. He glanced at me:

"You do not object to editing?"

"Yes, I do," I answered. "These are all Commerce Department figures, and I do not want this report to express any opinions. I want the figures to talk."

"I guess you are right," said the President, as he put down his pencil.

The official published copy contains this letter signed by the President: "Your letter of May 23rd and the figures you have presented are of tremendous interest to me and I am sure will be to others. I suggest that you make them public."

The report divided the years from 1896 to 1933 into four periods, thus: from July 1st, 1896 to June 30th, 1914 as representing the pre-war epoch; from July 1st, 1914 to December 31st, 1922 as representing the war and the post-war depression periods; from January 1st, 1923 to December 31st, 1929 as representing the post-war inflation period; and from January 1st, 1930 to December 31st, 1933 as representing the deflation period.

We discovered that during the whole thirty-eight years the country was a nominal creditor for its entire transactions in the enormous sum of $22,645,000,000. This had come about as follows, as given in the report:

We sold to the world goods in the amount of		$121,250,000,000
we bought from the world goods in the amount of		84,604,000,000
thereby placing the world in debt to us for goods in the amount of		36,646,000,000
Thus, the value of our imports of goods is, on the face of these figures, less than 70 per cent of our exports.		
As against this export excess we must in fairness deduct the amounts which our tourists spent abroad, and which our immigrants, charitable organizations, and others sent abroad		19,429,000,000
leaving an apparently favorable balance of		17,217,000,000
Services rendered by us to the world such as shipping and freight services, together with interest and dividend payments on our foreign investments, interest and principal payments on war debts, miscellaneous and other items, placed the world in debt to us for an additional		26,461,000,000
making a total owed to us of		43,678,000,000
Services rendered to us by the world such as shipping and freight services, together with our interest and dividend payments on foreigners' investments in the United States, miscellaneous and other items, in the amount of	$18,938,000,000	
together with net gold imports of	2,095,000,000	
reduced the world debt to us by		21,033,000,000
resulting in a net increase during the 38-year period in the debt owing to us amounting to		$22,645,000,000

This increase in debt is represented by foreign securities and other investments in foreign countries bought by United States citizens, net $14,398,000,000, and war loans advanced by the United States Government, $10,304,000,000, making a total of $24,702,000,000. From these figures must be deducted United States securities and other investments made by foreigners in the United States, net $2,057,000,000, resulting in the above net increase in debt of $22,645,000,000. Our national assets will be diminished by the amount of this debt which is not paid. (These figures represent net capital movement, and should be added to the estimated $2,500,000,000 which foreigners had invested in the United States in 1896, and the estimated $500,000,000 which we had invested in foreign countries in that year, to reflect the approximate present position.)

The first report showed how we managed, in our delusions of grandeur, to get ourselves owed by nearly every nation on earth—how we managed to work up a vast foreign trade on the formula of giving anything to anyone who asked for it. It was harvest time for the bankers, the exporters and the shipping men—the same groups who are now asking for a new Santa Claus and piously telling us how good the period was for everyone and that we must get back to 1929 levels of foreign trade. It is the American taxpayer, producer and investor who pay the bill. The second report showed the way that the book credit of $22,645,000,000 took refuge in various sorts of holdings and securities, and the third report—which will be given later—showed how our nation continued to follow and develop, against the plain records of the books, policies which have rid the credits of a large part of their asset value and may well return us to the status of a debtor nation. Here are summaries of what the accounts show for the periods.

I. The first period is of extraordinary interest because it throws light for the first time upon the dogma that before the War we were a debtor nation; that since the War we have become a creditor nation; and that we have come to disaster because, as a creditor nation, we persisted in retaining the policies we used as a debtor nation. From the account it appears that at no time since 1896 have we been a debtor nation except in a technical sense. The chief function of our foreign trade during the period up to the war was to provide funds for our immigrants to send to their relatives abroad. During the period from July 1st, 1896, to June 30th, 1914, we sold goods to the world in the amount of $31,033,000,000 and we took in exchange goods amounting to $22,180,000,000. This left the world owing us the sum of $8,853,000,000. We did not take goods in return for all the goods that we sold, because we neither needed them nor wanted them. We had no reason to import foodstuffs and we were building up our own factories. We thought we were doing a big business and, since everyone seemed to be getting paid, no one inquired how we were getting paid. It now appears from the account that the nation was not getting paid. Our immigrants and tourists (the tourist trade was comparatively small) sent or spent abroad funds to the amount of $6,080,000,000. This still left the world in our debt in the sum of $2,773,000,000. Adding to this debt the amount of our services to the world and deducting the amount of the interest payments we made and the cost of the services rendered to us, left us at the end of the period in debt to the world in the sum of one billion dollars.

During this whole period, the country was short of capital and the current notion was that we were progressing too fast to accumulate any capital. The fact is now revealed that, because we did not know the state of our accounts, we permitted our immigrants to send out a considerable portion of what should have been our national savings and we had to borrow from Europe what we should have been able to borrow at home. We closed the period a billion dollars more in debt to Europe than at the beginning—that is, our people freely presented six billion dollars to the world and then were compelled to borrow a billion of it back at interest. The net result of our foreign trade was to provide foreigners with money to lend to us. We were in the nature of a colony.

II. The second period, from July 1st, 1914, to the end of 1922, covers eight and a half years, and was abnormal. We sold the world goods, mostly foodstuffs and raw materials, to the amount of $46,952,000,000 and, in spite of most of the world being at war, we bought from it goods to the amount of $25,766,000,000—leaving the world in debt to us for goods in the sum of $21,186,000,000. Our tourist expenditures, immigrant remittances and the like amounted to only $3,500,000,000.

The world further went into our debt for a great new item of interest, dividends and principal payments upon the moneys owing to us both as a nation and as individuals, and these debt services, together with shipping and other services, increased the world's debt to us by $8,532,000,000. Our debt was offset by services rendered to us by foreigners, by payments made on account of debt interest and principal and by the shipping of gold to us in the sum of $1,746,000,000—making a total offset of $6,913,000,000. At the end, we had a net increase in the world's debt to us in the sum of $19,305,000,000.

Our government took obligations of foreign governments in the sum of $10,304,000,000. These are our war loans. In the payment of their debts, foreigners sent back to us securities they had previously purchased from us in the sum of $2,222,-000,000. As private citizens, we made investments abroad in the sum of $6,779,000,000. Public finance accounts for only somewhat more than half of the total of the financial transactions. Our citizens sold abroad a vast quantity of goods at very high prices because the world was hungry for goods and our people did not have the national bookkeeping facilities to know that the nation was not getting paid for what it sold.

III. The third period covers the years from the beginning

of 1923 through 1929. We entered the period owing practically nothing to foreign nations and being owed a great deal by them. We sold goods in the amount of $33,711,000,000—which was more than we had sold during the eighteen years of the pre-war period. But we also bought more from the world than we had ever bought—goods to the amount of $28,-735,000,000—leaving the world in debt to us on account of goods in the sum of $4,976,000,000.

During the eighteen years of the pre-war period, it will be remembered, our immigrants sent abroad nearly six billions, but during these seven years, 1923-29, our tourists and immigrants spent or sent abroad the sum of $7,021,000,000—leaving us in the hole on current transactions in the sum of $2,045,-000,000. This, however, was offset by the sum of $10,667,000,-000 due to us for service on our loans and for other services, against which was a counter charge by the foreigners for services rendered to us and for interest and the like owing to them, amounting to $5,875,000,000. They also shipped us gold in the net amount of $175,000,000. The result was a net increase in debt to us, for the period, of $2,572,000,000. Had we conducted our foreign affairs on the simple bookkeeping system, we should have known that we were selling goods for which we were unlikely ever to receive payment. But our bankers in this period floated loans and sold them to the American people in the net amount of $7,140,000,000. All the interest paid to us on war and private loans came out of our new lendings. The foreigners took the exchange provided by the loans and proceeded to buy our securities and build up demand bank deposits in the sum of $4,568,000,000. That is, we bought foreign long-term securities and the foreigners turned around and bought our securities, mostly short-term and highly liquid, thus creating for themselves a position of financial power and mobility that eventually contributed greatly to the wrecking of our banking system.

IV. The fourth period of four years from 1930 through 1933 shows the collapse of our house of cards. We sold goods to the amount of $9,554,000,000 and took goods to the amount of $7,923,000,000—leaving us creditors on the goods account in the sum of $1,631,000,000. The figures are not as small in volume of goods as they are in dollars, for world prices of raw commodities dropped vertically. Our tourists and immigrants at once wiped out our creditor position on goods by sending abroad $2,828,000,000—leaving us debtors in the amount of $1,197,000,000. Payments to us on account of interest and services offset by our payments of a similar character brought us out as creditors on the whole account of the period to the amount of $1,768,000,000. We managed to get back from abroad investments in the amount of only $521,000,000 while the foreigners during the same time were taking back from us their investments in the amount of $2,289,000,000. Thus, during a period of general default upon the foreign obligations held by us, the foreigners managed to take back more than two billions of the investments which they had made here with funds borrowed from us.

Bringing all the figures together, we find that in thirty-eight years we sold to the world goods in the amount of $121,250,000,000 and bought from the world goods in the amount of $84,604,000,000. The difference between what we sold in goods and what we took in goods is thus $36,646,000,000. This represents the amount of American materials and labor which has not been exchanged for foreign materials and labor.

Our immigrants sending home funds to their relatives and our tourists spending money for passage on foreign-owned steamships and in foreign countries cancelled payment in goods to the extent of $19,429,000,000. No other nation in the world would have allowed such a drain. Some nations have been so adversely affected by the effect of tourist expenditures upon their balance of payments that they have been obliged to subject them to the most rigid restrictions. In some instances they have even treated them as a specific object of barter transactions. I know of one agreement between two foreign countries whereby one of them traded tourists' revenues with another for carloads of hogs. The basis was about $40 per head for hogs and $60 per head for tourists. This is perhaps an extreme example, but it illustrates somewhat graphically the reality of the effect of tourist expenditures upon national economy.

The foreigners also paid us gold on account in the net sum of $2,095,000,000. There were on each side of the account charges for freight, insurance and other items incident to shipping, and for interest and dividends, so that at the end of the period and for the transactions of the period we found ourselves being owed the sum of $22,645,000,000. That is, we found ourselves unpaid for nearly one-sixth of all that we had sold. That is the net amount. The actual account stands thus:

Foreign securities and investments in foreign countries	$14,398,000,000
War loans	10,304,000,000
	$24,702,000,000
Foreign investments here	2,057,000,000
Net	$22,645,000,000

Our so-called investments fall into three classes:

1. Direct investments abroad—that is, American plants located on foreign soil and investments by Americans in foreign plants. These had a book value at the end of 1933 estimated at $7,767,000,000. However, this estimate was based on a 1929 Department of Commerce questionnaire, and there has been no reappraisal. The American factories abroad employing, as they must, foreign workmen are to be considered, not as a part of the American system, but as in competition with American products made in America. In part, therefore, our foreign trade has been used to finance the making abroad of goods formerly made in America.

2. The war debts, amounting to $10,304,000,000. The entirety of this debt, except for a small amount owed by Finland,

is in default and for the time being represents just so much wealth lost.

3. The balance of the debt is represented by securities issued by foreign nations and their political divisions and by foreign corporations which at the end of 1933 were estimated at $6,032,000,000. These are held by our citizens and institutions, and more than two billions are already in default.

Here is a summary of the debt transactions as given in my report of August 30, 1934:

The gross investments by the United States in foreign securities, loans to foreign governments (including war debts), and other investments during the 38-year period aggregated		$36,875,000,000
As against this sum there were repurchased, redeemed, and allowed as commissions, discounts, etc., the following:		
Repurchases	$4,466,000,000	
Redemptions	6,517,000,000	
Commissions and discounts	1,190,000,000	
an aggregate of		12,173,000,000
resulting in a net increase during the 38-year period in United States loans and investments in foreign countries of		$24,702,000,000
During the 38-year period the world bought from us, United States securities, etc., amounting to	$11,076,000,000	
During that period we bought or redeemed United States securities, etc., held in foreign countries	9,019,000,000	
resulting in a net increase during the 38-year period in foreigners' investments in the United States of		2,057,000,000
which amount, deducted from the net increase in United States loans and investments in foreign countries, makes up the net increase in debt for the 38-year period mentioned in my report of May 23, 1934, of		$22,645,000,000

In a section of "Comments" attached to the second report I made these observations, which are of importance because what happened in 1931 may happen again for, as will later appear, the country is being engineered around to much the same position it had in 1931. Here are the pertinent paragraphs:

We have found it impossible to realize upon many of our foreign investments. Foreign bonds (expressed in dollars) were not readily marketable outside of the United States. Our foreign direct investments were non-liquid. War debts had been funded on the basis of annual repayments. Finally, as a result of the German and other Standstill Agreements and exchange restrictions in various countries, only a limited withdrawal was possible of our short-term funds in foreign countries.

United States short-term (banking funds) in foreign countries, Dec. 31, 1929		$1,617,000,000
Increase in 1930	$185,000,000	
Decrease in 1931	563,000,000	
Decrease in 1932	186,000,000	
Increase in 1933	29,000,000	
Net decrease		535,000,000
Balance in foreign countries, Dec. 31, 1933		$1,082,000,000

On the other hand, foreign countries realized upon their holdings in our markets and withdrew short-term banking funds as follows:

Foreign short-term (banking funds) in the United States, Dec. 31, 1929		$3,037,000,000
Decrease in 1930	$ 300,000,000	
Decrease in 1931	1,272,000,000	
Decrease in 1932	595,000,000	
Decrease in 1933	383,000,000	
Total decrease		2,550,000,000
Balance in United States, Dec. 31, 1933		$ 487,000,000

The withdrawals by foreigners of $2,550,000,000 short-term banking funds were responsible for the heavy inroads upon our gold stocks from September 1931 to June 1932, inclusive. The withdrawal of this gold demoralized our banking system. The consequent pressure exerted by bankers to liquidate loans shattered prices. This situation was accentuated by interest defaults on many foreign bonds, accompanied by correspondingly low market prices.

The capital movements for 1922-29, inclusive, indicate that we ourselves made available to foreigners the funds which made possible in later years their withdrawal of our gold. With no responsibility for our national welfare, these investments were thrown on our market, converted into short-time balances, in turn into gold, and withdrawn at the most critical periods.

The report pointed out, among other things, that the discounts and commissions from foreign financing had amounted since 1914 to the sum of $1,190,000,000. It also showed in a table the growth in the part played by capital transactions in our whole trade as against goods transactions. In 1919 money transactions amounted to only 7.6 per cent of our whole trade as expressed in dollars, but in 1933 the proportion had risen to 41.6 per cent. This means that the trading in investments—that is, in promises to pay—had by 1933 reached almost as great a total as the goods exchanges.

My reports were received in many quarters with a curious resentment. The professional advocates of foreign trade and many others took the figure of $22,645,000,000 as my estimate of the losses on foreign trade. The total represented nothing of the kind. It simply showed the amount of credit the nation as a whole had extended in consequence of its international dealings. It followed as of course that the appraisal of the worth of that credit would be an appraisal of the effect of the international transactions on the national wealth of our country. At that time I did not attempt any appraisal.

There were some—chiefly those who had made money out of the exports—who set up that the country was better off as a result of the exports, regardless of whether or not the loans were paid, because thereby industry had been kept busy, wages paid and so on. It was of no concern to them that a great number of investors, rich and poor, were the involuntary angels of this trade, in that they bought the foreign bonds on the representation of banks and banking houses that the bonds were good. Not only were individuals involved but also insurance companies, savings banks and commercial banks. The report of the Comptroller of the Currency says that on June 30th, 1931 the active banks of the country held in their portfolios foreign government bonds and other foreign securities to the face amount of $765,152,000. It is difficult to comprehend the kind of reasoning which would condone such utter recklessness on the part of our bankers and others responsible for our orgy of foreign lendings. Yet it is not unusual to find the figures of our foreign trade covering these lending years given as the normal, healthy trade which the country might regain.

Some objected to the inclusion of the war debts as an extraordinary item outside the channels of trade. But excluding the war debts still left some twelve billion dollars outstanding, and the worth of an item of twelve billion dollars certainly merits inquiry. One commentator asked: "One wonders what Mr. Peek would make of Great Britain's £700,000,000 excess of merchandise imports in the five years before the War, or a similar surplus of £5,000,000,000 in the two past decades." That was an unnecessary question. Obviously Great Britain was able to pay for these through the sale of her shipping and banking services to the world and by income received from foreign investments. The Macmillan Committee had already tackled that exact problem and in consequence changed the whole British economy.

There was of course the conventional remedy of more imports to cure all our ills—but without any specifications as to how the country was to take more imports except at the expense of established American industries. It does not seem to be comprehended that all the major commodities used in industry and all the major quasi-necessities of life, such as coffee and tea, are already on the free list. As always, the argument came out that, if only we lowered our tariffs and took more goods from abroad, the foreigners would use their excess balances not only to buy our goods but also to pay their debts to us. The experience of England has been that in general the interest on foreign loans is paid very largely out of new lending and that when the lending stops the interest payments stop. There was practically no comment on the showing of the accounts that all the interest payments to us were made out of fresh borrowing and that at no time did our foreign loans sustain themselves.

And also there was almost no comment on the fact that our foreign loans, to the extent that they were converted into American securities and American bank deposits, gave to the foreign nations a claim upon our gold which they exercised in 1931. It does not take a long memory to recall that, while the stock market crash came in 1929, the real depression started when the withdrawal of gold forced our banks to contract credit. It does not seem too much to say that, if careful books and credit information had been kept upon the entirety of our international transactions on a country by country basis, the stupendous world credit smash would never have happened. For, had the accounts been public, it would have been seen that some of the countries of the world were over-lending and others were over-borrowing. This is confirmed by Fred I. Kent, a leading American authority on foreign exchange. In the course of an address he set out how Germany and Austria in 1924 found themselves without working capital and hence were forced to offer high rates. He said:

The great banking institutions of the world now began transferring funds for the accounts of their customers and themselves to Germany and Austria to take advantage of the high interest rates that were offered, but all without knowledge of what others were doing. The viciousness of this situation was so evident that, if I may refer to a personal activity, I endeavored to have the Bank for International Settlements develop a simple system that would make it possible for the bankers of the world to measure such operations on an intelligent basis. The bankers in London, Paris and New York, for instance, were not only unaware of the total transfers that were being made by other banks in their cities to Germany and Austria, but they had no knowledge whatsoever of the transfers that were being made from other countries. . . . The result was that in 1931, when the trouble started in Austria, with its repercussions upon Germany because of the close financial linking of many Austrian and German institutions, the world woke up one day and found that more money had been remitted to these two countries by the other countries of the world for short time investment than could possibly be returned unless it be over a long period of years, during which Germany and Austria must have a fairly continuing balance of trade in their favor.

It is scarcely conceivable that our own bankers would so freely have offered both short and long term loans had they known as much about our lendings and foreign borrowings as they demand to know about individual domestic borrowers.

The internationalists generally, including those within the Administration, refused to consider the accounts because they would not consider any facts which might interfere with their theories. They refused to face the realities that the trade of the world was everywhere based on selective imports and exports and that money generally was no longer based on gold but was simply managed public credit. Without going into the merits or the demerits of a managed money, it must be apparent that if the nations of the world, through exchange controls, import and export quotas and the like maintain one price for home consumption and another for export, the nation which does not know with exactness the state of its international accounts is in peril of having its resources drained away. For instance, Japanese industrial costs are abnormally low, but in addition to this Japan has one price for domestic consumption and another price for export. The price for export, by currency management, is so low that Japanese goods can pass any tariff barrier.

The purpose of my accounting was to obtain the facts on which a realistic policy could be built. I had my own very definite ideas as to the best policy, but the accounts as stated were accounts and nothing more. They were designed to take the discussion out of the air and get it down to the facts.

Of course I did not know that the internationalists had in mind only the lowering of all tariffs.

Chapter XII

The Star Chamber

The manner in which the reciprocal trade agreements have been negotiated gives a perfect illustration of the dangers inherent in substituting a government by men for a government by laws. Congress thought it was delegating the power to make trades. It did not realize that it was delegating the power to write a new tariff bill revising the present rates downward by 50 per cent. That is a more sweeping cut than any Congress in the history of the country ever dared to make —even though it had been elected on a low-tariff platform.

The Congress did not realize, in passing the Act, that its administration would be guided by other than the declared purposes of the Act. The Act was passed primarily to dispose of agricultural surpluses and to help domestic unemployment. But, once the internationalists got into the saddle, they found that trading was quite too commercial and sordid for their minds, and so gradually they fastened the Act to an internationalist program for world peace and sought to use it as an instrument to strike down the barriers of trade everywhere and to make the whole world into one great, happy family. The only important barriers which to date they have succeeded in striking down are those which have protected the United States.

They have, as will be shown, destroyed much of the power of the United States to bargain in international trade. For the traditional figure of Uncle Sam they have substituted Simple Simon with a nimbus. Congress thought it was putting the power to trade in the hands of the President. That was what Secretary Hull asked for. Before the Senate Committee he pleaded:

We have had as high as 14 to 15 million unemployed persons in this country who were accustomed to employment and who, with their families, would amount to 35,000,000 human souls, of our 120,000,000, living an utterly hopeless existence, out of employment.

Now, don't you think, if they were to choose, in this awful emergency, between continuing in their unemployed state on an increasing scale and trusting the Roosevelt administration to try to increase customers and increase demand for production and let them go back to work, don't you think they would be willing so to place their trust?

The Congress had no conception that those who were actively engaged in the trade of the country, foreign and domestic, and who might be helped or hurt by changes in the tariff, would have only a perfunctory opportunity to present their views and no opportunity at all to be heard on the actual terms of the agreements. It may be that truly scientific tariff-making requires the exclusion from the negotiations of all those who have commercial interests. It may be that the chief qualification for a tariff expert is that he never had any business or trading experience. It may be that the trading and log-rolling which attend the making of a tariff by Congress are very evil. Or again it may be that this is the method by which a democracy reaches its decisions. The proof of that lies in the agreements themselves—in what they are, as opposed to what they are said to be. If trade agreements have to do with trade, it does not seem apparent why those experienced in trade should be excluded from their making. If they have not to do primarily with trade, but are intended for some other purpose, why lug in the word "trade"?

It is reasonably apparent, from the terms of the bill, that Congress did not intend to grant a letter patent to the President or to the State Department to engage in a crusade to establish an international brotherhood of man. I doubt, for instance, if they felt as Secretary Wallace did one day when he said to me wistfully: "We will never get anywhere in this program until we change the hearts of men."

I thought we were going in for trading, and on June 9th, 1934, three days before the trade agreements measure became a law, I said over the radio:

We Americans have always believed that we are good traders. The tradition of Yankee trading goes back to the beginning of our history. I believe the President's ability as a trader is still as good as his ancestors', and that when he deals with other countries we need never be afraid that our citizens, man for man, and trade for trade, will ever in the long run get the worst of a bargain.

There are strong reasons why some of this trading skill of our forefathers is very much needed in the present situation of our foreign trade. Gone are the old days, on the farm especially, when as David Harum used to say "We eat what we raise and we raise what we eat." Now we live in a world where the farmer sells most of what he raises and buys much of what he eats. . . .

The long and short of it is that we have come to a point in our dealings with other nations where commodities, not dollars, or pounds or francs or any other form of currency, must be the basis of exchange if we are to resume this flow of business that is so important to us. We cannot continue the old practice of lending indiscriminately to our customers the wherewithal to conduct their trade with us and with each other. We must strike a balance somewhere, and that balance should be at some place where we can continue to sell our goods in the world and get in return something more tangible than promises.

We must determine upon the things we wish to sell and the things we wish to buy, and we must contrive, with due regard to other items that go to make up world trade, that these incoming and out-going accounts shall roughly balance. In other words, our task is to conduct our foreign trade with the world so that payments shall be effective in both directions. . . .

Our country now has an opportunity to enter into closer

commercial relationships with our neighbors based on reciprocal trade agreements. This is not a new opportunity. Other nations have been making these agreements among themselves for years. In fact, within the past three years more than sixty important agreements of this nature have been signed and put into effect between other nations. These agreements have had one striking characteristic in common. They have left American interests out of the picture except where they have affected them adversely. From this we may conclude that other nations know their own interest and have acted accordingly.

Clearly it is our duty then to know our interest and to act accordingly. But to know our interest requires that we shall construct and maintain a plainly understandable set of books for the United States. We must have a system whereby we may know the value to our country of the products offered to us in these reciprocal exchanges, and whether they involve a long-time arrangement or a simple "swap" of commodities in the form of a special transaction.

I do not apologize for that address. I sincerely thought that the Administration intended to act along these lines. Events have proved that I was mistaken. I was not unaware of the troubles which former administrations had run into in trying to make reciprocity treaties—a treaty differs from an agreement in that a treaty must be approved by two-thirds of the Senate. Through all the years before 1922 the United States as a matter of policy with but few exceptions made only conditional most-favored-nation treaties and thus left the way open to reciprocal bargaining. Over a period of sixty years, only three reciprocity treaties ever reached the point of becoming effective—Canada (1855-64), Hawaii (1875-1900), and Cuba (1902-34). (The preferential arrangement of 1904 with Brazil, terminated by the United States in 1922, was not a formal treaty.) Other proposals were turned down by the Senate, were withdrawn or failed to reach the Senate. The only reciprocal treaty in force when the trade agreements program was launched was the one with Cuba which was made in 1902.

Since political or other reasons had intervened to prevent the consummation of all previous negotiations, with the three exceptions noted, the new Act did not concern itself with treaties but only with agreements. As far as the public interest is concerned, there is no difference at all between the effect of a trade agreement and the effect of a reciprocity treaty.

The Trade Agreements Act was a delegation of powers to the President and the procedure was in his hands. Congress had provided in the Act: "Before any foreign trade agreement is concluded . . . reasonable public notice of the intention to negotiate . . . shall be given in order that any interested person may have an opportunity to present his views to the President, or to such agency as the President may designate."

Immediately the State Department took charge of everything and gave unmistakable evidence that it was going to run the show and write the agreements. The machinery for negotiating was most elaborate. Nominally it was devised by the Executive Committee on Commercial Policy which I have before mentioned. Actually all the arrangements were made by the State Department. In practice and effect all the agreements were written in the State Department and the imposing negotiating machinery was installed mainly to impress the public and Congress.

The actual formulation of the agreements was supposed to rest with an interdepartmental Committee on Foreign Trade Agreements, under State Department chairmanship, which was supposed to get its facts, before making any agreement, from an interdepartmental "Country Committee" of supposed specialists who made a study of the country in question and its trade relations with the United States. It was also supposed to get its information of a practical nature through the Committee for Reciprocity Information which held public hearings.

The Committee for Reciprocity Information was the show window and in theory gave all parties in interest a chance to be heard. When a Congressional committee holds a hearing, it nearly always has a bill before it and the witnesses have a chance to challenge the bill. The State Department evidently had no intention of giving anyone a chance to object to an agreement. It simply gave notice of an intention to negotiate a trade agreement with a certain country and set a day for a hearing. Neither the Committee nor those who chose to appear were given any information as to what kind of agreement was proposed. The witnesses had their say without interruption, filed six copies of any brief they happened to prepare and went on their way. The witnesses were seldom cross-examined, and if a witness misrepresented—and some of them did—little opportunity was afforded for any industry hurt by the statements to put in the real facts. Indeed, parties in interest seldom even knew what sort of statements the Committee was getting, for the briefs as filed were not open to inspection. Without any party who might be affected by the agreement having any knowledge of what kind of agreement was contemplated, the testimony and the briefs could not be to the point, and the hearings were essentially a farce. The Cuban agreement was practically consummated in advance of the hearing and I understand that the agreement was held up until the gesture of holding a hearing could be concluded. I am informed that even the members of the Reciprocity Information Committee did not all read the briefs as filed but merely transmitted them with a purely formal report to the Trade Agreements Committee. Those manufacturers and industries who spent thousands of dollars getting up briefs may be interested to know that only in the most exceptional cases were the briefs read or considered by anyone in real authority. It is not possible to prove how many agreements had been practically decided on before the hearings were held. They were generally regarded as a necessary nuisance to keep Congress and the business people from raising too much trouble.

Those hearings were the only point at which anyone with a stake in the trade of the country had the opportunity to appear and be heard. At the hearings, the members of the Committee could not answer questions concerning the proposed agreement because they did not know what the agreement would be. At no time after the hearing did anyone have an opportunity to get any information. It was as nothing to the internationalists that business firms with everything at stake in some instances could do nothing while the secret negotiations were in progress. It is impossible to say how much trade was hung up and how much unemployment was engendered by the uncertainty which was spread through the whole of industry while the internationalists in splendid isolation decided what the country ought to have. No man can plan ahead against an uncertain tariff.

Our own citizens could obtain not a word of information from the State Department or any other Department of the Government as to the terms of any agreement in the making. Not even the men who were supposed to be making the agreements knew much about their final form until they were announced by the State Department. It was quite different with many of the foreign governments on the other end of these agreements. They consulted with those most interested in the various products involved. If our own citizens wanted information, they could get it only from the foreign embassies or by sending men abroad. It has been told to me on good authority that the representatives of American watchmakers, while the agreement with Switzerland was pending, were very fearful that, through some technical constructions, tariff revisions of an apparently innocent nature would be made that might go far toward wiping out the American industry. They applied to the State Department for information and got nothing at all. Then they sent to Switzerland a representative. In discussions with a Swiss manufacturer, he turned the conversation to the pending agreement and the Swiss at once drew a digest of the agreement out of his desk. It showed classifications and reductions, I was told, which would have greatly hurt our industry. The representative had a photostat made of the memorandum and, as the story was told to me, presented that photostat at the State Department—but with what results I do not know.

The background of the members of the Committee for Reciprocity Information is interesting but not important. The Committee membership varied but these were the principal members: Professor Thomas Walker Page represented the Tariff Commission. He was a low-tariff Democrat of many years' standing. Thomas Hewes represented the Department of State. He had been a member of the Connecticut Bar until 1933, when he was appointed Assistant Secretary of the Treasury, and in April, 1934 he was appointed Special Assistant to the Secretary of State. Leslie A. Wheeler represented the Department of Agriculture. Mr. Wheeler was born in Iowa in 1899 and, after graduating from a college in California, took further work in foreign trade and marketing at Harvard and immediately entered the government service as a research worker. After three years of service in the Department of Commerce, he was in 1926 transferred to the Bureau of Agricultural Economics. He has done important work in the Department but has not had other than academic or bureau experience. Louis E. Van Norman represented the Department of Commerce. He was an older man, having been born in 1869, and, while serving on the Committee, held the post of Editorial Assistant to the Director of the Bureau of Foreign and Domestic Commerce. He had been a writer, a lecturer and a commercial attaché. John Lee Coulter, a former member of the Tariff Commission, represented me in my capacity as Special Adviser. He was a man of wide experience in agriculture and economics. This was a capable Committee but it had no power! Actually the Committee had no function other than to sit quietly at hearings and try to look interested.

For each country with which an agreement was proposed, an interdepartmental Country Committee of supposed specialists was appointed and, although I had a representative on each of these committees as long as the Special Adviser's office lasted, the complete membership of the committees was never announced, in order to guard the members against the possibility of undue outside pressure. That was a needless precaution because these committees were supposed only to find facts and make recommendations. They had no more knowledge of what the final agreement might be than had a complete outsider. These Country Committees of bureau specialists, had they been reinforced with a few practical foreign trade men, might have been very valuable. The first few committees worked very hard on their reports and recommendations. But they soon found that the agreements as drawn frequently were without regard to their recommendations and thereafter most of these committees, I am informed, followed the standard Washington bureaucratic practice and played safe. All the committees were made up of men from the bureaus.

They operated under instructions based on low-tariff principles—one was that if any import amounted to less than 10 per cent of the domestic consumption, the tariff amounted to an embargo and should be lowered. The textbook of the Country Committees was the "Economic Analysis of the Foreign Trade of the United States in Relation to the Tariff" submitted by the Tariff Commission in 1933 in response to Senate Resolution 325 of the 72nd Congress, Second Session. This report classifies imports and exports, with sources and duties, and gives a comprehensive statistical picture of the country's trade by tariff classifications. The committees simply picked out certain items, discussed them with a view to lowering the tariff and made their reports accordingly. I never heard any discussion of raising a rate, although the Act gave this authority. Some of the men were experts, in that they had taken courses in foreign trade or taught economics or foreign trade, or had been employed in a Washington bureau dealing with foreign trade, but, as far as I know, not one of them had ever bought or sold a nickel's worth of goods across salt water.

The center of the agreements was the Committee on Foreign Trade Agreements, which was headed by Professor Henry F. Grady, who was brought in on June 12th, 1934, the day the Trade Agreements Act became law, as a Special Adviser to the Secretary of State. He and Professor Sayre have been moving forces in shaping the agreements and especially in directing them away from the purposes intended by the Congress. He had been in teaching work or in government service all his life. He is a man of considerable ability and aggressiveness, but occasionally unfortunate in his manner and at all times dominated by his determination to put over the trade agreements program on an internationalist basis. Professor Alvin H. Hansen, also for the Department of State, has had wholly an academic career and was Professor of Economics at the University of Minnesota when he became Chief Economic Analyst in the Department of State. He had been largely responsible for the so-called Hutchins report which advocated general tariff reduction. Harry C. Hawkins, also for the Department of State, was a perfect type of the honest, capable, plodding civil servant. The Department of Agriculture was represented by Leslie A. Wheeler, whom I have already mentioned, and by Professor Carl C. Taylor, whose main job was in the Rural Resettlement Division of the Federal Resettlement Administration under Dr. Tugwell. Professor Taylor was born in Iowa, taught in various colleges and, at the time of being appointed to the government service, was a lecturer in adult education forums under the Public School Board of Des Moines, Iowa. The Department of Commerce was represented by Dr. Henry Chalmers, who, after graduating from college in 1914, had a year's experience in business as assistant to an export manager. He was Statistician to the New York State Board of Health, was attached to the Tariff Commission, and since 1921 has been in the Department of Commerce. His alternate was Louis Domeratzky. He was born in Russia in 1881, entered the Commerce Department in 1905 and has been there ever since. The Treasury was for a while represented by a bright and very young lawyer, Eli Frank, Jr., and afterwards by an economist, Professor Harry D. White. The representative of the Tariff Commission was Professor Oscar B. Ryder, whom I have previously referred to as a member of the Executive Committee on Commercial Policy, and by A. Manuel Fox. His (Fox's) career had comprised a year in the cost department of an automobile company, a season as an efficiency expert and an investigator, and a period as a lecturer and economist. In 1934 he became Director of Research of the Tariff Commission. The Office of Special Adviser was represented by James H. Edwards, who was born in 1878, had a public school education, served in the Spanish-American War, and held various important positions, public and private, in the Philippines, in the Dominican Republic, in Puerto Rico, in Ecuador, in Colombia and in Cuba. He had been in the foreign banking and exporting business and had an intimate knowledge of foreign trade, especially in the Latin-American countries. The N.R.A. and the A.A.A. were also represented.

My own opinion of the arrangements and the personnel was given in a letter to the late Colonel Louis McHenry Howe dated June 30th, 1934—the same month the arrangements were made. The letter was in response to a request for information. In it I said:

In connection with the setting up of the administrative machinery for carrying on the work under the new Act authorizing the President to enter into trade agreements with foreign governments, I have urged that emphasis must be kept constantly on the point that what we are concerned with here is commerce and trade. Diplomatic and political considerations cannot be ignored, but the agreements authorized by this new Act are not treaties in any formal sense. They are agreements for foreign trade. They are business arrangements. I fear that the importance of this is not yet fully recognized. Policies and plans must be formulated on the basis of full information and with sound trading judgment. . . .

This subject of foreign trade agreements is a volatile one. Both the authority and the responsibility for these agreements are placed squarely upon the President by the Congress. Success or failure in carrying out the purposes of this Act means much, a great deal indeed, to the Administration. As Special Adviser to the President on Foreign Trade I feel it my duty to speak plainly in regard to the plans so far made under the Act. . . .

In my opinion the machinery is adequate. My reservation is whether the Committee on Foreign Trade Agreements as now manned can function effectively. Trades are made by men, not machines. . . .

While the Act was in the making, the internationalists and the professors had insisted that the chief obstacles to increasing the trade and prosperity of the country were to be found in the stupidity of business men and Congressmen and that, if only the real experts had a chance, all would be well. It will be noted from the listing of the principal men brought into the making of the agreements that practically none of them were experts in other than a bookish sense. I doubt if any concern actually engaged in trying to make money out of foreign trade would have put any of them (Edwards excepted) at the head of a trading department. As the Macmillan Committee so well pointed out, the practical man and the academic man each has his weak and his strong points, and the best results are to be had only when affairs are under the direction of both kinds of minds. The making of the agreements was entirely in the control of one kind of mind—the academic. And so it is not surprising that these men never came to grips with the realities and thought that theories could be made to rule the world. They all held that, if only our tariffs were lowered in just the right way, imports would come in and these imports would give to foreign nations the purchasing power to buy our goods.

The method by which they proposed to do all this was fantastic in fact but plausible enough when explained to those who did not know the facts. Professor Sayre said: "After a careful study, it was found that each of some 29 nations was the leading supplier to the United States of at least one and in most cases of numerous important commodities." I never saw his list—and probably never shall. It was his idea that, if a concession were granted to a "principal supplier" in return for a concession, it would not matter if, by force of the unconditional most-favored-nation provision, our concession were also extended to all other nations without asking anything in return, because all those other nations could not supply us enough to matter either to them or to us.

It is curious that the internationalists base their view on trade, world peace and what-not on the conception of a static world. They seem to think that, since our South once supplied the world with cotton, it will always do so; that because Manchester once sent out cotton textiles to the Orient, some law of Nature ordains it always will. When they talk about restoring international trade, they have in mind going back to some period when this or that country had a supremacy. They do not seem to realize that the world is always moving and that trade is never "restored."

The "principal supplier" doctrine was an engaging classroom precept based on the world never changing. When the professors began to put the notion into practice, they ran into trouble. They then invented the term "important supplier." Some of the younger men, as negotiations went on, most irreverently suggested a new classification of "no supplier."

The theory was utterly amazing, in the light of the facts. Take just one commodity as an example—cement. Take the percentages of our total imports of cement as supplied by various countries during a period of six years. In 1928, 74.5 came from Belgium; 14.3 from Denmark; 4.4 from the United Kingdom; and 6.8 from all others. In 1929, Belgium supplied 60.7; Denmark, 21.4; the United Kingdom, 13.8; and all others, 4.1. In 1930, the percentages were: Belgium, 40.9; Denmark, 30.5; the United Kingdom, 20.5; and all others, 8.1. In 1931, Belgium sent 20.9; Denmark, 36; the United Kingdom, 22.4; and all others, 20.7. In 1932, Belgium sent 17.4; Denmark, 25.3; the United Kingdom, 42.9; and all others, 14.4. For 1933, the figures were: Belgium, 27.8; Denmark, 46.7; the United Kingdom, 10.8; and all others, 14.7. These figures show clearly the shifting nature of world trade and will apply to most commodities. During only two out of the six years was Belgium clearly our principal supplier of cement. During four of the years the importations were pretty well divided—Belgium leading in one of the years, Denmark in two and the United Kingdom in the fourth. Between 1932 and 1933 the United Kingdom dropped from 42.9 per cent to 10.8 per cent.

For the treaties then under consideration, my office prepared a list showing the principal imports from the countries in question and, if a concession were made to one country, what other countries would come in under the concession without the necessity of making any concession in return. Here is the list:

Country and Commodities	*Other Principal Countries Supplying U. S. Imports*
Brazil:	
coffee	Colombia, Venezuela, Mexico, Netherlands West Indies, Guatemala
cocoa beans	Gold Coast, Nigeria, Dominican Republic, Venezuela, Trinidad
cattle hides	Argentina, Canada, Uruguay, Australia, Colombia, Germany

Country and Commodities	*Other Principal Countries Supplying U. S. Imports*
Brazil—*Cont'd*	
manganese ore	Soviet Russia in Europe, British India, Gold Coast
Colombia:	
coffee	Brazil, Venezuela, Mexico, Netherlands East Indies, Guatemala
petroleum, crude	Netherlands West Indies, Venezuela, Mexico, Ecuador
bananas	Honduras, Jamaica, Costa Rica, Guatemala, Nicaragua
straw hats	Italy, China, Ecuador, Japan, France, Netherlands East Indies
Haiti:	
goat and kid skins	British India, China, Brazil, Mexico, Spain
cocoa beans	Gold Coast, Nigeria, Dominican Republic, Brazil, Venezuela
logwood	Jamaica, Mexico
rum	Cuba, Jamaica, Bermudas, United Kingdom, France
Belgium:	
manufacture of flax, etc.	United Kingdom, China, Germany, Czechoslovakia, Italy
leather gloves	France, Germany, Czechoslovakia, Italy, United Kingdom
plate glass	Germany, United Kingdom, France, Czechoslovakia
cement	Denmark, United Kingdom, France, Germany
Sweden:	
wood pulp, chemical	Canada, Finland, Germany, Norway, Esthonia
furs, undressed	United Kingdom, China, Germany, Canada, France, Japan
iron ore and concentrates	Chile, Algeria and Tunisia, Cuba, Australia
matches	Finland, Esthonia, Soviet Russia, Netherlands, Germany, Japan
Spain:	
cork	Portugal, France, Italy, Algeria and Tunisia, Morocco
copper ores	Canada, Chile, Mexico, Cuba, Venezuela, Peru
olive oil, edible	Italy, France, Portugal
goat and kid skins	British India, China, Brazil, Mexico, Argentina, Haiti

The Committee, under the guidance of Professors Sayre and Grady, did not seem to realize that they were out in a hard, cruel world and that things were not settled by giving bad marks to nations that did not answer in the way set down in their books. They had no conception whatsoever of practical trading. They thought that the agreements, arrangements and deals being made everywhere throughout the world were only emergency measures "to curb and control the ravages of the panic," as Secretary Hull put it, and not the emergence of a new and perhaps better arrangement of world trade founded on the solid and peace-making basis of reasonable self-containment supplemented by selective foreign trade on a basis of mutual advantage. There was no conception that science had changed the face of the world and that unnecessarily lugging goods about was only wasteful. Out in the world of affairs, beyond the atmosphere of the campus, from which these men could not free themselves, a new and different mode was forming.

Our State Department solemnly dedicated itself to the preservation of the unconditional most-favored-nation principle as though it were a fundamental American policy and not simply a device adopted in 1922. The foreign nations, while often giving lip service to the unconditional most-favored-nation principle, had for the most part abandoned it after the War or had nullified it by quotas, exchange controls and special exclusive agreements. All but a few nations use bilateral agreements whenever they consider it necessary. On June 30th, 1935 no less than 290 such agreements were of record in my office—and doubtless many more existed which had not been reported. These agreements are highly technical and fall into four general classes. First, the control of imports through controlling prices (i.e., tariffs, etc.); second, the control of imports by regulating the amount permitted to enter (i.e., quotas, etc.); third, the regulation of payments (i.e., exchange allotments, etc.); and fourth, the general control of the trade between the countries involved in the agreement. A favorite device is to make trick tariff classifications in the same fashion that specifications are drawn sometimes so that only one favored contractor can meet the conditions. In some cases the governments pledged the purchase of certain amounts of goods. In exchange agreements between creditor and debtor nations, the debtor agrees, for example, to set apart a portion of the funds realized for debt service, and it is by reason of such agreements that many of the debts in the world are in the way of being liquidated except those owed to the United States. In addition, all kinds of special agreements are made as the occasion demands. For instance, Japanese goods were flooding Argentina, while the Japanese were buying very little from that country because prices were too high. To meet this, Japan put a tax on exports to Argentina and applied the proceeds to subsidizing the import of goods from Argentina and thus made the prices low enough for Japanese pocketbooks.

On December 4th, 1934 I protested vigorously against the policy and, in a formal memorandum to the Trade Agreements Committee, I said:

It is said that by confining our concessions to the principal suppliers of commodities imported by us, the effects of automatic generalization of concessions will be minimized. However, in fact, there is usually not one, but a number of nations which may be regarded as principal suppliers of any given commodity and, furthermore, in many commodities the principal supplier or suppliers may differ in different years. This is particularly true in the case of commodities which are manufactured or controlled by cartels operating in two or more countries, of the type of the Swedish Match Trust. Moreover, such a policy of making concessions only to principal suppliers would virtually prevent negotiations with many of the smaller countries. An excellent example of this sort is that of Haiti which has no commodity of which it is a principal supplier to the American market.

I called attention to the fact that the State Department was not following the "principal supplier" formula and that keeping up the pretense could lead only to disaster. I called attention to these discrepancies between fact and theory:

(a) In the concession to Brazil on manganese. Brazil supplies less than 15 per cent of our manganese imports, the bulk of which comes from Soviet Russia, Gold Coast and British India, all of which will become the major beneficiaries through generalization of this concession;

(b) Concessions to Brazil on maté. Argentina is our principal supplier, sending us nearly three times as much as does Brazil, and consequently will get the major benefit of this concession;

(c) Concessions to Haiti on coffee. Nearly all of our coffee imports come from Brazil and Colombia, which, under the unconditional most-favored-nation policy are the principal beneficiaries of this concession. The circumstance that they are to receive this concession by virtue of the concession to Haiti may be the reason that Brazil and Colombia have delayed ratification of the trade agreements previously negotiated with them;

(d) Similar departures from the "Principal Supplier" formula may be found in the Belgian agreement (e.g., chalk, cement, steel ingots, waterproof cloth, oriental rugs, vegetable fibre fabrics, creosote);

(e) In the Swedish agreement attention is called to cellulose, knives, pliers, paperboard, matches. In the case of matches Russia and Japan will be the principal beneficiaries of our unconditional policy.

The internationalists kept to their theory and, as the negotiations went on, it became increasingly apparent that the United States, instead of being the most highly protected country in the world, was really the free trade country of the world—all the commodities we imported in large quantities were, except sugar, already on the free list. By the terms of the Act, the President had no power to touch the free list. In the case of Brazil, for instance, our chief importation was coffee which was on the free list. Therefore, the State Department instituted what may prove to be one of the most devastating of all its practices—the practice of what it called "binding on the free list." The State Department undertook to say, in making an agreement, that the United States would not during the term of the agreement put any duty on an article which was then on the free list. That was completely in line with the deadly scholastic concept that nothing should ever change. The full consequences of "binding" are yet to be revealed.

Had the kind of internationalists who made these trade agreements been in office a hundred years ago, the United States would now be a colony, for they would have pledged then, as they pledged in these agreements, that the United States would not extend the field of its domestic employment by taking up the making of anything it was not then making. In a subsequent chapter, I shall return to what this "binding on the free list" really means. This one innovation in American foreign policy is playing with a fire which will be very hard to put out.

The general idea, however, was exactly in line with Secretary Wallace's often-expressed delusion that our country could make more of everything than it could consume and that therefore our big task was to take imports and to build foreign purchasing power—and to do nothing at all in the way of building up new industries, although any one of these might provide more employment and more purchasing power at home than could be generated in a dozen little foreign nations. It may be recalled that he opposed the extension of the American Merchant Marine, on the ground that carrying goods in American ships would keep the shipping charges at home, whereas it was our high duty to give all the purchasing power we could to foreigners. The logic of this position may be grasped—if one has that kind of mind. But that kind of mind prevailed.

During the discussions on the Belgian agreement, it was brought out that certain reductions in steel and cement would be bound to lower American prices and affect net profits. "Suppose it does reduce net profits," piped up one professor. "What matters?" At the time, he did not know that profits in either steel or cement were few and far between and that the competition invited could not bear on profits, because there were none, and would therefore have to bear on employment and wages.

All through the discussions ran the thought that American prices were above world prices and ought to be reduced. That is part of the internationalist creed—a world scale of prices. They do not mention that this also involves a world scale of wages. While they were thus discussing the desirability of lowering prices, the N.R.A. and the A.A.A. were both trying to raise prices.

None of these theories could have taken a place on the stage, had the State Department given attention to the simple arithmetic of our foreign trade—which had been set out in a preliminary way in the accounts—and to reports supplied it by the Office of the Special Adviser. Especially, the Committee would not have clung like grim death to another extraordinary theory which was all right as a theory—except that it ran contrary to the facts. This was the theory of triangular trade. The phrase is innocuous enough, but the theory it stands for prevented the inclusion in any of the agreements of a provision for the collection of American debts, either war or private. Most nations, through their trade agreements, are collecting their debts. We are not collecting our debts. We are not getting income which we could have—and this at a time when every citizen of the United States is groaning under the weight of taxes. This point is so important that it seems necessary to quote the State Department position as presented by Professor Sayre at length:

The foreign trade of the United States from its very nature must be essentially triangular. Speaking in a general way, most of the European industrial countries produce goods competitive with our own. They need large quantities of our raw materials, such as cotton, wheat, hog products, and the like, whereas the United States being a manufacturing as well as an agricultural nation, naturally and almost necessarily buys less from these countries than it sells to them. In 1934 our exports to the United Kingdom, France, Germany, Italy, Belgium, and the Netherlands amounted to some $775,000,000; whereas, our imports from the same countries were but slightly over $335,000,000. In other words, our export balance to this group of nations amounted to some $440,000,000.

On the other hand our trade with the principal tropical countries is exactly the converse. From them we buy products, such as coffee, tea, rubber, etc., of far greater value than we can sell to them. To Cuba, Brazil, Colombia, Venezuela, British Malaya, Dutch East Indies, British India and Ceylon our total exports in 1934 amounted to no more than $225,000,000, in contrast to our imports of some $500,000,000. Our trade with this group of countries, in other words, showed an unfavorable balance of some $275,000,000.

Again, there is a third group of countries, primarily agricultural, competing with our own agricultural production, from which, as is quite natural, we can import considerably less than we export to them. In 1934 our total exports to the British Dominions and Argentina were about $400,000,000 and our imports $250,000,000, showing a balance in our favor of some $150,000,000.

From this it must be clear that any policy which proves destructive of triangular trade strikes at the very heart of American commercial interests. We have large export surpluses with Europe and the British Dominions. We have substantial import surpluses with the tropical countries. Our foreign trade is strikingly triangular. Preferential bargaining, as actual experience is proving, leads inescapably to the effort to equalize the value of exports and imports between each two countries; and bilateral balancing perforce kills triangular trade. Triangular trade cannot survive under a system of bargaining for special preferences. Its very existence depends upon most-favored-nation treatment and freedom from discriminatory practices in the movement of goods. So far as the United States is concerned, we must fight the system of preferential bargaining and bilateral balancing or lose a great part of our trade. . . .

If Professor Sayre had looked at the full accounts, as any man in business would, he would have discovered that he was talking nonsense—that he was reckoning only the balances in goods and forgetting entirely, as was pointed out in my reports, that a large share of international transactions consists of capital and other money transfers which have no relation to goods. Of course, Professor Sayre did not really mean "triangular trade." He had in mind triangular payments. But even in so far as goods are concerned he erred. Computations made by the League of Nations indicate that about four-fifths of the total world trade is bilateral and only one-fifth triangular, even in normal years. The trade of the United States shows nearly the same percentages. These figures are on a goods basis. When the money transfers are taken into account, the picture changes. My accounts showed that while we had a favorable trade balance with Europe in 1934 of $461,000,000, after full account had been taken of service, interest payments, gold movement, and capital transactions, we had an unfavorable balance of payments of $630,000,000. It is thus impossible to discuss triangular payments until full account has been taken of payments of all sorts. Any other course is both confusing and misleading. For example, the United States has a favorable balance of merchandise trade with the United Kingdom, yet, instead of giving rise to an equal volume of triangular trade, much of this is balanced by American dollars paid by tourists for British goods and services, and an additional amount is balanced by the purchase of British shipping services and the payment of interest to British holders of American securities. The United States has a favorable merchandise balance with Poland. However, Polish immigrants in the United States frequently remit a sufficient amount to cover the excess. In other words, American dollars are used to purchase the favorable balance of American goods.

"Triangular trade" is only a minor portion of the merchandise trade of the United States, and merchandise trade (plus service transactions) accounted in 1933 for only 41 per cent of our total international dollar settlements. A large amount of so-called triangular trade in merchandise is actually balanced bilaterally through non-merchandise transactions. This upsets the fundamental assumption in favor of triangular trade, and the trade itself, if it ever really existed, has been entirely upset by the direct and indirect governmental subsidy of exports and the direct and indirect restriction of imports by nearly all trading nations.

I protested repeatedly. I protested by letter, and my representatives in the negotiations protested against the concluding of any agreement with any nation exercising exchange controls against the United States, unless that agreement contained a provision for the liquidation of balances due us. These protests were from time to time brought to the attention of the President and were contained in my report to the President of December 31st, 1934 as Special Adviser. The protests were of no avail. The State Department people dominated the Trade Agreements Committee and they dominated a special committee set up to consider exchange control. Here is a memorandum of a part of one of the meetings of this committee made by my representative, Dr. John Donaldson, and which clearly shows the attitude of mind with which the internationalists and bureaucrats approached the practical problem of international trading:

Brazilian Exchange Control.

Messrs. Feis, Hansen, Pasvolsky and Jones continued the position they had taken at previous meetings. (Feis—wearily but definitely, Hansen—with stubborn academic dogmatism, Pasvolsky with doctrinaire passion). Mr. Hansen several times expressed the opinion that we should have no clause whatever regarding exchange in our agreements with other countries. In his zeal to prevent the placing of any pressure on Brazil, Mr. Hansen stated that it would be unfortunate for Brazil to be compelled to modify or abandon her exchange control system. His reasoning was briefly as follows: (a) Brazil's foreign trade is in disequilibrium. (b) If she should abandon her exchange control this disequilibrium would not only continue but would grow worse. (c) This would be especially true because American exporters would then export more material to Brazil. Mr. Donaldson pointed out the apparent inconsistency of this view, recalling that the majority of the committee, at the first meeting it had held, agreed that exchange controls were undesirable and should be eliminated, and that Mr. Hansen was now evidently arguing in favor of the Brazilian exchange control.

Mr. ——— expressed the opinion that American businessmen who export to Brazil are "damn fools." Mr. ——— concurred in Mr. ———'s judgment and stated that as early as 1931 in Cleveland he had warned American businessmen not to export to Brazil and if they now continued to do so whatever difficulty they encountered in exchange was their own fault. The idea that American businessmen are what Mr. ——— stated them to be seemed to find considerable support among several members of the committee. (This probably furnishes an interesting sidelight on the State Department attitude concerning American business.)

Mr. Chalmers' views were somewhat more realistic than those of some other members of the committee. While favoring no more than a promise of no discrimination at this time, he felt that we should make sure to have the promise and to see to it that Brazil lives up to it. He even remarked that later we might find it necessary to "crack down on Brazil." Mr. Gardner (Federal Reserve) argued for a view nearly approaching that of the Special Adviser's Office but did not, and indeed could not, by reason of the manner in which the meeting was conducted by the State Department, push his arguments to their logical conclusion. Mr. Donaldson reaffirmed the position of S.A.F.T., which he had previously recorded, in favor of definite provision by Brazil of American exchange requirements.

In like fashion, I opposed at every step the policy of generalization under the unconditional most-favored-nation clause. A whole sheaf of my protests is on file. I brought up the matter of the war debts and got nowhere. I talked with the President and, at his request, gave him full memoranda. For instance, in a letter dated November 14th, 1934 I said to him:

In accordance with your request of Monday, I am enclosing a table and accompanying memoranda covering certain specific instances which have come to light in the course of current trade agreement negotiations which appear to me to demonstrate unmistakably the impossibility, as a practical matter, of attempting to negotiate trade agreements contemplating the mutually advantageous exchange of goods for goods upon a reciprocal basis and at the same time to adhere to the unconditional most-favored-nation policy of the last twelve years. . . .

In conclusion I return to the recommendation contained in my letter of November 12th to the effect that, in view of existing world conditions, the unconditional most-favored-nation policy be revised and that we return to the traditional realistic policy of conditional most-favored-nation treatment which characterized American foreign trade policy from 1789 to 1922. In this manner I believe we can obtain a restoration of American foreign trade, with proper protection for the American domestic market, upon a foundation of mutually advantageous exchange of goods for goods upon a reciprocal basis.

And in my report of December 31st, 1934 I said:

Figures which I believe to be reliable indicate that the greatest gains in international trade have been made by those countries which have resorted to the employment of special trade agreements, notably Great Britain, France and Russia, and that these gains have been made largely at the expense of the United States. To cope with such conditions of trade we must retain in our hands the highest possible degree of bargaining power and the greatest freedom of action to deal with conditions as they arise.

The rebuilding of our foreign trade upon a sound and profitable basis will not be quick or easy. There is no short cut, no sovereign cure-all, but I do not doubt that it can be done if approached in a realistic and tenacious manner, in the spirit, shall we say, of our forebears who loaded their vessels and set sail in search of foreign trade—and got it!

The making of the agreements went on utterly without regard to facts or protests. Our internationalists sowed the seeds and the foreign nations are now reaping the harvest.

Chapter XIII

The Agreements

The declared purpose of the Trade Agreements Act was to further the interests of the United States through expanding foreign markets—especially for agricultural products. Nothing was said in the Act about giving a roving commission to the President or to the Secretary of State to adjust the affairs of the world. Let us therefore look at the agreements themselves and see what they are as opposed to what they pretend to be. It will not be necessary to go into all the agreements, for some are wholly trivial.

CUBA

The Cuban agreement was made hastily in order to "do something for Cuba." On its face the agreement is a good one and it differs from all the other agreements in that it is purely bilateral. Our country has a special arrangement with Cuba, and hence any advantages given to Cuba did not have to be generalized to the advantage of all other countries with whom we have most-favored-nation treaties. The agreement possessed possibilities, but so many considerations other than trade entered into its making that, instead of a trade agreement to further American trade, it turned out to be a subsidy to Cuban sugar plantation owners.

The agreement standing alone might well be a model—and I have publicly said so. But Secretary Wallace, under the sugar quota system of the Jones-Costigan Act, turned the thing into an expensive farce. The duty on sugar was lowered, but Cuba, being given a monopoly on the supply of a certain portion of the sugar for the American market, raised the price and got the benefit both of the duty cut and the higher price. The quotas of American producers were cut and an attempt was made to make up the difference in output and price through benefit payments by the A.A.A. Thus the American consumer was levied on in two directions for the benefit of Cuba. The increase in trade to Cuba has been negligible as compared to the subsidy granted. All of which goes to show the dangers of mixing diplomacy and trade without adding the priceless ingredient of common sense.

Cuban conditions in 1934 were grave. The island's peace and prosperity rises and falls with the price of sugar. Many great *centrals* owned by Americans through the large American banks and by British subjects through the Royal Bank of Canada were on the point of failure. The American bank loans to the Cuban Government were uncollectible. Upwards of $300,000,000 in Cuban securities were outstanding as a result of American flotations, and an unknown number of these was held in the United States. These issues were largely in default.

The basic sugar tariff under the 1930 Act is 2.50 cents a pound for 96° (degree test sugar). Under the Reciprocity Treaty of 1902, Cuba got a 20 per cent reduction below other countries, bringing her rate to 2.00 cents. On May 9th, 1934, President Roosevelt further reduced the rate, giving to Cuba a duty of 1.50 cents. The Tariff Commission had recommended this rate. In the agreement as proclaimed on September 3rd, 1934 the rate was cut to .90 cent—without explanation. The agreement gave certain concessions to the United States on both agricultural and industrial products.

Now let us see what happened. We are the largest buyers of Cuban sugar and have had special trade arrangements of sorts ever since we set up the island as an independent state. In 1932 we sold goods to Cuba in the amount of $28,755,000. In 1933 we sold $25,093,000, in 1934 we sold $45,323,374 and in 1935 we sold $60,152,732. Of the 1934 exports, $17,614,000 were accounted for in the September-December period after the execution of the agreement—therefore apparently proving that the reciprocal trade agreement was a success.

The Cuban agreement in no way involves the most-favored-nation clause yet it has been exhibited as the star example of what we may expect to gain through reciprocal trade agreements. The State Department took the extraordinary course of issuing a press release of Cuban opinion to show what a great success the agreement was from the Cuban viewpoint. But apparently the American effects were not important.

After the Cuban agreement went into effect, duty was paid on about 1,100,000 tons of raw sugar and about 200,000 tons of refined. The loss in duties to the United States between the trade agreement rates and the old tariff rates amounted to $32,323,000.

Under the quota system for sugar as fixed by the A.A.A., the Cubans had a practical monopoly of sugar shipments for the balance of 1934. Our insular possessions had sugar, but they had exhausted their quotas. The Cubans demanded a fancy price for sugar shipped to the United States. This price was brought down by negotiations to an average of 1.97 cents per pound (f.o.b. Cuba)—although at the same time Cuba was selling to the world other than the United States at an average of .80 cent. The result was that the American consumers of sugar—because of the coincidence of the trade agreement and the A.A.A. quota system—paid for about 500,000 tons of their sugar the sum of about $15,000,000 over and above what they would have paid, had our Government not intervened ostensibly to help American trade.

Taking the loss of duty which went into the pockets of the Cuban producers and which was not reflected in the retail prices and the additional sum exacted by the Cuban producers owing to their fortunate situation under the quota, the American people paid a total of about $47,000,000 in order to sell $45,323,374 in goods.

Since these total sales were only $20,000,000 in excess of the low sales of 1933—which minimum of sales would likely have been made anyway—the American people as a whole paid over $2.00 to promote each dollar's worth of gross sales to Cuba.

To summarize: Our sales to Cuba in 1934 amounted to $45,323,374. To obtain this amount of business, we granted a subsidy of $47,000,000.

This, however, is not all. For the year 1935 the Cuban sugar quota was 1,658,055 tons. On this amount, at the new duties, we lost the sum of $40,726,000. The Cuban price to the United States for sugar averaged about 1.19 cents a pound above the world price. We paid about $43,000,000 extra on our sugar for the exclusive benefit of Cuba. Adding the loss of duties, the new tax amounts to over $83,000,000.

Thus for $60,000,000 of exports to Cuba in 1935 we paid a subsidy of around $83,000,000. At the same time, the A.A.A. was paying American beet and cane sugar producers not to produce. The average tax on Cuban sugar land is 29 cents an acre. The average tax on American beet sugar land is $2.59 an acre. The retail price of sugar in the United States as of December 31st, 1932 was 5.10 cents per pound; in 1933 the price rose to 5.50 cents and stayed at that figure through 1934, rising to 5.80 cents in 1935.

From these figures the cost of the agreement to American citizens may be estimated. Instead of promoting trade with Cuba through Government action of this sort, it would be cheaper for us to take a census of everyone who wants to sell anything to Cuba, have him set the largest profit he can think of on his sales, and then pay him the profits directly on the promise that he will stay out of business.

Our general imports from Cuba were $78,928,916 in 1934 and $104,638,523 in 1935—an increase of $25,709,607. Our exports to Cuba were $45,323,374 in 1934 and $60,152,732 in 1935—an increase of $14,829,358, or about $5,000,000 less than the increase of 1934 over 1933. We are steadily importing more from Cuba and exporting proportionately less.

What is Cuba doing with the great balance to her credit in the United States over and above what she buys from us? Paying debts? Not at all. The American bondholders were not provided for in the agreement. They are still unpaid. In the absence of a comprehensive accounting of our trade and money relations with Cuba, it is not possible to say exactly what Cuba is doing with the money.

Taking the dollar value of Cuban imports as a whole, they show an increase for 1934 over 1933 of $31,026,000—or less than the amount of our subsidy. Of this increase, the United States obtained a slice amounting to $18,551,000 (Cuban figures) while all other nations together obtained $12,475,000. We did all the subsidizing but got only a part of the new trade. During the years 1931-1933, without subsidy we supplied 57.4 per cent, 54.2 per cent and 53.5 per cent of the Cuban imports. In 1934 with the subsidy we supplied 56.2 per cent. In 1934 Cuban imports from the United States increased 82 per cent over 1933, but at the same time Cuba increased her purchases from Japan by 265 per cent over 1933.

The current figures are not now available to me, but it would appear that we are providing a subsidized purchasing power for Cuba which is being used only in part in the United States. We are subsidizing Cuban trade with Japan and Germany.

Cuba has been faced with two great problems—the overproduction of sugar and the overproduction of debt. Our contribution seems to have been the augmenting of both kinds of overproduction. And the country has been put in a position where a change in our sugar arrangements will cause great hardship and possibly another revolution in Cuba.

BRAZIL

An agreement was negotiated in February, 1935 with a mission from Brazil which also endeavored, without result, to float a loan in New York. The mission then departed for London on a similar errand where they were more successful. The agreement was not ratified by the Brazilian Congress for many months and did not become effective until January 1st, 1936. Hence the agreement has been in effect too short a time to determine what, if any, influence it has had on trade. Our exports to Brazil increased $3,242,544 in 1935 over 1934, but our imports from Brazil increased $8,202,755 for the same period.

We are the principal takers of Brazilian coffee, but we sell less to her than we buy. Brazil and the United States have always been on very friendly terms, and during the big lending period Brazil borrowed heavily in the United States. Practically all of these loans went into default with the drop in the price of coffee, and exchange troubles caused the blocking of about $20,000,000 in sums due to Americans who sold goods in Brazil.

Our balance of payments with Brazil for the period 1914-1933 were as follows:

Balance of Payments Between the United States and Brazil
1914-1933 Inclusive

(Based on Information Available December, 1934)

During this 20-year period:	
we bought from Brazil goods in the amount of	$3,085,000,000
and we sold to Brazil goods in the amount of	1,333,300,000
leaving an unfavorable balance with Brazil for goods in the amount of	$1,751,700,000
We paid for gold imported from Brazil the net amount of	37,900,000
making a total unfavorable balance of	$1,789,600,000

Interest and dividends received on our investments in Brazil	240,000,000
reduced our unfavorable balance to	$1,549,600,000
Also during this 20-year period:	
we made new long-term loans and new direct investments in Brazil in the net amount of..........	516,000,000
resulting in an unfavorable balance of payments with Brazil during the 20-year period amounting to	$2,065,600,000

The concession on coffee was meaningless, for that already was on the free list, and had subsequently been bound there as a result of the agreement with Haiti concluded before the Brazilian Agreement had been ratified. Brazil makes some unimportant concessions in tariff rates to the United States and the United States reduces some tariffs on the products of Brazil—among them, manganese. The agreement made no provision whatsoever for the claims of American creditors, in spite of the large balance of trade that each year accrues to Brazil.

The reduction of the duty on manganese gives an impressive example of the dangers of theorists drawing up national documents in secret and without the benefit of free and open discussion. It so happens that Brazil had exported little or no manganese to the United States for several years. The principal supplies of the United States come from Russia, India and Africa, and the price at the American seaboard is the world price plus the tariff. The amount of manganese that we use is small, but it is vital in the manufacture of steel and is listed by the War Department as a war necessity.

There are ample deposits of manganese ore in the United States, but they are mostly of a very low grade and cannot be worked under present methods to sell at a profit in competition with the Russian and Far Eastern ores—even with the duty added. Cuba, however, has manganese ores of the same general character as the American but of a somewhat higher grade. These ores have been worked by an American company, buying American products, and, as a result, methods have been developed which give promise of making not only effective use of the Cuban deposits but also of the American deposits. The tariff protection heretofore granted has been about enough to make the Cuban company able to continue its experiments. It has not been enough to put and keep the American industry on its feet.

The reduction of the tariff on Brazilian manganese, if it applied only to Brazilian manganese, would not greatly affect the situation, for the Brazilian capacity to produce is small and the known deposits there are owned by a single American corporation.

Here is where the unconditional most-favored-nation policy comes in. The reduction of the duty to Brazil automatically reduces the duties on imports from India, Africa and Russia. Brazilian manganese cannot compete on a level with African and Indian manganese and so the reduction in tariff means absolutely nothing to Brazil. She is exactly where she was before the reduction.

But the reduction wipes out the Cuban and the American industries and, in the event of war, makes the steel industry of the United States subservient to the will of foreign nations from which the manganese comes, and therefore compromises the defense of the United States. In the event of war, it might be possible to revive the American manganese industry—but that could not be done over night.

The net result of the Brazilian trade agreement will be the loss to the United States of an industry which, although not financially great, is vital to our defense.

Apparently unconscious of what he had actually done, Secretary Hull blithely announced:

I have just had the pleasure of signing a trade agreement between this Government and the United States of Brazil. . . .

Having once started on the road away from the medieval mercantilism which was strangling the commerce of a new world, progress should now be more rapid and the movement gain momentum.

I am confident that in our dealings with other countries we shall encounter the same spirit of reasonableness and co-operation for the general welfare that we have experienced with Brazil and that soon by the expansion of this program we shall be casting a broad beam of light and hope into the existing economic darkness.

The most important feature of the Brazilian agreement, aside from the manganese question, was the introduction of the practice of "binding on the free list." The effect of such action has previously been noted. Secretary Hull agreed that during the life of the agreement the United States would place no duty upon coffee. It is implied in this that Congress will not place an excise tax upon coffee. In short, the undertaking was to put coffee out of the jurisdiction of the Congress of the United States. Any and every domestic foodstuff may be taxed. A tax on coffee would probably fall on the producer—or at least be divided between the foreign producer and the American consumer. But in the high interests of something or other the foreign producer is exempted.

In spite of the large balance of merchandise trade in favor of Brazil and the consequent fund at the command of Brazilians in New York, the agreement, as I mentioned, made no provision for debt service or blocked exchange. On the general subject, I wrote to Secretary Hull on September 22nd, 1934:

I have received and read with the closest interest your letter of September 15, regarding the question of proceeding without delay to the negotiation of clearing agreements where desirable and possible. I note that you are of the opinion that amelioration of the difficulties now being experienced by Americans trading with countries exercising exchange controls is to be found in the application of diplomatic pressure and the negotiation of general trade agreements rather than in the establishment of clearing agreements with such countries. While not wishing to ignore the valuable results which may be achieved by diplomatic pressure, it is clear that in the nature of things, this cannot always hope to be uniformly successful, as trade, including international trade, is dominated by economic and financial pressures rather than those of sentiments of good or ill will. Moreover, the negotiation of trade agreements is a process that must necessarily involve a considerable space of time, and while such agreements will undoubtedly lead to a gradual improvement of the difficulties to which I have referred, our exporters will in the meantime lie under the disadvantage of having to choose between taking a chance on ultimate payment for the goods they sell to "exchange restriction" countries or of surrendering their markets in those countries to other nations having exchange agreements with the countries in question. . . .

It is not my contention that clearing agreements will necessarily develop trade. They do, however, provide what is of prime importance, namely a method of insuring payment for what goods we do ship to "exchange restriction" countries, and they may thus operate to preserve a foothold in markets which might otherwise be lost to American exports. . . .

On the specific agreements, I wrote to Professor Sayre on October 19th, 1934:

My reasons for voting against the memorandum in connection with Brazil presented at the meeting this morning are:

First, I am opposed to a declaration of policy with respect to clearing, compensation, and other special agreements, for the reason that there are many nations employing these devices and I think that under existing conditions each case must be considered on its merits. Our position is quite different with nations having an unfavorable balance of trade with us than it is with those having a favorable balance. Any such declaration of policy at this time may prove embarrassing later. Furthermore, this whole subject really relates to the question of payments; it is unnecessary to say that our own record in this regard requires little apology or explanation.

Second, I am of the opinion that these subjects should be considered in advance of a general trade agreement or at least at the same time, and not after that event.

I feel that the procedure suggested is quite the reverse of the one which would be followed in good business practice, and may weaken our position in the negotiations now taking place.

We had many arguments in the meetings. But the agreement went through without making any provision at all for American debts.

BELGIUM

The Belgian agreement is a very extraordinary document. It was signed on February 27th, 1935 and in announcing it the State Department, through Acting Secretary of State Phillips, made this statement:

> The lowering of some of these extremely high duties should prove of benefit to wide circles of American users. This is particularly important in connection with the duty changes on various building materials such as cement, plate glass, and low priced or tonnage grade iron and steel products because of the importance of these materials in building construction. In all these instances, a lowered price should help to stimulate both urban and rural building, make it less costly to enter upon new building and repair operations, and thereby facilitate the general spread of business recovery. It is believed that whatever new competition may present itself can be ably met by the American industries.

There is nothing in the Trade Agreements Act which suggests that it was intended to authorize the President to use it as an instrument for regulating domestic prices. At the time, the N.R.A. was raising prices. The Belgian agreement lowered duties on cement, plate glass and certain grades of iron and steel at a time when these American industries were working at a very low production, with many thousands of unemployed. If only Belgium had been concerned, the agreement would have been sufficiently destructive, but all the rates were generalized to all the important foreign steel-producing countries with the exception of Germany. Our tariff rates on iron and steel products have been practically unchanged since the Tariff Act of 1922 and they were not high as compared with the tariff rates in other leading countries. For instance, our tariff on pig iron was $1.125 a gross ton, while in France the duty was $5.14 and in Germany was $4.03. On structural shapes, our import duty was $4.48 a gross ton; in France it was $48.38; in England it was $19.20; and in Germany it was $6.04. On sheets, our duty was $10.08; the French duty was $22.40; the British duty was about $13.80; and the German duty was $18.36. The foreign duties were higher than ours, in spite of the fact that their wages were lower. The average American steel-mill wage was then 65 cents an hour. The corresponding Belgian wage was 17 cents an hour. In the other leading producer countries the wages were: Czechoslovakia, 23 cents an hour; France, 20 cents; Germany, 26 cents; Great Britain, 25 cents; Italy, 28 cents; Sweden, 29 cents; Japan, 10 cents; and India, somewhat under 9 cents. The same relative conditions obtained in cement and glass. Therefore the Belgian agreement cannot be considered as other than an attack upon American wages and employment.

It contained certain other extraordinary provisions. In 1933, foreign-made rugs flooded the country because American costs were increased by the N.R.A. The American manufacturers applied for relief and on June 10th, 1934, the President, after an investigation by the Tariff Commission, imposed a fee of 23 cents a square yard in addition to the tariff duty of 35 per cent ad valorem. This fee became inoperative when the Supreme Court declared the N.R.A. unconstitutional. In the trade agreement, the duty on cotton imitation Oriental rugs was reduced from 35 per cent to 20 per cent. The Belgian agreement contained a provision for the adjustment of rates in the case of currency devaluation. On March 31st, 1935, the Belgian Government devalued its currency by 28 per cent. Our State Department made no adjustments to meet the devaluation, with the result that the duty on Belgian rugs went far below the 1933 figure which the President, on the advice of the Tariff Commission, had found destructive.

Take another instance. A very small quantity of a special type of vegetable parchment paper made in Belgium was ordinarily imported into the United States. In the agreement, the rate of duty, not only on this type imported from Belgium but also on vegetable parchment not produced in Belgium, was reduced. These reductions were immediately generalized to all the other foreign paper manufacturers excepting the German. The foreign manufacturers at once announced lower prices in the American markets. These lower prices were below those which the American manufacturers could meet—paying the existing wage scales. In order to keep the factories open, I am informed, the employees voluntarily agreed to lower wages and longer hours.

Consider the accounts. In the case of Brazil we bought more than we sold, but we sold more to Belgium than we bought. The full account of the transactions with Belgium from 1919 to 1933 stands:

Balance of Payments Between the United States and Belgium 1919-1933 Inclusive

(Based on Information Available December, 1934)

During this 15-year period:	
we sold to Belgium goods in the amount of	$1,888,000,000
and we bought from Belgium goods in the amount of	776,700,000
leaving a favorable balance with Belgium for goods in the amount of	1,111,300,000
We received for gold exported to Belgium the net amount of	98,300,000
making a total favorable balance of	$1,209,600,000

Our tourists spent in Belgium		$52,000,000	
our immigrants sent to Belgium		48,000,000	
and the U. S. Government paid to Belgium net (War Debt)		126,000,000	
a total of		$226,000,000	
less shipping services rendered by us	$ 34,000,000		
and interest on our loans to Belgium	113,000,000		
a total of		147,000,000	
or net payments from service items in the amount of			79,000,000
reduced our favorable balance to			$1,130,600,000
Also during this 15-year period: we made new long-term loans in Belgium in the net amount of			196,000,000
resulting in a favorable balance of payments with Belgium during the 15-year period amounting to			$ 934,600,000

This net favorable balance represents goods sold to Belgium and paid for by Belgium with dollars obtained from other countries for interest or Belgian exports.

A part of the favorable balance is represented by the "war debt," Belgian bonds held in the United States and other American investments in Belgium. At the end of 1933 it was estimated that Belgian bonds held in the United States amounted to $166,000,000. However, it is now known that from $90,000,000 to $100,000,000 of the dollar bonds of the Government of Belgium have been repatriated or purchased by other countries and are held outside of the United States. Thus Belgian bonds held in the United States have been reduced to about $70,000,000 and the annual interest charge ($12,000,000 in 1926) has been reduced to about $4,000,000.

The agreement went into effect on May 1st, 1935. From May 1st, 1934 to December 31st, 1934, we imported from Belgium goods to the amount of $17,577,446 and exported in the sum of $31,434,470. From May 1st, 1935 to December 31st, 1935, we imported in the sum of $28,242,259 and exported in the sum of $41,013,354. This represents an increase in imports of $10,664,813 and of exports in the sum of $9,578,884. If these figures mean anything, they mean that the effect of the agreement has been to increase our imports without a proportionate increase in our exports. And the increase in imports comes in those lines where American unemployment has been greatest—the industries depending on the revival of the durable goods trades.

The agreement made no provision at all for the payment of the war debts or for any other financial matters. In fact, no particular reason existed for the making of the Belgian agreement—other than that it provided the first opportunity for the lowering of our tariffs in a big way. Belgium was simply a dummy on which to hang a lot of tariff reductions—that would have attracted unpleasant attention if they had been granted directly to any of the major producing nations.

SWEDEN

The main point in the Swedish agreement was lowering the duty on matches. On this point the State Department announced:

> A recent investigation by the Tariff Commission showed that the profits of a principal manufacturer of strike-on-box matches in 1933, in which year the imports were the largest since 1930, were enormously high. Although the reduced output of 1934, and some increase in costs resulting from operation under the code, cut down the profits last year, they were still far higher than in most industries. If the small reduction in the duty on matches which is made by this Agreement should have a tendency to increase imports, a moderate reduction of the profits of the domestic producers and of some of the high salaries paid to their officials should enable them to meet this competition without putting a single American workman out of employment.

The Trade Agreements Act contains no authority for the President or the State Department to pass upon the salaries of officers of domestic corporations. That is not among the reasons given in the Act for making agreements. The document was supposed to be a trade agreement with the object of increasing American exports through taking imports that would not hurt the American economy. If, as the State Department asserts, the American match industry can meet the foreign competition by reducing the salaries of officers, there will be no imports of matches and the sole purpose of the agreement will be the reduction of some executive salaries. Among the several new theories concocted by the State Department, the regulation of domestic earnings by solemn international agreements has at least the merit of being quite unusual.

The concessions to Sweden on matches apply also to Russia and Japan. The wages in the Japanese match industry rise to the extraordinary heights of three cents an hour. That is, for men. The rate for children is .4 cent per hour. Sweden and Japan are managed currency countries; Russia trades as a state. It is for the benefit of that sort of competition that the American markets are thrown open.

Our whole balance of transactions with Sweden has been unfavorable. Here is the account:

Balance of Payments Between the United States and Sweden
1919-1933 Inclusive

(Based on Information Available December, 1934)

During this 15-year period:		
we sold to Sweden goods in the amount of		$760,400,000
and we bought from Sweden goods in the amount of		541,900,000
leaving a favorable balance with Sweden for goods in the amount of		$218,500,000
Our tourists spent in Sweden (net)	$ 59,000,000	
our immigrants sent to Sweden (net) ..	120,000,000	
shipping services rendered to us (net) ..	65,000,000	
or net payments for service items in the amount of ...		244,000,000
leaving an unfavorable balance of		$25,500,000

We paid for gold imported from Sweden the net amount of	101,000,000
making a total unfavorable balance of	$126,500,000
Also during this 15-year period:	
we made new long-term loans in Sweden in the net amount of	42,000,000
resulting in an unfavorable balance of payments with Sweden during the 15-year period amounting to . .	$168,500,000

This unfavorable balance represents dollars used by Sweden (1) to buy in other countries (the dollars in turn being used by such other countries to buy American goods, American securities, or foreign securities held in the United States), and (2) to buy back Swedish dollar securities held in the United States.

Further, a part of the unfavorable balance would be represented by Swedish securities held in the United States. However, in October, 1934, following substantial repatriation of Swedish bonds during recent years, the remaining bonds outstanding in the United States were called. We have, therefore, no longer any bond investments in Sweden.

Now for the results. The Swedish agreement went into effect on August 1st, 1935. During the period from August 1st, 1934 to December 31st, 1934 we bought goods from Sweden in the amount of $16,290,548 and sold goods in the amount of $15,618,813. From August 1st, 1935 to December 31st, 1935 we bought goods to the amount of $21,774,691 and sold goods to the amount of $18,134,641. That is, under the agreement we had an increase of imports amounting to $5,484,143 and an increase of exports amounting only to $2,515,828. In other words, we did not meet the Swedish competition—and gave up a certain number of American jobs in order that foreign workmen might be employed.

COLOMBIA—HAITI—RUSSIA

The Colombian agreement was signed on September 13th, 1935 but was only recently ratified by the Colombian Government and so its results cannot be estimated. Our chief purchases from Colombia are coffee and bananas—the latter coming largely from American-owned plantations. Coffee is bound on the free list as in the case of Brazil.

We have always bought more from Colombia than we have sold. The outstanding reason for making an agreement with Colombia should have been to collect some of the debts owing to Americans on defaulted bonds and blocked exchange. Nothing that might benefit American creditors was included in the agreement, and the mystery is why it was made. The Office of the Special Adviser sought to gain some benefits—but the agreement went through on its original lines. The account of our transactions with Colombia is of interest—as showing a lost opportunity; it was available to the negotiators.

BALANCE OF PAYMENTS BETWEEN THE UNITED STATES AND COLOMBIA 1914-1933 INCLUSIVE

(Based on Information Available December, 1934)

During this 20-year period:		
we bought from Colombia goods in the amount of...		$1,115,700,000
and we sold to Colombia goods in the amount of ...		537,000,000
leaving an unfavorable balance with Colombia for goods in the amount of		$578,700,000
We paid for gold imported from Colombia the net amount of		77,500,000
making a total unfavorable balance of		$656,200,000
Shipping services rendered by us	$46,000,000	
and interest received on our loans to Colombia	63,000,000	
a total of	$109,000,000	
less Treaty payments to Colombia under the 1922 Treaty	25,000,000	
or net receipts from service items in the amount of..		84,000,000
reduced our unfavorable balance to		$572,200,000
Also during this 20-year period:		
we made new long-term loans and new direct investments in Colombia in the net amount of		183,000,000
resulting in an unfavorable balance of payments with Colombia during the 20-year period amounting to		$755,200,000

By an exchange of notes between our Ambassador and the Soviet Government, the U. S. S. R. was admitted to most-favored-nation status. This means that tariff concessions granted under any trade agreement are opened to the products of the forced labor of Russia. In return, Russia agrees to buy $30,000,000 worth of American goods—and a much larger amount, if only sufficient credits can be had. This amounts to an unenforceable agreement to buy about the same amount of goods as usual. The agreement makes no mention of the estimated $700,000,000 owed to us by Russia.

The agreement with Haiti by itself is of slight economic importance, for the buying power of Haiti is trivial. Coffee was bound on the free list—which means that Brazil and Colombia had no need to make their agreements to secure coffee concessions, for their coffee was bound free by the compact with Haiti!

Chapter XIV

More Agreements—Canada

The trade agreement with Canada was announced on November 15th, 1935 with a larger volume of "publicity" than has ever attended a Government announcement. The President called a special conference of correspondents on Sunday; the Departments of State, Agriculture and Commerce issued several pounds of press matter of a complicated and supposedly profound nature; and Secretary Wallace went on the air to tell the country in general and the farmers in particular how great would be the benefits under the agreement.

All of these statements, I regret to say, were disingenuous. The vast publicity had as its objective, not the clarifying of the agreement, but the covering up of the fact that it represented a complete shift from the President's pledge not to reduce the tariffs on agricultural products. The agreement gave important concessions to Canada on agricultural products of which we normally have a surplus. Most of the concessions granted by Canada were illusory or unimportant. In the main they had to do with our industrial exports. The plain intent of the agreement is to trade a share of the American farm market for industrial export trade. This intent is concealed in a mass of schedules which are utterly unintelligible to other than an expert.

The agreement was made just before I left the Government service, but under date of December 8th, 1935 I finished an analysis of the schedules and, at the request of the President, sent a copy to him at the same time that I made a release to the press.

The agreement not only reversed the President's pledge, but also it was made without regard to the state of the accounts between this country and Canada. The agreement was based on the assumption that, because of the Hawley-Smoot Tariff Act of 1930, Canada had put on retaliatory duties, that we had lost a great amount of trade by reason of these duties and that, by refusing to buy Canadian goods, we had withdrawn from Canada a purchasing power which would have been used to buy our goods. The official announcements failed to state that in 1932 Canada, through the Ottawa Agreements, had adopted the Empire Preference scheme by which the units of the British Empire gave preferential treatment to imports from one another. The announcements also failed to state that Canada, through selling us gold and silver, had plenty of purchasing power in this country but was using it, not to buy our goods, but to buy their and our securities and to buy British goods. Our official announcements concerned themselves only with the exchanges of goods and did not touch the gold, silver and capital transactions which changed our balance of payments with Canada from the credit to the debit side.

The profound importance of basing trading agreements, tariffs and all foreign trade policies on the sound foundation of accounts was never better illustrated than in the agreement with Canada. Had the State Department proceeded on the accounting facts instead of on scholastic theory, it could never have made an agreement so adverse to American interests. The Canadians knew their accounts. That is why they got concessions while we got pictures of concessions. Here are the facts of our trade with Canada in simple bookkeeping terms:

	1929	1934	1935 (9 months)
	(Thousands of Dollars)		
United States sold merchandise to Canada	948,400	302,400	243,700
United States bought merchandise from Canada	503,500	231,600	203,100

	1929	1934	(9 months) 1935
	(Thousands of Dollars)		
Leaving us with an export merchandise surplus of	444,900	70,800	40,600
We bought gold and silver from Canada net	77,500	87,100	77,900
Leaving us with a visible export or import (—) surplus of	367,400	—16,300	—37,300

In the light of the facts, this statement by the Department of Agriculture on November 19th, 1935, is incomprehensible:

A large part of the decline in our agricultural exports to Canada from $50,000,000 to $15,000,000 in the past five years should be recovered in consequence of the Canadian trade agreement, and, in addition the domestic market for farm products should expand on account of increased domestic payrolls, the U. S. Department of Agriculture estimated today. Canadian imports of American farm products, upon which duty reductions are secured, in the year ending March 31, 1930, were valued at $50,000,000; in the year ending March 31, 1935 they had dropped to $15,000,000. With the aid of an improved price level, the new trade agreement should do much to recapture that lost trade, the Department declared.

The new agreement will benefit "the whole of agriculture," in the opinion of Henry A. Wallace, Secretary of Agriculture.

"The United States has always had a greater volume of trade with Canada than with any other country except the United Kingdom," Mr. Wallace pointed out. "This extremely profitable mutual relationship, amounting on the average to over a billion dollars a year, was rudely broken by our Tariff Act of 1930 and by the retaliatory Canadian tariff shortly thereafter. It is my opinion that the new trade agreement with Canada is beneficial to all people of the United States, and especially to farmers.

"There are a few farm groups which will fear they are being hurt by the new agreement, but actually in those cases the tariff reductions are moderate and in addition there are quota restrictions of such a nature that imports from Canada cannot affect the American price structure by more than 1 per cent. This small effect, in my judgment, will as a rule be more than offset by the increased payrolls of industries established along the northern border and in the Northeastern States. These increased payrolls will stimulate the demand in the United States for most of the farm products in which there has been a slight reduction in duty. I am thoroughly convinced that the Canadian treaty will prove of benefit to the whole of American agriculture, and that no particular branch of farming will be seriously, if at all, disadvantaged."

Equally incomprehensible is this somewhat ill-tempered release by Secretary Hull on November 21st:

The reaction of the country to the trade agreement between the United States and Canada has been overwhelmingly favorable. I have noted a number of protests, confined almost entirely to professional partisan politicians or to some of the specially privileged individuals benefiting from excessive tariff rates, with a notable division of opinion, however, among the latter.

Such protests as have been made are confined almost exclusively to a very few particular interests. No one questions the broad economic benefits which will result to the nation as a whole. From the standpoint of both agriculture and industry the soundness of this trade agreement is clear. A few months of practical operation will demonstrate the value of the agreement in terms of increased trade to the mutual benefit of both countries. . . .

This administration, in striking contrast with the log-rolling method of the past, is at present carrying on in the most careful manner a temporary program to meet the depression emergency by seeking to restore the large volume of trade between this and other countries lost during the years of depression. This extremely important program is being conducted in a strictly non-partisan manner and thus far with the support of probably 85 per cent of the press of the nation.

It means mutually profitable trade, greater employment of labor and a fuller and more stable measure of domestic prosperity.

The methods employed in formulating agreements and the conduct of the program are open, careful and thorough. In the case of each agreement hearings are given to all interested persons. Invitations are submitted to all to submit data and arguments concerning every tariff item in question. During the succeeding six to twelve months in which trade proposals are being studied each detail pertaining to each tariff item is, in the light of the data submitted, of independent study and of informal consultation, fully and carefully examined by capable, non-partisan specialists from the various government departments concerned.

Consideration of the Canadian Trade Agreement began in January last and its preparation comprised more than ten months of strenuous labor and consideration. Scores of briefs and statements were submitted, both at the oral hearings and in writing at other times. All received the most careful attention. The final outcome represents a judgment based largely on this material. Few legislative hearings have afforded such ample and systematic opportunity for effective presentation of all views and interests.

Our agricultural exports slumped from $1,884,000,000 in 1927 to $694,000,000 in 1933. In other words, we lost markets for some $1,200,000,000 of our farm surpluses. Either we can seek a restoration of most of these foreign markets or we can abandon the idea of increased sales of surpluses and move straight and steadily along the pathway of a regimentation of our processes of production, transportation and distribution.

If we cannot sell surpluses abroad, we must inescapably restrict our production to our domestic consuming capacity. This means new waves of unemployment and a permanent dole to many millions on a steadily increasing basis.

The many millions of wage-earners thrown out of employment from 1929 to 1933 and of farmers thrown into conditions of bankruptcy during the same period, who know their present improved and steadily improving condition, will, I imagine, think twice before giving heed to the small but powerful Hawley-Smoot wrecking crew that dominated the agricultural, business and economic affairs of the nation during the years prior to 1933.

Now let us examine the facts. Canada has a three-column tariff system: the British Empire Preferential rates, which are the lowest; the Intermediate rates, which are used principally for bargaining purposes and are accorded to nations making trade agreements with Canada; and the General or highest rate. In addition there are certain "conventional" rates below the intermediate rates established in trade agreements with foreign nations, including France, Italy, Belgium, Netherlands, Spain, Switzerland, and Japan, which are generalized on a limited most-favored-foreign-nation basis. The United States alone, among the leading commercial countries, has paid the highest scale of Canadian duties.

An important exchange of notes between Canada and the United States took place late in 1934, which was made public in September, 1935, in which Canada proposed that the United States accept more agricultural, cattle, forest, fishing and mineral products in return for numerous minor concessions on American fruit and other agricultural products and extensive concessions on American industrial products.

Canada's chief exports are of agricultural, forest, fishery and mineral products, including gold and silver, from the proceeds of which she imports principally manufactured goods to supplement her as yet incompletely developed industrial production. Her objective was simple and understandable—to exchange her surpluses for increased industrial products, including the importation of productive machinery which might increase her own industrial self-sufficiency. Her proposals were a perfect example of what I have called the policy of selective exports and imports.

As against this, the United States is an exporter of both agricultural and industrial products. The circumstance that a great part of Canada's exports are competitive with American products sharply limited the trading possibilities. Nevertheless the Administration decided to go ahead along the lines proposed by Canada. The negotiations lasted over ten months, being briefly interrupted by the change of government in Canada which put out of office Mr. Bennett and the Conservatives, and put back in office Mr. MacKenzie King and the Liberals. Mr. MacKenzie King made a flying visit to Washington shortly after his return to power, and on November eleventh President Roosevelt announced that an agreement had been reached which was subsequently signed on the fifteenth and made public on the seventeenth, to take effect at the beginning of 1936. It is not impossible that political exigencies on both sides had much to do with the sudden signing—and perhaps with the differences between the announcements and the facts.

In my analysis I presented a thorough statistical tabulation of the main features of the agreement and made these observations—all of which was presented to the President:

The striking changes which have taken place in our trade and financial relations with Canada between 1929 and 1934-5 (which were noted in my Letter to the President of April 30th, 1935, on Foreign Trade and International Investment Position of the United States, Exhibit III) are to be attributed not only to the passage of the Tariff Act of 1930 and the enactment of subsequent new tariff legislation by Canada, but more particularly to such developments as the negotiation of the Ottawa agreements, higher prices of gold and silver, and the general breakdown of international exchanges.

Tables II and III indicate the following situation with respect to concessions made and bound by us to Canada, and those made and bound by Canada to us until December 31st, 1938:

Distribution of concessions by commodity groups	Value of 1929 trade in articles upon which concessions are bound	
	Concessions by United States	Concessions by Canada
	$307,894,400	$244,653,000
Agricultural and forest products	83.8%	22.6%
Fishery products	2.9%	0.2%
Mineral products	7.1%	3.4%
Manufactured and miscellaneous products	6.2%	73.8%

In substance this results in giving Canada an increased share of our markets for agricultural and forest products, in the expectation that certain of our industries will obtain larger markets in Canada for their products especially of productive machinery. The reason advanced in the official statement of November 17th, 1935, for this procedure is that our farmers will gain much from the numerous and important concessions obtained for manufactured American goods. In the words of the statement:

"The increase in the exports of our factories which seems bound to result will so add to the purchasing power of the wage earners that they can buy more of the products of American farms."

This, I am led to observe, is precisely the theory upon which three Republican administrations acted during the 'twenties when American agriculture progressively declined. The Democratic party adopted an opposite policy for its successful campaign of 1932 and for its subsequent requests for farm legislation. President Roosevelt stated the issue unequivocally in his Baltimore and Boston speeches in 1932. . . .

Increased agricultural imports can have only a depressing effect on farm prices, and one which tends to continue the necessity for restriction of production. While quotas on some commodities have been provided, they are tariff quotas only. There is no limit on the quantity which may be imported at the regular tariff rates. Moreover the importation of even small quantities at lower rates may have a depressing effect on general market prices.

In the face of these facts and of President Roosevelt's assurances in his Baltimore speech of October 26th, 1932, that agricultural tariffs would not be reduced, it may be asked whether it is wise or fair to ask agriculture at this time to accept the sacrifices involved in the Canadian agreement. . . .

I have pointed out repeatedly, as the trend of the present trade agreements program gradually became apparent, that the adoption of the unconditional most-favored-nation principle for the Canadian and other trade agreements means a general reduction of the tariff. It has been minimized or obscured in some instances, notably in the case of the Canadian agreement, by the skill with which our negotiators have in part nullified the operation of the most-favored-nation principle through the selection of commodities supplied solely by one nation, by "trick" classifications, by employment of quotas, and by inclusion of "escape" clauses. Nevertheless sufficient of the unconditional principle has remained to make the substantial effect of the tariff concessions in the individual agreements one of general tariff reduction in exchange for scattering concessions from the countries concerned. One has only to point to items such as the inclusion of Scotch and Irish whiskies in the Canadian agreement to see how this operates. . . .

As I said above, the agreement was announced with a tremendous fanfare, and the suspicion is unescapable that the publicity was designed by its very volume to confuse rather than to elucidate the facts. The comparisons of the loss of trade with Canada were based on the year 1929 as though that were a representative year and somehow the agreement would restore the big business of that boom period.

Government Departments ordinarily use the years 1923-25 or the year 1926 as base periods. A well-known, but not very respectable, statistical device is to select whatever base period will give the result desired. If one wants to show a great improvement under one's administration, the trick is to take some very low period in the past as a base—for instance, March, 1933 when the wheels of the country had stopped. If, on the contrary, one wants to show disaster during the administration of a predecessor, the trick is to take a high base period like 1929 and show the decline. An honest statistician takes a normal base period and reckons from it regardless of the consequences.

The Secretary of State took the utterly abnormal exports to Canada of 1929, amounting to $902,144,000, and contrasted them with the equally abnormal period of 1933 when our exports to Canada were only $197,930,000. An average of these periods gives the round figure of $550,000,000. An average for the period 1923-25 is about $600,000,000. Hence, in any ethical presentation, $600,000,000 would have to be considered as a high on the 1923-25 price level. But if we had exported in 1934 the same goods in the same quantity as during the base period, the value of our exports to Canada would have been $480,-000,000—because of the drop in prices. Our actual exports were about $300,000,000. That is a heavy decline. But it may well be asked how much of the trade is recoverable and how much, owing to the industrial development of Canada, must permanently be marked off.

The Dominion has been considered primarily as a raw material producer. Under the peculiar concepts of the internationalists, once a raw material producer, always a raw material producer. With them the world never changes. But Canada has changed. Over the ten-year period 1920-29 we exported to Canada a total of about $750,000,000 of equipment for the building and furnishing of a manufacturing industry. Under no circumstances could such an exporting of machinery be considered as a continuing trade. Canada is now able to make many of the machines for itself. Therefore logically, in considering trade possibilities, $75,000,000 a year should be deducted from the figure of $450,000,000 a year, leaving $375,-000,000 a year as the highest normal trade expectation. But the machinery we shipped to Canada is making in Canada much of the goods we formerly exported. For instance, in 1929 we exported more than 16,000,000 pounds of wrapping paper and 15,000,000 pounds of paper boxes and cartons. Now they make their own. In 1929 we shipped about 15,000,000 pounds of binder twine. Now they buy their fibres in the country of origin and make their own. In 1929 we shipped 22,820,000 pounds of canned soups. Now American branch factories make these soups in Canada. In 1929 we shipped 38,-

692,000 pounds of refined copper. Now we ship none. Formerly we shipped a great deal of refined petroleum products. Now Canada does its own refining.

Canadian home industries are producing at least $50,000,000 a year of the goods we formerly exported. That reduces our potential export trade from about $375,000,000 a year to $325,000,000 a year. Therefore our exports in 1934 of around $300,000,000 were not as low as represented.

It must be noted that Secretaries Hull and Wallace, in making their statements about the loss of Canadian trade, were either misinformed or less than candid. The Canadian authorities have no intention of wrecking their industries to promote world peace or world prosperity or whatever it is that Secretary Hull and his internationalists think that they are after. It is of interest that the Canadian Automobile Chamber of Commerce takes no stock in the theory that lowering Canadian import duties will promote the Canadian export trade and aid in Canadian prosperity. In a brief presented to the Canadian Tariff Board, the automobile makers said:

> Other countries have not been content to allow the United States to control this industry, although if price were the only consideration consumers throughout the world would probably have been better served by the purchase of American-made cars than those manufactured at home. Every major country adopted practically the same policy in regard to the industry, and this policy was to encourage its establishment and development. Numerous reasons, both commercial and political, led to the general adoption of protection. Primarily, the production of motor cars is a great industry in itself but even further does it stimulate and build up subsidiary and affiliated industrial activity. It permeates the whole industrial life of a nation. Indirectly, it exercises an enormous influence socially and commercially. It affects transportation, road construction, merchandising, areas of population and domestic comfort and safety. The great war showed in a spectacular way the importance of motor transport in military operations.

In Great Britain one of the early departures from the traditional policy of Free Trade took place in connection with the motor car. In 1915 by The Finance (No. 2) Act a general Customs Tariff of 33 1-3 per cent was imposed on motor cars and certain other industrial products. It was then and has since been customary to speak of the selected industries covered by the 1915 Tariff as Key Industries, which are so essential to modern industrialism that exceptional tariff protection is advisable to ensure their establishment and development.

In other countries where there is no manufacturing of motor cars and no likelihood of this taking place, customs Tariffs have nevertheless been established. There can be no element of protection in these duties and presumably the object is revenue only. The motor car has always been a favorite object of taxation, partly as a result of the earlier conception that it was largely a luxury product. The Duties in a number of these wholly importing countries run from 32 to 60 per cent. . . .

Production for the export market is an indispensable and profitable complement to production for the domestic market. The automobile export business makes a valuable contribution to international trade and the maintenance of Canada's credit abroad. . . .

If the industry is to prosper it is necessary that protection be maintained and that the growing burden of taxes on the manufacturer be substantially lightened.

The Canadian Automobile Chamber of Commerce is made up of: Chrysler Corporation of Canada Limited, General Motors of Canada Limited, Hudson Motors of Canada Limited, International Harvester Company of Canada Limited, and The Studebaker Corporation of Canada Limited.

The American companies, which largely own and direct the Canadian companies, are the leading members of the Automobile Manufacturers Association of the United States and control its policies. But in the United States these same automobile manufacturers are the leading backers of the theory that reducing tariffs and taking more imports will produce more exports and add to the general prosperity. And this in spite of the fact that Canada is primarily a raw material exporting nation and the United States is not!

The Dominion is a part of the British Empire and as such it is bound by the preferential trade agreements which seek to make the Empire an economic as well as a political entity. In a fashion, the Dominion is going through the same stages of progress toward industrialization that our own country went through. In the course of that progress, it will be mutually profitable to exchange many products, but the present agreement does little to promote that exchange and is, on the part of Canada, a skillfully drawn paper to dispose of Canadian agricultural surpluses in the United States. In view of the Ottawa agreements, the concessions granted to the United States amount to little or nothing because in only limited instances are our rates as low as the rates given to the British Empire.

For instance, in 1929 we shipped to Canada 3,015,000 tons of anthracite coal. This has dropped a million tons. Coal exports are very important to Great Britain and it is not likely that she will permit her Canadian market to be taken away. We may be able to provide the Canadian cotton requirements, but the Empire is going in heavily for cotton. The same applies to petroleum. In 1929 we were furnishing Canada with most of the bauxite and other aluminum ores and concentrates —125,545 tons in that year. Now we are shipping only about two-thirds of that amount. Tremendous branch plants have been built in Canada, and the raw materials come in from other parts of the British Empire.

The agricultural concessions to Canada are real. Under the Tariff Act of 1922, our tariff on cream was 20 cents a gallon, and during the years 1925-29 Canada shipped us from a high of more than 5,000,000 gallons to a low of just under 3,000,000 gallons a year. In 1929, by Presidential proclamation, the rate was raised to 30 cents a gallon and the imports dropped to under 2,000,000 gallons. By the Tariff Act of 1930, the rate was raised to 56.6 cents a gallon and in 1933 our imports were only 24,797 gallons. Under the trade agreement, the rate is lowered to 35 cents per gallon for the first 1,500,000 gallons. This means the displacement of that much American production. The decrease in lumber tariffs on woods directly competitive with the American means the displacement of production in the depressed American lumber industry and also seriously affects American-owned shipping. Under a trick classification, we admit cattle weighing over 700 pounds at a reduced duty up to 250,000 head. The quota is in excess of what Canada would ordinarily be able to ship and displaces production in the depressed American cattle industry. It is likewise with potatoes.

Take some of the supposed concessions granted to us:

In 1930 Canada imported raisins in the amount of $2,433,000, of which we furnished $1,572,000 and Australia furnished $718,000. In 1934 Canada imported raisins to the amount of $2,094,000, of which we furnished $452,000 and Australia $1,474,000. Under the agreement, Canada "reduced" the tariff on American raisins from the general rate of 3 cents per pound to the intermediate rate of 3 cents a pound, or exactly nothing, and since Australian raisins come in free, the concession is meaningless.

In 1930 Canada imported canned peaches and apricots to the amount of $1,040,000, of which we furnished $851,000 and Australia furnished $188,000. In 1934 Canada imported only to the amount of $133,000, of which we furnished $9,000 and Australia furnished $124,000. Under the agreement, we secured a reduction from the general rate of 5 cents to the intermediate rate of 4 cents. The Australian rate remains at 2 cents.

In 1930 Canada imported print cottons to the amount of $3,777,000, of which we furnished $2,209,000 and the United

Kingdom $1,384,000. In 1934 Canada imported print cottons to the amount of $1,576,000, of which we furnished $405,000 and the United Kingdom $1,077,000. The general duty on print cottons was 32½ per cent plus 4 cents a pound. Under the agreement, we secured the intermediate duty of 27½ per cent plus 3½ cents a pound. The Empire preferential duty remains at 22½ per cent plus 2 cents a pound.

In 1931 Canada imported tin-coated sheets to the amount of $496,000, of which we furnished $76,000 and the United Kingdom furnished $420,000. In 1934 Canada imported $7,-036,000, of which $221,000 came from the United States and $6,812,000 came from the United Kingdom. The general tariff rate was 20 per cent and the intermediate rate was also 20 per cent. Under the agreement, we got the intermediate rate—or exactly nothing. Under the Empire preference, tin-coated sheets are free.

In 1930 Canada imported vacuum cleaners in the amount of $270,000, of which the entire amount came from us. In 1934 Canada imported to the amount of $297,000, of which we furnished $27,000, the United Kingdom furnished $13,000 and Sweden furnished $256,000. The general rate of duty was 25 per cent and the intermediate rate 20 per cent. Under the agreement, we got the intermediate rate along with Sweden. The preferential rate is 12½ per cent.

In other words, we got no concessions that Canada was not already giving to a considerable number of nations and no concessions (barring minor exceptions) which touched the Empire rate. The doctrine of the "principal supplier" has already been brought out. It will be recalled that Secretary Hull said that concessions would be granted only to the principal suppliers and therefore the generalization of these concessions would not matter. As has already been explained, this theory did not hold water. But in the Canadian Agreement the principle is apparently abandoned, for concessions were made on the following products where there is no pretense that Canada is the principal supplier: cherries in their natural state; peas, green: duty reduced only from July 1st to September 30th; by-product feeds and mixed feeds dutiable at 10 per cent; smoked herring (boned, whether or not skinned); talc, steatite or soapstone, ground, etc. (except toilet preparations), valued not over $12.50 per long ton; ferromanganese, containing not less than 4 per cent carbon on manganese content; cobalt oxide; whiskey (aged not less than 4 years in wood containers); cobalt and cobalt ore; sodium cyanide; and undressed furs: mink, beaver, muskrat and wolf.

These concessions, being generalized, mean that the Canadian agreement was used to make a general tariff reduction on the above items.

Newsprint is bound on the free list—which means that the building of a newsprint industry in the United States is at the mercy of the Canadian producers. A newsprint industry founded on slash pine grown on exhausted cotton lands in our South would be of great economic benefit to the United States and give a cash crop to farmers who no longer can profitably raise cotton. The hazards of making ourselves dependent on a foreign source of supply through binding any article on the free list were well brought out at the meeting of the American Newspaper Publishers Association in New York on April 24th, 1936. After the agreement was signed, the Canadian producers of newsprint made a coalition with the Dominion Government to control prices. It so happens that the intention is to lift prices but, were an American industry established, the same machinery could be used, as it has often been used before, to make a dumping price to ruin the American industry. For these reasons, the remarks, at the meeting, of William G. Chandler of the Scripps-Howard newspapers are especially interesting:

Now, under the Marketing Act, upon application to the Minister of Agriculture, a scheme for controlling marketing of newsprint may be put into operation. This scheme would be administered by a local board, and according to the Toronto Financial Post of July 20, 1935, the newsprint industry would undoubtedly nominate the members of the local board. The board would have complete control over export of newsprint. It has power to ration markets, regulate prices and eliminate excess capacity.

Recent events and statements lead to the inevitable conclusion that the time is near when United States publishers who may purchase Canadian newsprint will not have to deal alone with the manufacturer of their choice but with a coalition of the Canadian Government and of the Canadian manufacturer. . . .

The day does not seem to be far distant when Southern newsprint will be a reality. Perhaps the reason it is not a reality today is because there was only a moderate advance in the price of newsprint at the beginning of this year. As an answer to the apparent determination of the Canadian Government to become a party to negotiations for the purchase of newsprint, it seems that it would behoove every publisher to give his encouragement to the founding of a new, important newsprint-producing center.

The Canadians made a good bargain and they know it. In a despatch from Toronto to the *New York Times,* dated November 23rd, 1935, it was said:

But if the trade pact works out according to Canadian expectations, it will result in much wider markets in the United States for Canadian farm products. That would not only advance the price locally, but would increase the general total of sales. The theory, at least, has it that the heavier purchasing power of Canadian farmers would not only place Canadian agriculturists in a position to buy farm machinery more freely, but would let them pay off some of their back debts to the implement makers. Those accounts are material in the case of all Canadian farm implement manufacturers.

By lowering the American duty on live stock, cream and seed potatoes, though a quota will be in effect, benefits should come to the wide sweep of Canadian farmers from coast to coast. That background has encouraged so much hope for Canadian farm implements that stock markets have been advancing the price of the stocks of such companies.

The precise manner in which the Canadian trade agreement is going to help the American farmer or the American industrialist or anyone in the United States, according to the fervent promises of Secretaries Hull and Wallace, is not evident in the agreement or in its surrounding circumstances.

THE NETHERLANDS AGREEMENT

The agreement with the Netherlands (also covering insular possessions), signed on December 20th, 1935 to take effect February 1st, 1936, is in the spirit of the Canadian agreement —that is, it is not a trade agreement but so palpably a general revision of our tariffs downward as to lead the *New York Times,* on December 24th, 1935, jubilantly to remark:

> The significance of what is happening should not be overlooked. The Government is not merely negotiating a series of bilateral trade pacts. Because of the practice of generalizing all reductions, it is gradually rewriting the Hawley-Smoot tariff of 1930. About 150 of the rates established by that celebrated "tariff of abominations" have already been scaled down, to the advantage of all nations which trade with us without discrimination. Secretary Hull is accomplishing indirectly, and with some compensation in each case, what the advocates of a unilateral reduction of our tariffs have long urged but long regarded as politically impossible.

The agreement, as in the case of Canada, again sacrifices American agricultural interests and does exactly what President

Roosevelt, in his election campaign said he would not do. Agriculture, however, is not sacrificed to the advantage of industry —it is just sacrificed.

In 1934 our imports from the Netherlands and its possessions amounted to $80,035,000. The agreement made concessions on items making up $25,582,045 of these imports. These concessions were divided as follows: 66.3 per cent consisted in binding on the free list; 20.1 per cent in duty reductions of 35 per cent or less; 0.7 per cent in duty reductions of 36 per cent to 49 per cent; while on 12.8 per cent of the items on which concessions were made we reduced our duties to the full limit of the Act—that is 50 per cent. The Netherlands duties were in most cases not high, but the trade was covered by quotas and other restrictions which are modified—although not to the point of giving the United States any price preference—and a somewhat elaborate concession is made admitting American wheat and flour provided it meets competitive world prices. This concession is trivial at best and comes close to being no concession at all.

The State Department announcement is both apologetic and disingenuous and is built upon comparing our trade with the Netherlands in 1934 with that in 1929. This was the trick used in the Canadian agreement, but in the Netherlands announcement, in addition to selecting non-comparable bases, the Department uses dollars instead of quantities and presents a condition which does not in fact exist. For instance, in binding tapioca imports on the free list, the State Department shows that tapioca imports declined from $4,548,000 in 1929 to $2,834,000 in 1934, thereby creating the impression that the imports of tapioca were declining. The Department of Commerce gives the tonnage in 1929 as 173,000,000 pounds and the tonnage in 1934 as 176,000,000 pounds. Therefore the Department of State, by choosing dollar figures instead of tonnage figures, gave an impression exactly contrary to the truth.

In addition to binding tapioca on the free list, the agreement also binds sago. Both of these are directly competitive with domestic corn and potato starches. Not only that, the policy enunciated goes directly contrary to the Government policies of promoting the potato starch industry.

Making starch from corn is one of our established domestic industries. The State Department announcement accompanying the agreement said that the competition by the imports from the Netherlands would not amount to over 5 per cent of the domestic production. But 5 per cent of the domestic production amounts to three or four million bushels of corn—which means several million dollars less cash income for the corn states. The competition of imported tapioca and sago had already been felt by these states and a measure known as the Thompson Bill, proposing an excise tax on tapioca and sago, was pending in Congress at the time the agreement was signed—and had been brought to the attention of the State Department. The Illinois State Legislature had passed a resolution favoring the bill and it also had been endorsed by a number of farm groups.

The imports of tapioca and sago do a great deal more than withdraw income from the corn farmers. The imported tapioca and sago arrive in prepared form, and the only labor that they absorb in this country has to do with repackaging and selling. The domestic wet corn milling industry uses a large quantity of direct and indirect labor and, I believe, about a million and a half tons of coal a year. Thus the competition invites displacement not only in corn growing but also in coal mining and transportation—all of which are in a depressed condition.

The agreement makes a reduction of duty on potato starch and potato dextrine. This reduction runs directly counter to other Government policies. When the agreement was signed, the Potato Act of 1935 was in force and that Act had, among other purposes, the encouragement of the diversion of surplus potatoes. It may be recalled that at the time of the passage of the Act, representatives of the potato growers of New England were called to Washington to see what they could do about turning more cull potatoes into starch. The farm representatives stated that a two-years' supply of starch had already dammed up on them because of the low prices of foreign potato starch. At the same time, the Government had established at Laurel, Mississippi an experimental factory to make sweet potato starch and thus aid the sweet potato growers by industrializing a part of their product. All of these facts were presumably called to the attention of the American negotiators.

The duties were reduced on cigar wrapper tobacco, and on this point the Department of State announced:

> Cigar wrapper tobacco is largest in value among the dutiable commodities imported from the Kingdom of the Netherlands on which concessions have been granted.
>
> The duty on unstemmed cigar wrapper tobacco is lowered by this Agreement from $2.275 per pound to $1.875 per pound until June 30, 1936, and thereafter to $1.50 per pound. Stemmed wrapper tobacco, because of the greater loss through breakage, is not an important article of trade. The rate on the stemmed is reduced from $2.925 per pound to $2.525 per pound, and later to $2.15, in order to preserve the 65 cent differential between it and the rate on unstemmed wrapper.
>
> Wrapper tobacco is grown only in limited areas in the Connecticut Valley and on the Georgia-Florida boundary under artificial shade. The ad valorem equivalent of the duty has ranged from 119 to 184 per cent in recent years. Our climatic and other conditions are not nearly so favorable for the production of wrapper tobacco as are those of Sumatra, where artificial shade is not needed.
>
> The reduction in duty on wrapper tobacco will be of considerable benefit to American producers of filler and binder tobacco. These tobaccos are combined with the imported wrapper in the manufacture of low-priced cigars. Binder and

filler tobaccos are grown principally in the states of Pennsylvania, Ohio, Massachusetts, Connecticut, and Wisconsin. The growers of these classes of tobacco greatly outnumber the producers of wrapper tobacco with which the imported Sumatra tobacco competes. Moreover, the producers of shade wrapper tobacco will still be accorded substantial protection since the rate of $1.50 per pound, which will be in effect after June 30, 1936, will be equivalent to about 80 per cent ad valorem.

The American cigar wrapper tobacco growers do not feel that the duty reduction is quite so trivial a matter. They believe that they are going to be put out of business. The wages in Sumatra are a few cents a day. The wages in Connecticut, where most of the tobacco of this type is grown, are substantial. In Sumatra, artificial shade is not needed. In Connecticut, it is needed. There is no comparison in the expense of growing. The Connecticut Valley Tobacco Growers Association members have approximately 6,000 acres under cultivation, and the shade is obtained by stretching cotton cloth on poles over the fields. This takes about 35,000,000 square yards of cotton cloth and about 100,000 pounds of cotton string. In addition, the Connecticut cultivation uses 7500 tons a year of cottonseed meal as fertilizer. Thus the reduction in duty under the agreement hits not only directly at an important New England industry but also indirectly at both cotton growing and the textile trade.

The agreement, by reducing the duty on tulip and other bulbs, hits the growing domestic industry, particularly in the Northwest where 600 varieties are grown. Duties are reduced on rose stock, garden and field seeds, on the ground that reducing the cost of these seeds will benefit agriculture—although growing the seeds is a part of agriculture.

The principal concessions granted to the United States are contained in Schedule 3, under which the Dutch Government undertakes to purchase annually a quantity of wheat flour equivalent to not less than 5 per cent of the annual total wheat flour consumption of the Netherlands and also to purchase annually a quantity of milling wheat equivalent to not less than 5 per cent of the annual total consumption of foreign milling wheat—provided the prices to the Netherlands are "competitive with the world price." A careful survey in Washington disclosed no official facts in the possession of anyone as to what this 5 per cent figure meant in bushels, and there is strong reason to believe that our negotiators took the figure without knowing what it meant. The population of the Netherlands is somewhat over eight millions. That is, it contains slightly more people than Greater New York City. This important concession, if it be a concession, amounts to little more than the right to provide 5 per cent of New York City's bread requirements. However, it may not mean even that, for the American flour and wheat must be as cheap as foreign flour and wheat and therefore the imports, if any, are to be taken at the world price instead of at an American price.

It is for concessions such as these that a substantial portion of the production of American agriculture and agricultural industry was given away.

Chapter XV

The Sell-Out

The Roosevelt Administration adopted two major policies with the declared intent of aiding domestic prosperity and employment. Both policies were designed to dispose of surplus agricultural production through export channels and thereby to bring domestic agricultural prices up to a point where the farm and the factory could freely exchange their products upon an equitable level and go forward to a prosperity based upon the sound foundation of mutual interest.

That was the intent, in part, of the devaluation of the dollar. That was the whole intent of the Reciprocal Trade Agreements Act. Both policies have been so slightly comprehended and so unskillfully administered that they have brought results exactly opposite to those intended, and the country has been put into a desperate condition—which would be more generally realized, were it not for the violent official and unofficial propaganda to cover up and confuse the facts.

It is not necessary to be a student of foreign affairs or of international exchanges or to have special knowledge of any kind to understand the facts. It is necessary only to have a knowledge of elementary arithmetic equivalent to that taught in the first grade of the public schools.

The Reciprocal Trade Agreements Act and the devaluation of the dollar are not connected in the public mind. It is not generally realized that we are today living in a most extraordinary world in which money is not what it seems to be—it is being made a servant of government rather than a servant of goods. That is, nowadays money is being manipulated to carry out political and economic policies and only incidentally acts as a medium for the exchange of goods or the storing of hours of labor.

Gold and silver are no longer money metals in the old sense—not even in the gold or silver blocs. They are simply readily salable commodities of high value. The management of money and the management of trade go hand in hand. But, most unfortunately for the nation, the Roosevelt Administration, after equipping itself with the tools, refused to learn how to use them. Others have picked up those tools and used them against us.

To be concrete. When in 1933 the President removed the country from the gold standard, he also changed all our tariff rates—he changed the value of money, and tariff rates are reckoned in money. An ad valorem rate is a percentage of the value of the imported product in dollars. A specific rate is a definite charge in dollars or cents against a unit of the imported article. When the President, on January 31st, 1934, devalued the dollar by approximately 40 per cent and authorized the Secretary of the Treasury to buy all the gold offered at the rate of $35.00 a Troy ounce, he put the country upon the system that most of the world had been using since the British left gold in 1931, i. e., upon managed paper money. This means that a price in paper money is maintained in the domestic market, while exports are sold at world prices. The object of the system is to keep domestic prices in paper independent of world prices and to facilitate the export of surpluses at world prices. For instance, the average export price of our cotton was 11.8 cents a pound in 1934 and 12.1 cents a pound in 1935, but to countries on the gold standard the prices were 40 per cent less in terms of gold currencies. To maintain a paper money price at home thus requires a governmental control over exports and imports and over the movement of capital in and out of the country. Maintaining these prices is a problem in management which requires an immense skill.

The Administration elected to play a game without first learning how.

And so it has come about that the devaluation of the dollar (the book profits of which created the stabilization fund) and the offer to buy gold at $35.00 an ounce result simply in a sell-out of the United States. Our nation has been offered to the world at a bargain.

The Reciprocal Trade Agreements Act had as its avowed purpose "expanding foreign markets for the products of the United States" to the end of "restoring the American standard of living, in overcoming domestic unemployment . . . and in establishing and maintaining a better relationship among various branches of American agriculture, industry, mining and commerce." The purpose of the Act cannot too often be repeated. The Act was a necessary supplement to the devaluation policy, for it gave to us the means of protecting and extending our markets according to the circumstances in each case, providing we kept an eye on the books of account. Secretaries Hull and Wallace, with their associates, could not comprehend the program on which the Administration had embarked. Evidently neither the President nor the Cabinet knew what they were doing when they devalued the dollar.

I well remember attending several meetings of high Treasury and other experts, at which took place very profound discussions as to the point at which the dollar ought to be valued. If I remember rightly, the final meeting resolved on some point in the sixties—the exact point does not matter. Knowing nothing at all about such matters, I innocently asked how the decision was being arrived at and why pick on, say, 65 instead of 55 or 75. Immediately it seemed convenient for everyone to go to luncheon, and I am still without an answer. I am reasonably certain that the President settled on his figure by intuition.

Devaluation having been accomplished, our tariff structure

took on a different meaning. Since the value of money was being managed, everything connected with foreign trade had to be managed. The first principle of management is an accounting system so that one will know what one is doing. Secretary Hull and Secretary Wallace, never having had any managerial experience, simply could not get through their heads the kindergarten relation between accounting and management. They refused to play the game as it was being played throughout the world. It makes not the slightest difference whether it was a nice game or less than a nice game. It was the game that the Administration, for better or for worse, had elected to play. Instead of playing, Secretaries Hull and Wallace got out their school books, gathered around them a group that owned the same school books, and started to play a game that was in their books instead of the game that was in progress. Secretary Hull could not recognize that the elaborate system of exchange controls, quota systems, restrictions and regulations on trade which had sprung up through the world were not panic expedients but were reasoned attempts to preserve monetary systems and domestic economies. He did not know that the tariff principle, including our own, had been shot to pieces by money manipulation. He thought that what he read in his book was right and that everyone else was wrong and that, if he followed the letter of his book, everyone else would change and be as right as he knew he was.

The sincerity of his position is not in question, but the intellectual honesty of maintaining such a position within an Administration that was specifically pledged to do something else is most decidedly open to question. And that applies with equal force to Secretary Wallace and their academic associates. Instead of using the authority under the Act to trade, these men took that authority as a license for an evangelistic crusade. They have refused to face the realities. In consequence of none of those in authority really knowing what they were doing and of hiding their lack of knowledge behind an uproar of positively untruthful propaganda, these things have happened to our country:

(1) In the two years 1934 and 1935, foreign citizens, taking advantage of the price our Government was offering, have sent us $2,872,931,000 in gold and $421,904,000 in silver. These imports are almost entirely unconnected with any movement of goods. Very curiously, this is universally recognized in the case of silver, but since the movement of gold formerly had an intimate connection with the balancing of the trade in goods, there are those who refuse to admit that the tie between gold and goods has been broken and that gold, like silver, is simply a commodity. These imports of gold and silver have changed us from creditors to debtors on current transactions.

(2) By reason of these and other uncontrolled capital transactions, foreign citizens have built up tremendous holdings in this country. These holdings extend through most of our large corporations, and we are today on security investments probably a debtor nation. This means that we have lost a great deal of control over our own affairs. Only time can demonstrate the ultimate consequences, but today we are not a free nation. We do not control our destinies.

(3) The program started out to increase our foreign trade by disposing of those products in which we presumably had a surplus production. This is what has taken place:

In 1935 our exports increased by only 7 per cent over 1934 expressed in dollars. The increase in quantity was only 5 per cent. But our general imports increased 24 per cent in dollars and 22 per cent in quantity.

Our largest export was, as usual, cotton, but it increased over 1934 by only 4.9 per cent. This increase was mostly in price, for only 150,000 more bales went out than in the previous year. The 1910-14 cotton export average was 8,532,000 bales and the 1922-26 average was 7,154,000 bales. The 1934 cotton export of 5,943,000 bales was the record low for recent years—the exports in 1933 being 8,532,000 bales (the same as the pre-war average), while in 1932 the exports amounted to 9,060,000 bales. Cotton exports have not been helped by the policies. The cotton export reveals what dollar devaluation means to the cotton farmer in terms of world prices. Contrast 1930 with 1935. In 1930 the country exported 6,597,000 bales for which it received $496,798,000. The average price was 14.2 cents a pound. The 1935 exports brought in $390,899,000 at an average price of about 12.1 cents a pound. The 1930 exports gave a claim on 24,035,000 Troy ounces of gold at $20.67 an ounce. But the 1935 exports gave a claim on only 11,168,000 Troy ounces of gold at $35.00 an ounce. This means that for each bale of cotton exported in 1930 we received 3.6 ounces of gold, as against 1.8 ounces received for each bale in 1935.

Our other great export increases were in iron and steel scrap and in petroleum. These were bought for war purposes, and the Secretary of State under his neutrality plan would have stopped the sales.

The export of manufactured foodstuffs decreased by $11,000,000. The whole increase in agricultural exports was only $14,000,000, more than accounted for by the $18,000,000 increase in cotton exports, while the increase in non-agricultural exports was $128,000,000.

That is, aside from a slight increase in cotton, the Administration's program did not dispose of surplus products. Industrial establishments may and normally should have an amount of unused capacity, but to speak of surplus industrial products is to evidence a comprehensive unfamiliarity with industrial practice.

(4) The imports tell a very different story. For the year 1935 our country became dependent on foreign food imports to an extent unparalleled in our history. Still we curtailed production! Our imports of agricultural products increased by $248,000,000, while our imports of non-agricultural products increased $155,000,000. We are no longer feeding and clothing

ourselves. The change in our agricultural position is clearly brought out in the following table:

		Annual Average		*Year*	
		1921-1925	1926-1930	1933	1935
Cattle—exports	No.	97,292	13,437	2,912	3,348
" —imports	"	177,000	378,000	65,000	365,000
Hogs (swine)—exports .	"	83,472	32,936	14,207	303
" " —imports.	1M lbs.	—	11,614	8	3,414
Meat products—exports	"	838,927	425,286	231,439	155,347
" " —imports	"	67,805	144,782	60,684	115,059
Bacon, hams and shoulders—exports ...	"	642,692	265,932	100,169	61,691
Canned meats—imports.	"	—	51,206	41,476	76,653
Animals oils and fats, edible—exports	"	1,035,892	835,262	640,054	111,914
Animals oils and fats, edible—imports	"	—	2,049	287	18,895
Butter—exports	"	7,680	4,080	1,191	958
" —imports	"	15,175	5,279	899	22,675
Animal oils and greases, inedible—exports	"	82,986	78,336	81,806	24,990
Tallow—imports	"	—	10,629	239	245,851
Corn (grain)—exports .	1M bu.	73,180	20,481	5,365	177
" " —imports.	"	1,135	1,808	160	43,242
Oats (grain)—exports ..	"	13,972	8,032	1,476	568
" " —imports..	"	2,465	205	132	10,107
Wheat (grain)—exports.	"	159,222	116,155	7,983	233
" " —imports.	"	18,973	15,858	10,318	38,865
Barley—exports	"	21,274	28,527	7,142	7,507
Barley malt—imports ..	1M lbs.	—	—	109,183	320,623
Rye—exports	1M bu.	34,453	13,216	40	5
" —imports	"	—	—	8,006	9,643
Oil cake and oil-cake meal—exports	1M lbs.	1,165,577	1,199,315	760,478	469,878
Oil cake and oil-cake meal—imports	"	112,848	284,480	124,513	301,750
Cottonseed cake—exports	"	403,867	393,002	163,925	6,616
" meal—exports	"	156,065	183,310	63,596	6,734
Cottonseed—imports ...	"	—	32,923	7,004	59,744

		Annual Average 1921-1925	1926-1930	*Year* 1933	1935
Vegetable oils and fats, edible—exports	"	109,012	33,938	18,163	16,575
Vegetable oils and fats, edible—imports	"	79,910	94,569	91,108	397,634
Cottonseed oil, refined—exports	"	74,244	11,876	9,292	3,655
Sunflower seed oil—imports	"	—	—	14,082	37,052
Peanut oil—imports	"	6,384	6,935	1,323	80,723
Cottonseed oil—imports.	"	—	—	—	166,687
Corn oil—imports	"	—	—	9,160	25,746

(5) Comparing the first three months of 1936 with the first three months of 1935, the same trend continues. Our exports of agricultural products increased by only $9,941,000, but our imports of agricultural products increased by $33,164,-000. Our exports of non-agricultural products increased by $41,591,000 and our imports of non-agricultural products increased by $40,888,000.

(6) It was solemnly asserted by Secretary Hull, Secretary Wallace and their fellow internationalists that, our country being a creditor nation, it was essential that we take a large volume of imports and these imports would be used not only to buy the surplus goods that we most wanted to sell, but also to pay the service upon the debts owing to us.

In the years 1934 and 1935, we took an immense volume of gold and silver imports and we took also a large volume of merchandise imports—particularly in competitive agricultural lines which displaced American production. But we made a very slight increase in our exports, and this increase was almost wholly in non-agricultural products in which there was no surplus.

Now as to service on our debts. In 1931 we received net $536,000,000 as interest and dividends on foreign investments. In 1932 we received $393,000,000. In 1933 we received $384,-000,000. In 1934, with the new program partially under way, we received $327,000,000. In 1935, with the new program more fully under way, we received only $286,000,000.

Such are the facts. They are all of public record. It is therefore somewhat surprising to discover Secretary Hull, on April 30th, 1936, saying before the Chamber of Commerce of the United States exactly what he has said many times before and during the execution of the program—just as though his whole program had not proved a dismal failure. It is also surprising to find his chief assistants, Professors Sayre and Grady, repeating the same thing at various places with phonographic exactness. Mr. Hull said:

The foreign trade program of this Government is based fundamentally upon what to us is an indisputable assumption —namely, that our domestic recovery can be neither complete nor durable unless our surplus-creating branches of production succeed in regaining at least a substantial portion of their lost foreign markets. Our production of cotton, lard, tobacco, fruits, copper, petroleum products, automobiles, machinery, electrical and office appliances, and a host of other specialities is geared to a scale of operation the output of which exceeds domestic consumption by 10 to 50 per cent. In his message to Congress recommending the passage of the Trade Agreements Act, the President urged the need of restoring foreign markets in order that our surplus-producing industries may be "spared in part, at least, the heart-breaking readjustments that must be necessary if the shrinkage of American foreign commerce remains permanent." . . . There are some in this country who, without waiting for the economic emergency to be brought under control, demand the immediate repeal of the Act and the abandonment of the trade agreements negotiated under its authority. Let us face squarely what that would mean. We would automatically go back to the Smoot-Hawley Tariff and face once more the vicious discrimination against our trade which it caused and the virtually suicidal effort at economic self-containment which it represented. This futile and fatal course backward would involve a steadily increasing aggravation of regulation and regimentation in our economic life. Yet some of those who voice loudest their opposition to regimentation in general demand, at the same time, a commercial policy that would inevitably lead to such regimentation, and to a permanently increasing dole as well.

It may or may not be true that our permanent recovery depends upon our extending the foreign outlets for our surplus production. It may or may not be true that, unless these foreign outlets be found, the whole economy of our country must be regimented and controlled. Secretary Hull seems to have recently borrowed this latter idea from Secretary Wallace, who is now engaged in twisting that idea into something else. But whatever the merit of these contentions—and I shall shortly examine into their merit—the plain fact is that the program Secretary Hull advocates and desires to continue is doing very little toward furthering the export of these so-called surplus products and is not only doing a great deal to aggravate the conditions which he deplores but is also bringing about a very critical financial condition, of which he appears to be totally ignorant.

This is not a question of aligning theories against theories. What is being done to our country through the Administration's inability to comprehend its own policies need not rest on anyone's word. The accounts speak for themselves. Here is the record as compiled from the preliminary Government sources.

During 1934—

1. We sold to the world goods in the amount of	$2,133,000,000
we bought from the world goods in the amount of	1,655,000,000
thereby placing the world in debt to us for goods in the amount of	$ 478,000,000
2. Our tourists spent abroad and our immigrants, charitable organizations and others sent abroad the net amount of	352,000,000
leaving a balance owed to us of	$ 126,000,000

3. Services sold to the world and miscellaneous items amounted to	$264,000,000	
services bought from the world and miscellaneous items amounted to	274,000,000	
decreasing the balance owed to us by		10,000,000
leaving a balance owed to us of		$ 116,000,000
4. Interest and dividends received from:		
foreign bonds held in United States	$217,000,000	
foreign bonds, interest funded	13,000,000	
direct investment abroad	125,000,000	
short-term banking funds abroad	25,000,000	
stock transfer taxes, commissions, etc.	10,000,000	
a total of	$390,000,000	
less interest and dividends paid	125,000,000	
increased the balance owed to us by		265,000,000
leaving a balance owed to us by the world for goods, services, interest and dividends of		$ 381,000,000
5. We bought gold (including earmarking) in the net amount of	$1,217,000,000	
we bought silver in the net amount of	86,000,000	
we bought paper currency in the net amount of	48,000,000	
a total of		1,351,000,000
thereby placing us in debt to the world in 1934 in the amount of		$ 970,000,000

The results are very plain, and they utterly dispose of the hypothesis that any definite relation existed between the amount of our imports and the amount of our exports. The principal items of the income account are these:

We exported more goods than we imported, leaving the world in debt to us for goods in the amount of $478,000,000.

Against this we paid for services rendered to our tourists

and made charitable and other contributions to the net amount of $352,000,000, reducing the balance owed to us to $126,000,000.

We sold shipping services and the like to the world to an amount of $10,000,000 less than the world sold to us, reducing the balance owed to us to $116,000,000.

We received on our foreign investments certain interest and dividends, together with other payments growing out of financial transactions not connected with the flow of goods. These amounted to $390,000,000. Against this we made payments of the same nature to foreigners amounting to $125,000,000, thus increasing the balance owed to us by $265,000,000.

The grand total, therefore, owed to us by the world for the year 1934 for goods, services, interest and dividends was $381,000,000.

We bought gold in the net amount of $1,217,000,000. We bought silver in the net amount of $86,000,000. We bought back our paper currencies circulating abroad in the net amount of $48,000,000. These imports together amounted to $1,351,000,000.

The imports of gold, silver and paper money wiped out our creditor position for the year and left us in debt to the world for the year in the amount of $970,000,000.

Our transactions in the year 1934 provided foreigners with an unprecedented amount of exchange, i.e., purchasing power to buy our goods. The internationalist theory is that imports breed exports. The foreigners did not buy our goods. They bought securities.

This is what happened to the $970,000,000 credit the foreigners had with us:

1. Foreigners bought and redeemed (*a*) foreign stocks and bonds held in the United States and (*b*) American direct investments and private and commercial balances in foreign countries		$1,090,000,000
Foreigners bought American stocks and bonds and made new direct investments in the United States		615,000,000
Foreigners' banking funds and short-term investments in the United States were increased		103,000,000
Our banking funds and short-term investments in foreign countries were decreased		92,000,000
a total of		$1,900,000,000
As against this sum:		
2. We bought American stocks and bonds	$480,000,000	
We bought foreign stocks and bonds and made new direct investments in foreign countries	450,000,000	
a total of		930,000,000
leaving net capital assets transferred to foreigners in 1934		$ 970,000,000

As far as trade was concerned, the effects of the imports of gold and silver were negligible, but the trend was away from agricultural exports and toward non-agricultural exports —away from the objectives of the Administration's policies. The warning was plain that devaluation without control would make possible a raid on our national assets.

Our exports during 1934 were 27 per cent greater in value than in 1933 but only about 8 per cent larger in volume, while the imports were 14 per cent higher in value than in 1933 but the volume was practically unchanged. The chief change in exports was the sharp drop that occurred in our shipments of crude materials and foodstuffs. These declined 16 per cent in physical volume. The quantity increases were in semi-manufactures, which were 26 per cent larger than in 1933, and in finished manufactures, which were 31 per cent larger. The quantity of cotton exported in 1934 was 30 per cent smaller than in 1933. Our volume of exports was drawn, not from the agricultural products of which we are presumed to have a surplus, but from our manufactured products.

As a result of paying no attention to our national books, the nation went in debt for the year 1934 in the sum of $970,-000,000. By 1935 it became evident to the world that our Administration would interpose none of the controls or protective devices that all the leading countries were using. And so in 1935 we were raided in the enormous sum of $1,929,000,000. This is how it came about:

During 1935:

1. We sold to the world goods in the amount of....		$2,282,000,000
We bought from the world goods in the amount of		2,048,000,000
Thereby placing the world in debt to us for goods in the amount of		$ 234,000,000
2. Our tourists spent abroad and our immigrants, charitable organizations, and others sent abroad the net amount of		379,000,000
Leaving a balance owed by us of		$ 145,000,000
3. Services sold to the world and miscellaneous items amounted to..	$309,000,000	
Services bought from the world and miscellaneous items amounted to	303,000,000	
Decreasing the balance owed by us by		6,000,000
Leaving a balance owed by us of		$ 139,000,000
4. Interest and dividends received from:		
Foreign bonds held in United States	$185,000,000	
Direct investments abroad	225,000,000	
Short-term banking funds abroad and interest funded on foreign bonds	16,000,000	
A total of	$426,000,000	
Less interest and dividends paid	140,000,000	
Decreased the balance owed by us by		286,000,000
Leaving a balance owed to us by the world for goods, services, interest and dividends of		$ 147,000,000

5. We bought gold in the net amount of	$1,739,000,000	
We bought silver in the net amount of	336,000,000	
We bought paper currency in the net amount of	1,000,000	
A total of		2,076,000,000
Thereby placing us in debt to the world in 1935 in the amount of		$1,929,000,000

The account for the year 1934 was made by me in my official capacity as Special Adviser to the President on Foreign Trade and, as is the case with the other accounts, it was made in cooperation with the appropriate Departments of the Government and is a public document. The 1935 account is my own summary as a private citizen and is based upon the preliminary Balance of International Payments of the United States in 1935 by Amos E. Taylor, Assistant Chief, Finance Division of the Bureau of Foreign and Domestic Commerce. For some unexplained reason, Dr. Taylor's account was not issued until May 4th, 1936—that is, the country had to wait over four months to learn the results of 1935's international transactions.

The reception given to the 1934 account was curious, in that it showed the ends to which the internationalists would go to dodge the plain figures. The inclusion of gold as an import was especially disconcerting to them, although, as I remarked above, those who objected to the inclusion of gold as a commodity import did not object to the inclusion of silver. Some said that it was absurd to talk about buying gold. It is equally absurd to buy silver. But that is precisely what the Treasury was doing. Another school of thought, trying to dodge the realities, claimed that the gold imports represented the repatriation of American funds which had fled abroad and therefore the item had to be considered as a non-recurring one and put in a special account all by itself. The prophecy of a non-recurring item died with the publication of the 1935 Balance of

Payments—for the imports of gold in 1935 were more than half a billion dollars greater than in 1934. Others tried to dodge the facts by claiming that capital was fleeing from Europe. The Federal Reserve Board went as far as it could toward telling the truth by saying that the foreign gold was seeking an opportunity for profitable investment. The contention that these gold imports represented the repatriation of American funds and also the contention that the imports had any relation to trade have now been dropped. The compelling truth of the 1934 account has been dodged, but at least it is no longer denied by responsible critics.

The facts show that in recent years the movements of gold have had no particular relation to the movements of goods. In 1932 we had an excess of merchandise exports over imports amounting to $288,000,000; in 1933 the excess of exports was $226,000,000. In 1932 we lost gold (in old dollars) amounting to $446,213,000 and in 1933 we shipped out gold amounting to $173,455,000. In these two years we sent $657,684,000 in gold to France—we gained gold from certain other countries offsetting part of our losses to France.

The international movements of gold are tabulated, and it is hardly possible that any large amount of gold belonging to American citizens should have been sent abroad without appearing in the records. The rumors of an immense gold flight by Americans are based on fancy.

According to the trade balance, gold should have flowed in to us in 1932 and 1933. Instead it was shipped out. There is no reason to believe that in 1934 these same nations would have rushed to pay their debit balances in gold. They had credit balances available. The reason for sending us gold in 1934 was the gold buying policy of the Treasury, by which a foreigner could get more for his gold here than anywhere else.

The gold we bought did not come from the central banks. During 1934 the gold reserves of Europe, reckoned in devalued dollars, increased $48,000,000; of Latin-America, $18,000,000; of Asia and Oceania, $24,000,000; and of Africa, $40,000,000—a total of $130,000,000. In 1934 we took gold in the amount of $1,217,000,000—in devalued dollars. This is a greater weight of gold than we lost in 1932 and 1933. From England we took $499,870,000; from France, $260,223,000; from the Netherlands, $94,348,000; from Canada, $86,829,000; and from British India, $76,820,000.

The estimated gold production of 1934 (at $35.000 an ounce) was $942,374,000. It is evident that, to get our gold, we bought the production of the year and called out some gold hoards to take advantage of the bargains. Our 1934 bonanza buying created a gold boom, and in 1935 world production rose to the record height of $1,042,221,000. In 1935 we again bought the world's output.

What happened to this gold? The figures show that our export trade has had a negligible increase. The gold did not promote trade. Where did it go?

That is a vital question. It concerns our position as a creditor nation. My office drew this account which speaks for itself:

On December 31, 1933:

1. Our gross foreign creditor balance amounted to		$25,202,000,000
Based on a census conducted in 1934, the estimate has been increased by		17,000,000
making the revised estimate of our gross creditor balance		$25,219,000,000
Foreigners' investments in the United States were estimated at	$4,557,000,000	
Based on the 1934 census, the estimate of these investments has been increased by	2,795,000,000	
making the revised estimate of foreigners' investments in the United States as of December 31, 1933		7,352,000,000
resulting in a corrected net creditor balance on December 31, 1933, of		$17,867,000,000

2. Net capital assets transferred to foreigners during 1934 represented:		
A decrease in our investments in foreign countries	$ 732,000,000	
An increase in foreigners' investments in the United States	238,000,000	
A total of		970,000,000
Thereby reducing the net creditor balance of the United States (including war debts), on December 31, 1934, to		$16,897,000,000

This account shows that the $970,000,000 was used by its holders to buy back their own bonds and to buy stocks and bonds of American companies. In so doing, the foreigners committed no crime. A good share of the foreign bonds floated in the United States during the boom years were in default and kicking around at well under fifty cents on the dollar. They were in default for many reasons, and our Government made no arrangements of any kind looking toward the resuming of service on these securities. Our war debts were all in default, with the exception of the small sum owing from Finland, and the internationalist group objected to any action looking toward their collection. A number of Americans seem more interested in promoting foreign solvency than in preserving the solvency of the United States. It seems to mean nothing to them that the American tax burden might be considerably lightened by a resumption of foreign debt service. The foreigners simply took advantage of the great gold bargain offered by the Treasury, just as they would have taken advantage of a similar bargain if the Treasury had engaged to buy wheat instead of gold. They took the proceeds of their bargain sales and put them to the most profitable uses they knew. They bought up their own bonds at a discount and picked up such American securities as seemed to be a good buy. On the whole, it was rather a neat operation, and our internationalists, disregarding the obvious trends, stood blandly by with only a hazy comprehension of what was going on.

From a broad national standpoint, these operations and the facts disclosed by the previous accounts made imperative the casting of a balance sheet to discover whether or not we were a creditor nation. If the world owes us more than we owe the world, we are a creditor nation. If the debts which the world owes to us are uncollectible and the debts we owe to the world are collectible, we are in fact a debtor nation. The collectibility of a debt may be, up to a point, a matter of argument, but the significance of the status of a debt is not a matter for argument. It is a matter of bookkeeping. We do not actually know either our assets or our liabilities—that is, we do not know how much of America is owned by foreigners or how much of the world is owned by us. A census of foreigners' holdings of securities in this country was imperatively needed and I managed to get one under way. I am informed it is nearly completed. At the very outset, it disclosed that the figures with which we had been working were absurdly low and that foreign holdings were much greater than had been imagined.

Here is the balance sheet (based upon the preliminary figures) as of December 31st, 1934:

Assets

1. Foreign bonds held in the United States—face value (market value $4,016,000,000)	$ 5,270,000,000
2. Deposits and short-term funds of American banks in foreign countries	990,000,000
3. American funds "blocked" in foreign countries	100,000,000
4. American branch factories and other direct investments in foreign countries—book value	7,823,000,000
5. War debts as	10,304,000,000
	$24,487,000,000

LIABILITIES

1. American stocks and bonds held in foreign countries—market value for shares; face value for bonds		$ 6,000,000,000
2. Deposits and short-term funds of foreign banks in the United States		590,000,000
3. Foreign branch factories and other direct investments in the United States—book value		1,000,000,000
4. United States net creditor:		
Balance Dec. 31, 1933	$20,645,000,000	
Adjustments	2,778,000,000	
Corrected balance Dec. 31, 1933	$17,867,000,000	
Decrease during 1934	970,000,000	
Balance Dec. 31, 1934		16,897,000,000
		$24,487,000,000

That account shows that we were a creditor nation on December 31st, 1934 only if our direct investments abroad and our war debts had a value as assets sufficient to overcome the foreign investments in our own country. The results of 1935 show that the bargain sale which began in 1934 continued at a quickened pace. At this time of writing figures sufficient to detail the 1935 capital transactions are not available, but should be forthcoming at an early date as a result of the census of securities now nearly concluded by the Department of Commerce.

However, taking the official published records, it appears that on December 31st, 1935 foreigners had on deposit in this country over a billion dollars, while against this Americans had on deposit in foreign countries about half a billion dollars, making this country a net debtor on current demand deposits of over half a billion. That is, the Administration's conduct of its international financial and trade affairs has been so unskilled that the foreigners can take about half a billion dollars out of our banks merely by writing checks.

We know that, as a result of 1935's transactions, we gave

to foreigners claims upon our assets amounting to $1,929,000,-000. We do not know exactly how they used the claims. It is a matter of common knowledge that the brokerage offices of Wall Street are full of foreign accounts. We know that in our principal corporations foreign holdings are at a record high. We do not know what these holdings amount to and we shall not know until the census of foreign holdings is completed. The stock lists of our corporations show only such foreign holdings as are registered as being in foreign hands. They cannot tell how many of the shares standing in the names of brokers or nominees belong to foreign citizens.

We do know, however, that an immense quantity of foreign bonds has been repatriated at low prices and that the figure used in the 1934 balance sheet as to the amount of foreign bonds held by our citizens was overestimated. Since there is no movement to convert the war debts into assets, the war debts must be considered as presently frozen. Most certainly they are not current assets. The figures given as to the book value of American branch factories and other direct investments abroad are based on 1929 values. An actual appraisal might disclose them as worth much less.

Therefore, it definitely appears that as a nation we are a net debtor on international banking accounts. Our exact position on the whole account is unknown.

Such matters as these should not in good conscience be left to estimates or guesswork. We ought to know the facts and then take whatever action the facts warrant.

Chapter XVI

Internationalism Gone Wild

The executed agreements have been in effect too short a time for the public to learn the full consequences of the policy to which they are being involuntarily committed. The scheme of the agreements is now quite apparent, and it is a very strange scheme—so strange and so destructive to everything our country has cherished that it took a long time to uncover the motives behind it.

The manner in which the dollar was devalued and the buying of gold at $35.00 an ounce without compensating controls have served no American purpose. They have served only to sell out our country by creating an immense foreign interest in our corporations and in our financial structure. That interest is so great that, as things now stand, the liquidation of only half the foreign holdings of our stocks and bonds and the withdrawal of the proceeds, as well as the bank balances, might wreck our country. What happened in 1931 can happen again. Everyone knows the stock crash of 1929 started with selling orders from abroad.

The Reciprocal Trade Agreements Act provided a method by which the situation might have been saved. But the agreements to date do not concern themselves, except in a perfunctory way, with the interests of our country. Each of them is a piece in a jig-saw puzzle which, when put together, will disclose that the agreements have broken down the protective tariff system, have made impossible adequate defense of our economy and, by inference, will have prejudiced the possibility of collecting anything on our defaulted war and private debts.

These agreements are trade agreements only in the sense that they promote foreigners' trade by throwing open our great home market for the easy entry of foreign manufactures and foodstuffs. They have not promoted and by their very nature cannot promote, the only kind of export trade that might be valuable to us. Indeed, opportunities for profitable trade have been rejected because they seemed to those in charge somehow to conflict with the plans they were promoting.

It is now an acknowledged fact that Secretary Hull and his associates in the State Department, aided by Secretary Wallace and with the implied approval of the President, are using the Trade Agreements Act to break down the American protective system and to involve the country in the affairs of the world—to do precisely what all our great statesmen, from George Washington down, have steadily fought against.

The project may have great merit. The internationalists have the plain right to urge their point of view upon us at any and every opportunity. Our nation may some day want to join the low-wage family of nations—although all the more prominent members of that family seem to be trying to get out of it. The nation may want to abandon the American System. That, however, is a question for the nation to decide at the polls and through the Congress it elects. The right to decide for ourselves has been taken away from us and has been assumed by Secretary Hull and his associates. They have set up a State Department dictatorship over our internal economy which was not delegated to them by the Congress.

The question of deciding between nationalism and internationalism may or may not be up for decision in academic circles. It is not up for decision in the State Department. Whatever may be the personal views of Secretary Hull and his associates, their plain duty is to obey the laws and intent of Congress—not to concoct philosophical excuses for ignoring them.

By successive steps, the State Department officials have departed from the legal authority granted under the Trade Agreements Act; until now they are acting practically without relation to that authority. This they have admitted. I shall quote them.

(1) Before the Senate Committee in 1934, Professor Sayre testified in support of the Reciprocal Trade Agreements Bill which was then pending:

MR. SAYRE. I can say this, sir, and I am speaking for myself alone, that no blanket tariff revision is contemplated. It is not, to my mind, a proceeding which will mean a tariff revision. It is a proceeding which will mean finding bargains which will prove of advantage to foreign trade, without undue injury to American producers. Now, those responsible for this program will have the program, and a real problem of finding just how trade can be increased, without undue injury to American producers.

I have studied the problem enough myself to be convinced that we can secure a substantial increase of foreign trade without injury.

SENATOR WALSH. In other words, the ideal purpose to seek here is to increase our export business without increasing our imports.

MR. SAYRE. No; I would not say that; because I do not think one can permanently increase exports without increasing imports, but the object is to increase our exports without increasing those kinds of imports which will work undue injury to American domestic producers.

Secretary Hull said:

A vast and ever-increasing foreign trade is easily within the grasp of this country, unless we fritter away the opportunity.

The proposed reciprocity policy would, on the whole, enhance these benefits by increasing commerce, which would result in increased production and increased employment at home.

(2) As the scheme developed and the agreements disclosed that they could not substantially increase trade, the

State Department shifted its position and came out more frankly for internationalism. In January, 1936 Professor Sayre said that the agreements were for the purpose of stabilizing world financial conditions, thus:

One of the important underlying causes of the existing financial difficulties which are so grievously delaying the return of prosperity is the failure of international trade, due to its diminished proportions, to offer a sufficiently broad base to support the volume of international debts and credits and thus to stabilize the financial situation of the various countries. Without an increased international trade it is difficult to see how to meet the problems of international finance which press us in on every side.

The trusts and combinations of the end of the nineteenth century, with their soulless unethical practices and their "public be damned" attitude are in the way of becoming eclipsed today by profoundly more powerful units. Today great nations, competing relentlessly one against the other for the business of the world, with armies and navies at their command, resorting too often to methods which the courts would not tolerate in private life, manifest far too frequently an attitude of "the world be damned."

Professor Henry F. Grady, writing in the January issue of Foreign Affairs, stated in effect that the State Department was not following Professor Sayre's declaration before the Senate Committee but was using the authority to force a general tariff revision downward. He said:

Our objective is the general amelioration of the world situation. . . .

We have already lowered many rates, which have been generalized to other countries. When we shall have gone the rounds of most of the important countries of the world, reducing in each case the duties on commodities of which it is the principal or important source, we shall have lowered our tariffs on a great many items where the case for lowering is justified. As a result of extending these reductions to virtually all countries, we will obtain, it would seem, what the proponents of unilateral tariff reduction desire; but we will do it more carefully and scientifically than is possible by legislative action.

Dr. Grady made the objective doubly clear in a speech at Riverside, California, December 20th, 1935, when he said:

This new policy is of an importance that can hardly be exaggerated. We are to a greater degree than ever before meshing our domestic economy into world economy.

(3) In the same month, Secretary Hull, being then preoccupied with neutrality plans, found that the purpose of the trade agreements program was to promote the peace of the world. He then said:

The primary purpose of American foreign policy is the maintenance and promotion of peace, not only between the United States and foreign nations but throughout the world.

In March, 1936, still being held by the same thought, he said:

Our program, essentially, consists in replacing the regime of commercial conflicts with instruments of commercial peace, to constitute an effective element for the preservation of peace itself.

These statements, taken together, constitute a flat declaration for an internationalist policy as opposed to an American policy. The speeches and articles containing these declarations are cluttered with discussions of the perils of isolation. Whatever the perils may be or may not be, the issue is not up. The Act provides neither for an isolated nationalism nor for a chummy internationalism. It provides for trade.

Also a considerable number of words are used to describe the exquisite care and skill which the Administration uses in making the agreements. I have already described the nature and quality of that care and skill. The defense of the doctrine of "principal supplier" has been present in most of the addresses by officers of the State Department. I have already shown that the phrase "principal supplier" is meaningless.

To get at the true meaning of the whole policy, one must look at the possibilities inherent in the countries with which negotiations were initially undertaken. None of them were principal markets for the products of American agriculture, and there was no possibility that, even if the agreements had granted real concessions to the United States, any appreciable amount of farm or factory products could have been sold. The countries selected for the first agreements were Cuba, Brazil, Belgium, Haiti, Sweden, Colombia, Canada, Honduras, Netherlands, Switzerland, Nicaragua, Costa Rica, El Salvador, Guatemala, Spain, Finland and France. All these countries together in 1935 took only 24.3 per cent of our agricultural exports in value. The big takers of our agricultural products—which means cotton—have been Great Britain, Germany and Japan. Hence at the very outset it was plain that getting rid of agricultural surpluses was not the major objective of the program as administered.

Our greatest national problem was then—as it is now—to give the farmer an American price in the American market with the best price obtainable in the world market for such part of the production as could not be consumed at home. It is evident that the basic reason for the Act was never taken seriously by the State Department. That was my own view and it is supported by many others, including Professor R. L. Adams of the University of California, who, after spending some time in Washington in the fall of 1934, wrote:

There is no gainsaying that a new and different theory of tariff-making is being developed in Washington. Instead of open Congressional hearings, the new order is done in secrecy, behind closed doors, and those most vitally affected are left in ignorance until the deal is consummated. While the old way was bad enough, the tariff in fact being written by experts and advisers from the Tariff Commission sitting with the formulating groups, yet I am wondering if this new way isn't worse. Handled by a group of economists, graduates in theory, they lack business or other experience, and in their youthful enthusiasm are willing to try anything, no matter how novel or weird. I heard of proposals being considered that were startling but, told in confidence, cannot be broadcasted. As one outspoken opponent (a former member of the Tariff Commission) said, "This plan is selling us out . . . but the faster and further it goes the quicker will be the reaction to get it back." If the results cause industry or agriculture to arise in consternation and indignation, then I look for Congress to again initiate a revision of the tariff of its own volition.

The first issue that I met in the making of the agreements was the stubborn insistence by Secretary Hull and his associates that the concessions given by the United States be generalized to all nations. Under the "unconditional" most-favored-nation clause in a treaty, the parties to the treaty are entitled as of course to all the benefits given to any third party; under the "conditional" clause such concessions to third parties need be given only in return for equivalent or corresponding concessions. The United States had "unconditional" arrangements with thirty-two countries, but they supplied in 1934 only 18.8 per cent of our total imports and took only 14.2 per cent of our total exports. The total trade of the United States with these countries—that is, the sum of the imports and exports—amounted to only 16.2 per cent of our total trade with the world. Secretary Hull insisted on granting the concessions we made in the agreements to all nations except Germany regardless of the nature of our treaty arrangements with them. That is, by the process of generalization, he made a plain gift to everyone of the duty reductions.

It has been said that any other policy would have required the rewriting of a large number of treaties. That is not true. Belgium, Czechoslovakia, Norway and Spain were the only important European countries with whom we had "unconditional" most-favored-nation commitments. We had none with our biggest customers after Germany terminated her treaty with us. It is impossible to believe that the objective of generalizing, without regard to what we got in return, was animated by any other desire than to effect a general tariff reduction by subterfuge.

The nations to whom we have granted the concessions through the process of generalization have not materially relaxed any of their own quotas or restrictions. The statement frequently made by officials of the State Department that our trade agreements are breaking down restrictions everywhere is without foundation in fact. The only exception to the generalization benefits was Germany. The Germans renounced their treaty with us, and ostensibly for that reason Secretary Hull has withheld from Germany the benefit of our concessions—although Germany has no more restrictions upon our trade than have many other countries.

The result of this policy has been first to bind upon the free list to everybody a very large number of items. On these items, during the life of the agreements, we cannot put duties, quotas, excise taxes or any charges. They have been put beyond the jurisdiction of Congress. They have been, in effect, put in a class of sacred articles upon which no American hand shall be laid.

The second effect has been to rewrite downward a large number of the schedules of our tariff. I do not know the exact number today, but as of January first, general reductions of duty had been made upon over 242 items.

Although the State Department in practice generalized the concessions to everyone (except Germany), it reserved the right to withhold concessions and established what the newspapers called a "black list." This policy, it seemed to me, was extremely dangerous and an open invitation to commercial war. I recorded my protest to Professor Sayre as Chairman of the Executive Committee on Commercial Policy in a letter in which I said:

With respect to the question of withholding from certain nations concessions granted by us under the Brazilian and other trade agreements, I wish to go on record as expressing my extreme misgiving as to the method which appears to have been adopted to accomplish this result, which has been described in the press and elsewhere as "black listing." I can conceive of no method of procedure better calculated to arouse distrust and ill will abroad and to invite direct retaliation if not to precipitate open trade warfare.

As I understand it, it is proposed that refusal to generalize concessions is to be based upon the sole ground of clear-cut discrimination against the United States. While I consider this policy a mistaken one, I would entertain greater hopes for its effective success if it were applied consistently and firmly. This does not appear to be the case at present as I am informed that the only nations from whom it has been so far suggested that concessions might be withheld are Canada, France, Netherlands, Denmark, Germany, Poland, Czechoslovakia, Spain and Portugal. I would remind the Committee of the Ottawa Agreements entered upon by the various countries composing the British Empire, which I believe have been found by the Tariff Commission to constitute discrimination within the meaning of the Tariff Act of 1930. In this connection I would further remind the Committee that the Tariff Commission has from time to time, in accordance with its prescribed duties, submitted to the President a number of other cases of discrimination. Furthermore, I enclose a list as of January 31, 1935 of known bilateral agreements entered upon by various nations in recent years, from the benefits of which the United States is excluded and which place the commerce of the United States at a disadvantage as compared with the commerce of the nations party to them. If discrimination is to be made the test and if we are to be consistent I fail to see why all these nations under reference should not be included in the proposed "black list."

However, as I have stated, I consider the "black list" to be wrong in principle and dangerous in practice. I believe that the whole question can be avoided by reversing the action taken by the Harding Administration and by taking appropriate steps to return to the traditional conditional most-favored-nation policy of the United States. I have endeavored to lay my views on this subject before this Committee and to secure a free and open discussion of the principles and policies involved both in this Committee and in the Trade Agreements Committee, thus far without success. Nevertheless, it is not too late for us to retrace our steps.

In conclusion, I would state that the present proposed "black list" policy appears to be laden with grave possibilities for our foreign trade, the responsibility for which has been placed upon the President by Congress. Moreover, the policy of extending concessions without compensation will give rise to serious political and economic difficulties within the United States. I wish to be numbered among those advising the President against pursuing such a course as appears at present to be contemplated. I would, therefore, request that you have this letter read to the Executive Committee on Commercial Policy and incorporated in the minutes of the Committee, and that in any recommendation which may be made to the President by this Committee appropriate reference be made to my position.

The only nation actually black-listed was Germany and, although the technical explanation had to do with the German discriminations against American trade, the actual reason appears to be found, in part at least, in the anti-German movement of some groups in the United States because of the Nazi persecutions. Those persecutions were deplorable, and no right-minded citizen can countenance them. But primarily it was an affair of the Germans, and our Government as a government had declined to interfere. The question came up on a proposal to export cotton to Germany. Some of our cotton exporters worked out an arrangement with German merchants and spinners whereby Germany would take American cotton up to eight hundred thousand bales, paying 25 per cent in cash, and for the balance would send to us a wide range of German articles which we had been in the custom of importing from Germany and which would not have affected our home industries.

The proposal was presented to me, and it seemed a very good trade and exactly along the lines which both the A.A.A. and the Trade Agreements Act were designed to further. Germany had been one of the best of our cotton customers and in fact had been second only to Great Britain in taking agricultural products. Under the exigencies of the German economic system, the country could not take cotton from us and pay for it in dollars, for exchange was lacking. Germany had been bartering all over the world. Some of our Jewish citizens protested when they heard of the contemplated trade, but one of the most prominent of them, B. M. Baruch, when I explained that turning down this deal might mean the loss of the great German market for American cotton, said at once that no consideration other than the American interests should enter and that I ought to go ahead with the business. I was at the time President of the Export-Import Banks. I was also holding the office of Special Adviser. Under the terms of the Executive Order establishing the office I was authorized, in connection with foreign trade activities, "to carry on negotiations with respect to specific trade transactions . . . (with those) interested in obtaining assistance from the Federal Government through (1) financing transactions, (2) barter transactions, or (3) other forms of Governmental participation authorized by law." This put the German business right down my alley.

The Executive Order further provided "The Special Adviser shall bring such proposals . . . before the departments or other agencies affected by or having an interest therein for appropriate action and shall keep me (the President) advised concerning the action taken or proposed by such department or other agency." In handling the German negotiations I was scrupulous at all times to keep both the Departments of State and Agriculture as well as the President informed in detail as to developments, and the deal was unanimously approved by the Executive Committee of the Bank on which the State Department was represented. The project then went to the President.

At this point Professors Sayre and Grady stepped into the picture and took the position that the project was inconsistent with their trade agreements program. The principal basis for this position, judging from Professor Sayre's later testimony on the subject before the Senate Committee on Agriculture and Forestry, seems to have been the State Department's touching solicitude for so-called triangular trade, which they felt would somehow be endangered by a direct trade with Germany of such magnitude. The fact of the matter was that the amount of cotton involved was entirely in keeping with our normal trade with Germany, and the deal was primarily designed to prevent our German trade from dropping to an abnormal low.

This opposition did not stop me. I took the question to the President. Apparently others did, too. The President did not rule against me at the time, but he refrained from acting on my recommendations, and in consequence the deal went dead.

Because of that refusal to trade and a similar one in 1935, our country may have lost the German cotton market. According to an article by George W. Hirschfeld, writing in the *Weser Zeitung* and quoting official sources, the share of the United States in the German cotton supply was 80 per cent in 1933, 55 per cent in 1934 and only 29 per cent in 1935. These figures represent the cotton as used in Germany and exclude the trans-shipments. Germany is now buying the major part of its cotton from Brazil, Peru, East India and Egypt under agreements more or less the same as our Administration rejected. This one action turned down more export business than the trade agreements as made to date would generate in a hundred years.

All of these matters I set out very fully in testimony before the Senate Committee on Agriculture and Forestry early in 1935. The German projects were the most important of those which I had up as Special Adviser. But there were many other opportunities to trade, and some of them I set out in my testimony. They were all rejected because of the preoccupation with advancing the cause of internationalism.

Secretary Hull and his associates, just as they insisted on generalizing the concessions in our agreements without regard to the consequences, as steadfastly refused to make debt settlements a part of any trade agreement. Cuba, Brazil, Haiti and Colombia were heavily in debt to our citizens for private loans. Belgium was a war debtor. The reason given by State Department officers for the refusal to make debt-servicing arrangements in these agreements was that to do so would interfere with trade and particularly triangular trade.

What they really meant was that exchange agreements would interfere with the working of a peculiar creed that goes under the name of "world economy" as distinguished from a "national" or "American" economy. The conception inclines to the fantastic, but it is held by our internationalists and, when understood, explains many of the odd and un-American things they advocate and do.

I have previously noted that Secretary Hull and his associates talk a great deal about certain sections of the world being peculiarly adapted to the growing of certain products and that other sections of the world have acquired mechanical skill, and that the world functions best when the raw material nations exchange their products with the manufacturing nations. Such was the division of the world in the first half of the past century, when Great Britain repealed her Corn Laws and decided to take raw materials and food in exchange for factory products. If the cost of the British navy be added to the price Great Britain paid for her food, her bargain on the whole was not a particularly good one. That is unimportant, for Great Britain has abandoned those policies, is no longer a free trade nation and is trying to raise her own food. Secretary Hull and his associates have not noted the changes that science and invention have made in the world during the past one hundred years.

Great Britain's trade supremacy was challenged by Germany. Her financial supremacy was challenged by us. The war disposed of the German challenge. Our financial challenge is now being disposed of through the operations of our internationalists, combined with an extraordinary shortsightedness on the part of some of our bankers and industrialists.

The position of the British Empire today depends, to quote the Macmillan Report, "on very large imports to maintain our standard of living and on very large exports to maintain employment; but to pay for these imports we have become largely dependent on our interest from foreign investments, and on our profits as international bankers, merchants, and so forth."

Now take the following from the publication *Balances of Payments—1933* issued by the League of Nations:

> . . . the transfer of amounts due to the United Kingdom is but one—though undoubtedly the most important—operation involving triangular or many-cornered trading transactions. . . .
>
> The bulk of the British income from foreign investments is derived from other countries, and its transfer involves large triangular operations . . . that "each year, the United Kingdom collects in the form of American merchandise about $500 million of the revenues from its oversea investments and its merchant marine," and that, accordingly, to that extent the United States export trade depended upon the prosperity of British shipping and foreign investments.

Triangular trade—by which is meant triangular payment—is of high importance to the United States, but its exact effect cannot be comprehended without a complete bookkeeping system—the kind of bookkeeping system that I attempted to put into effect as Special Trade Adviser. The internationalists believe that it is very important for the peace of the world that the British investment fund operate smoothly. That is more important to them than the interests of the United States. It is impossible to explain why. Probably it is a complex.

All the debtor nations of the world today have exchange controls. Nearly all of them are debtors to Great Britain and many of them have their currencies hitched to managed sterling. Take a specific case. Brazil owes the citizens of the United States a great deal of money on defaulted bonds and blocked exchange. We buy more from Brazil than we sell. Therefore I insisted that in any agreement with Brazil provision be made for the payment of the debts owing to American citizens. Our State Department flatly rejected that proposal. Under Brazil's exchange control a part of the money that accumulates in New York to the credit of Brazil, and which arises out of our coffee buying, goes to the service of British debts! The same is true of Cuba, Colombia and practically all the countries from whom we buy more than we sell. This is the fund which the League of Nations refers to. This fund, supplemented by the addition of American payments of interest, is available to Great Britain to buy our goods or our securities. That is the reason why Great Britain is our largest customer.

When our State Department officers talk about not disturbing triangular trade, what they really mean is not disturbing the accumulation of British credits in New York. When Secretary Wallace made his now famous speech about not encouraging the American Merchant Marine because to do so would decrease foreign purchasing power, he was really aiding —although I doubt if he knew what he was doing—the accumulating of British funds from shipping and other services.

The policy of Secretary Hull and his associates, as expressed in the trade agreements written to date, is to give British debt claims precedence over American debt claims and of course utterly to ignore the war debts. The Act, in Section 3, specifically says: "Nothing in this Act shall be construed to give any authority to cancel or reduce, in any manner, any of the indebtedness of any foreign country to the United States." It does not preclude an effort to collect our debts.

A comparison of the interest and dividends received on foreign investments by the United States and by Great Britain is instructive. The numbers represent millions of dollars:

Year	United States	United Kingdom
1930	616	1,070
1931	536	771
1932	393	526
1933	383	678
1934	327	882
1935	286	907

It is also instructive to note that the United States paid out $16,000,000 for shipping in 1933 and $40,000,000 in 1935, while the British shipping income increased from $275,000,000 in 1933 to $368,000,000 in 1935. It is of further interest to note, in connection with the following paragraph taken from the League of Nations World Economic Survey, 1934-35, that, while our agricultural exports increased by only $85,392,000 in 1935 over 1932, our agricultural imports during the same period increased by the very substantial sum of $438,026,000.

In the first half of 1934, the strong demand for, and high prices of, industrial raw materials gave a great fillip to the exports of the raw-material-producing countries. Special factors operated in certain areas. The successful schemes for the restriction of production or marketing of tin, rubber and tea greatly assisted many tropical countries. British Malaya, Ceylon, the Netherlands Indies, the Belgian Congo, increased their exports substantially. The rise in wool prices in the season 1933-34 was a great gain to Australia, the Union of South Africa, New Zealand, the Argentine and Uruguay; but the subsequent fall in 1934-35 was embarrassing, especially to Australia. The Argentine shipped much larger quantities of wheat and also profited from higher maize prices. Egypt, Peru, Brazil, the Anglo-Egyptian Sudan and other cotton suppliers profited from the restriction of the American cotton crop. Brazil, in particular, made great strides in substituting cotton for coffee production. Finland, Sweden, Canada, Yugoslavia, Latvia and Estonia and other timber producers exported more timber at higher prices because of the reduction of Russian competition and the demand for building materials in the reflating countries. Gold production advanced in Soviet Russia, Mexico, Canada, Chile, Brazil, Colombia, Japan, Chosen and Australia. Under the stimulus of American demand, silver production also increased in Mexico, Canada and Peru. There was a very substantial export gain also in the petroleum-producing countries—Venezuela, Peru, Iran, and especially Iraq, where exports trebled in 1934 because of the opening of the pipe-line constructed to the Mediterranean.

In view of these facts, I trust that it may not be amiss briefly to set down the record:

February, 1934—Treaties signed with Cuba and Colombia but withheld from Senate so they could be put through as trade agreements.

June, 1934—Trade Agreements Act passed. Cuban treaty renegotiated as a trade agreement. Negotiations with Colombia reopened but difficult. Case of Colombia first raises question of payment on debt and blocked exchange.

July-August, 1934—G. N. P. raises question of most-favored-nation with Sayre who defers discussion until fall. G. N. P. raises question of clearing agreements with Hull (later declares in New York speech for settlement of exchange problems as prerequisite to agreement).

November-December, 1934—G. N. P. raises most-favored-nation question with President and in memorandum to Trade Agreements Committee. Head-on collision occurs over German cotton deal which State Department regards as inconsistent with trade agreements program. President rules against G. N. P., or at least State Department has its way. (See Senate testimony of G. N. P. and Sayre re "Causes of Loss of Export Trade.")

January, 1935—Brazilian mission arrives. G. N. P. insistent upon settlement of blocked balances through authority to tie up coffee receipts. State Department concludes agreement with unconditional most-favored-nation clause and without adequate financial provisions (see memo to President), and keeps Brazilian financial mission from seeing G. N. P. Mission makes perfunctory effort to obtain refunding loan in New York and then goes to England where it negotiates an exchange agreement with British Government and obtains Rothschild loan. Brazil defers ratification of trade agreement.

March, 1935—Haitian agreement binds coffee on free list and agreement is generalized, thus removing incentive for Brazil and Colombia to ratify their agreements.

April, 1935—Belgian agreement. First industrial country and first war debt country. President believed to have devised "escape" clause (showy but impracticable) to prevent major benefit of concessions going to third nations. Belgium devalues but makes gentleman's agreement not to ship abnormal quantities.

May, 1935—Swedish agreement (matches).

July, 1935—Russian agreement made to give Russia advantage of manganese and match concessions.

July, 1935—G. N. P. tries to resign.

June-November, 1935—Canadian negotiations. (Germany blacklisted October, 1935.) Canadian agreement regarded generally as crux of whole program; signed November 15th, 1935.

November 26th, 1935—G. N. P. resigns.

December, 1935—G. N. P. attacks Canadian agreement and whole program in public memorandum.

That is where we are at. What can be done about it?

Chapter XVII

What Can Be Done

Let us get clearly in mind what we are about. Our objective is to afford the opportunity for employment to all our people of working age in such fashion that man hours of labor may be exchanged for man hours of labor on a basis which will permit the free exchange of goods and services.

Mere employment is of no consequence. Employment paid for by public funds raised through borrowing or taxation and which does not create wealth or useful services has no exchange value, and hence those who are thus employed are only burdens on the creatively employed. Those who found employment as a result of the great foreign lending of the war and post-war period were not usefully employed—although they seemed to be—because the country, in return for their labor received to a large extent only scraps of engraved paper. Very little wealth was exchanged.

Exchanging goods and services for goods and services takes our standard of living up in an ascending spiral. But if any large section of our population cannot exchange its man hours of labor on a reasonable basis with the other groups, the process of exchanging will be interrupted and an unnatural surplus of goods and services will appear. That means unemployment and low prices.

Agriculture has for some years been unable to exchange its production on a reasonable basis with industrial production, and hence the nation has been out of balance. Our objective is to secure a balance in a manner permitting the individual to have the largest possible freedom and to give complete freedom to the play of science and invention. Life without freedom is not worth living. Fortunately freedom is also an economic necessity. The American System has demonstrated that freedom is necessary for the greatest good to the greatest number.

The Roosevelt Administration pledged itself to achieve a balance in our economic system by taking measures to increase agriculture's share in the national income. To that end, Congress passed the Agricultural Adjustment Act. The Act was not administered to restore a balance under the American System, but was seized as an opportunity to socialize farming. Fortunately for the country, the Supreme Court nullified the Act which should have prevented those in charge of it from doing any further harm in this direction.

The socialization of farming is not a way of meeting the farm problem. At the best, it would merely replace our present serious problem with a much more serious one. In spite of the fiasco of regimentation under the A.A.A., the Administration remains committed to the principle of acreage limitation and control—that is, for planned and dictated economy as applied to agriculture. The Soil Erosion Act is an example of how a good principle can be distorted and made to serve a bad purpose. The conservation of the soil is one thing, but using the principle of conservation to enforce socialized farming is another thing. There is pending a tobacco act—evidently inspired by the present heads of the Department of Agriculture—in which a plan is set out to restrict tobacco production through interstate compacts. It is the A.A.A. regimentation wearing false whiskers.

The farmer ought to know—and I think he does know—that through regimentation he has everything to lose and nothing to gain. The example of Russia should be enough, and on this point I am permitted to quote from a memorandum prepared for me by my friend Charles Stephenson Smith on the socializing of the Russian farms. He was in Russia for many years, before and after the revolution, as a correspondent and he knows the situation at first hand. He has this to say:

> . . . in the ruthless use of famine as a means of crushing peasant opposition to his intensive industrialization plan Stalin was following the teachings of Lenin, who regarded the prosperous peasants as the most formidable enemies of Communism.
>
> "Land, Bread and Peace" was the slogan of the Bolshevists which drew peasants into line with industrial workers during the revolution which brought the Soviets into power. Yet in the All-Russian Soviet Congress the following year Lenin urged the poor peasants to take property away from the rich peasants. He exhorted the men who had no livestock to take animals away from those who had two cows or two pigs.
>
> This speech brought a fiery protest from Maria Spiridonova, the Social Revolutionist who had long been the most beloved leader of the peasants.
>
> Shaking her fist at Lenin she shouted: "Lenin, the thrifty peasants will never endure such a policy. It favors the ne'er-do-well and loafer and penalizes the industrious."
>
> This speech sent Maria Spiridonova into exile, and she has lived in obscurity ever since, in spite of the fact that she was one of the great heroines of the revolution. . . .
>
> Herded into collectives, the peasants have been robbed of all their individuality and turned into robots who carry out the plans of the leadership of two million Communists who dominate one hundred and sixty-seven million Russians.
>
> Firing squads silence the protests of men and women who fail to carry out the paper plans of the Moscow government. With an army of more than a million, Soviet leaders in the Kremlin feel secure and give no quarter to those who ignore official orders.
>
> Terrible examples are made of members of collectives charged with neglect of duty. Failure to irrigate crops at the proper time, refusal to make plantings in accordance with official orders or the misdirection of motive power are charges punishable by death under Soviet law.
>
> Children are encouraged by Communists to spy and report

on alleged derelictions of members of their own families, and Soviet newspapers have reported the execution of many parents on the testimony of their own children.

The Reciprocal Trade Agreements Act gave the authority to help achieve a balance between agriculture and industry by profitably disposing of agricultural surpluses through the use of our bargaining power in the international field. The purpose of this Act was distorted in its administration and an attempt was made to commit the United States to a "world economy" as alien to the American System as the socialization attempted under the A.A.A. The Act has not been an aid to trade and, as it is being administered, cannot be an aid to trade, unless we mean by trade the displacement of American workers by foreign workers.

The devaluation of the dollar, supplemented by the refusal of the Administration to use the Reciprocal Trade Agreements Act as a trade aid, has resulted in transferring several billion dollars' worth of our capital assets to foreign control, while at the same time tying our hands against taking any defensive measures. In consequence of the maladministration of these acts, not only are we losing control over our financial system, such as it is, but also the foreign farmer is displacing the American farmer in the domestic market. The American farmer is no longer supreme in the American market, and, in the manner in which the agreements are being written, the American workman will shortly not be supreme in the American industrial market.

The Agricultural Adjustment Act and the Trade Agreements Act, while not the best acts which could have been drawn, contained sufficient authority to help alleviate the conditions they were designed to correct. Neither act was administered in accordance with the intentions of Congress. Instead, both acts were considered by their administrators as roving commissions to carry out theories which had not been passed upon by the Congress. The question is not, in so far as the executive officers of the Government are concerned, whether "America Must Choose" or "America Must Act." The question is whether the executive officers of the Government, sworn to support the Constitution, shall or shall not carry out the laws as made by Congress. The question is whether we shall have a government of laws or a government of men. If the Congress intended in these two acts to delegate all its power and all its discretion with respect to the subjects covered, it is up to the people to say whether or not they want that kind of Congress. That is more fundamental than any decision of the United States Supreme Court passing on the Constitutionality of the legislation.

Previously it has been a principle of our Government that its officers should act within the laws as written. There seems to be no good reason for changing that principle.

* * * * * *

How can we expect to attain the balance which would result in the largest amount of profitable domestic employment in all branches of agriculture, industry and service? Before a definite answer can be given to that question, we must know with reasonable exactness the size and character of the national income, how it is earned and how it is distributed. We must also know how many persons are employed, and where, and how. And how many are unemployed, and where, and why. These are essential facts that we ought currently to know. The accounting facts of the nation are as important to the management of the nation as they are to a business and, as I have set out on previous pages, our position cannot be rightly comprehended until we have detailed books on our international transactions, both as a whole and by countries.

Back in 1922, Mr. Martin J. Gillen of New York prepared at his own expense an exhaustive international balance sheet showing the then condition of the United States and presented it to the Republican Administration then in office. It was plainly evident from those accounts that already we had granted too many foreign credits and we stood to lose a great deal of money. That Administration paid no attention to those accounts and encouraged a great, new, private foreign lending. As a result, we have as a nation a great deal of money out that we cannot now collect and may or may not ever be able to collect. As Special Adviser to the President on Foreign Trade, with the counsel of Mr. Gillen and others, I laid out an accounting on our foreign trade, the results of which I have given. The Roosevelt Administration paid no attention whatsoever to that accounting—else the fiscal and trade policies which are selling out the country would not be continued. Dodging the facts is not a monopoly of either political party.

In the absence of the full accounting facts, it is still possible to advance these propositions as self-evident truths:

1. If we exchange one hour of American labor for one hour of foreign labor, we have done a useful thing only if the hour of foreign labor could not have been performed by an American.

2. If we exchange one hour of American labor for an hour of foreign labor that might have been performed by an American, we have done a harmful thing, for we have withdrawn the opportunity to create wealth in this country.

3. If we exchange one hour of American labor for two or more hours of foreign labor that might have been performed by an American, we are doing a harmful thing, in that we are postponing the opportunity to create wealth in this country until such time as our wage rates can be lowered to the foreign level. And, in the meantime, in depriving the American workman of his opportunity, we also deprive both industry and agriculture of his spending power. That spending power, expressed as it is in houses, transport, food, clothing and a thousand other directions, means more to us than getting cheap foreign goods.

4. If any integral part of our economy depends upon goods imported from abroad, then to that extent our whole economy becomes dependent on the pleasure of the foreign producers.

5. If any integral part of our economy depends upon exporting goods, then equally our whole economy hangs on the will of the foreign buyers.

All of which means that we must start our efforts at home—what we may do abroad can, at the best, only supplement what we do at home. This cannot be better expressed than as Henry Ford has put it:

> Whatever we do, we shall need to do at home. The place to revive the standard of living of the United States is within the United States, and the idea that we can revive our own industries and promote a higher level of domestic exchange by foreign trade is without foundation. In the first place, the world could not offer us enough sales to make any material difference in our home production, and in the second place, business founded upon foreign markets, instead of our own markets, is only temporary.
>
> It is a precept of modern industry that goods should be made as near as possible to where they are consumed. The old idea of dividing the world into raw-material and manufacturing nations does not hold now; it was based on the presumption that foreign peoples would always be dependent on us, but all of them are learning more and more of self-maintenance. We can help raise the standards of foreign nations and help to preserve world peace by teaching them our methods. We can aid neither the foreigners nor ourselves simply by trading.

There is here a larger implication, which has to do with preserving the peace of the world. We talk a great deal about preserving the peace of the world. But would it not be more to the point to remove the causes of war? The desire for commercial aggrandizement has been, since the beginning of the world, one of the chief causes of war. Any effort to preserve a division of nations into raw material and manufacturing countries is a certain inducement to war. We have only to look at our own history to know that. We fought the Revolution principally because England insisted on keeping us producers of raw material. The Colonists were forbidden to engage in other than the most elementary manufacturing. With the spread of science and invention, more and more countries are achieving a measure of independence through self-containment, and in the natural course of events, if the program be not interrupted by the internationalists' drive for a world economy, the earth will divide itself naturally into economic areas and a chief reason for war will tend to vanish. It is probable, with the higher standards of living which such an arrangement will bring, that international trade of a non-competitive and mutually profitable character will be far greater than the abnormal international trade which rests on keeping the raw material countries in a state of industrial subjection.

Internationalism does not and cannot make for peace because it seeks to keep intact all of those elements which have always made for war. Fortunately that is now becoming apparent. The League of Nations, had it been able to carry out its ludicrous peace policy of enforcing economic sanctions against Italy, would have started a general war in the name of peace!

And had it not been for the vigilance of Congress, our country would have been involved in that adventure!

It is scarcely necessary to dwell at length on some of the absurdities which have been brought out to support the internationalists' program for abandoning the American System. None of the assertions are supported by facts and none can be. Take a few of the more common whim whams.

(a) That the world suddenly started to put up trade barriers and retaliate against American exports because of the Hawley-Smoot Tariff Act.

The present restrictions began almost immediately after

the war, as the nations of the earth recovered sufficiently to set about making themselves independent of other nations for the necessities of life. The Great War taught a lesson which no self-respecting nation will ever forget.

(b) That from seven to ten million American workmen depend on our export trade, and that, unless our imports be greatly increased, these people in the export trade will be out of work.

It is impossible to determine how many people depend upon exports, for we have no exclusively export industries of any consequence. Our chief agricultural export is cotton. Our chief industrial export is the automobile. Very few men are employed in making automotive vehicles. The big employment is in servicing them after they are made—all of which is lost in foreign sales. If we take 350,000 as the normal employment in motor vehicle factories and 10 per cent as a normal export figure, we should have only 35,000 men employed as the result of the manufacture of automobiles for export. The Automobile Manufacturers Association estimates that the domestic employment generated by the automobile is upwards of five million. So even our largest industrial export absorbs a trifling number of people. Be that as it may, since increasing imports, as has been demonstrated, serves only to displace American workers in American industries without adding to those in the export industries, the solution proposed gets down to suggesting pneumonia as a cure for a common cold.

(c) That domestic production increases with imports and also that more employment is created by imports than by domestic production.

Both of these whimsical notions go directly counter to common sense. It is possible, by mixing both the free and the dutiable imports together and comparing them with the Federal Reserve Board index of industrial production, to get the same sort of result as may be obtained by multiplying horses by apples. The only possible comparison is between the free imports and industrial production. From the free imports must be deducted coffee, tea, newsprint and certain other articles which, although processed or packaged, are scarcely the raw materials of industry. Having deducted these, it appears, taking the monthly figures, that the industrial production and the free imports for use in industry move very closely together except during periods when the industries are obviously stocking up on raw materials. As to the second thought, that imports employ more men than domestic production, it would follow that our greatest happiness would be gained by importing everything and making nothing at all.

(d) That unless we increase our exports and depend more largely upon world trade it is necessary intensively to regiment the country.

The United States, within its continental borders, does about one-half of the business of the whole world. A 5 per cent increase in domestic business means as much as a 100 per cent increase in our export business, and the notion that regimentation must follow unless export increases evidences a profound conviction that the tail wags the dog.

* * * * * *

What can be done toward achieving the desired balance in our economy? Here are some elementary suggestions:

(1) Put an embargo on all competitive farm products or limit them by quota to actual requirements. The American home market belongs to the American farmer.

(2) Terminate the buying of gold and silver at improvident prices from abroad.

(3) Renounce the existing trade agreements and rebuild the American protective system. Repeal or amend the Reciprocal Trade Agreements Act to provide for Congressional approval of all general trade agreements. Set up a Foreign Trade Board or reorganize the Tariff Commission, somewhat along

the lines proposed in the Lewis Foreign Trade Board Bill, which will separate the control of commercial policy from diplomatic policy. This board or commission would need a considerable latitude, but its activities should be confined to the area of fact. It should have the power, under a new or amended Trade Agreements Act, to consummate barter transactions, to impose quotas and restrictions and otherwise, whenever necessary, to aid and protect the interests of the United States. Its policies should be defined by Congress and, although in certain cases it might be given the power to act according to its own judgment, no major action should be taken without the full opportunity for all parties in interest to be heard. Return to the "conditional" most-favored-nation treaty policy and renounce all our "unconditional" treaties.

(4) Set up as soon as possible a statistical organization to tabulate how the country makes its living and how it distributes it. Most of this machinery is already in existence and needs only coordination. Not until we have the bookkeeping facts on our country currently published can we determine our national policies with any surety.

(5) Set up accounts on all our international transactions and keep them with the same accuracy as we now use in accounting for the exports and imports of goods. Compel the registration of all foreign holdings in the United States and of all American holdings abroad, in order that we may always know our exact international position and act accordingly.

(6) Include in every trade agreement an exchange provision for the collection of debts due to American citizens or to our Government. It is necessary, for the preservation of our own financial system, that a part at least of the large foreign holdings in the United States be applied to the liquidation of the war debts. This adjustment should be particularly easy at the present time because practically all the foreign governments have assumed a measure of control over the foreign in-

vestments of their nationals. A method of liquidating the debts due to us could be worked out along the lines which the British Government used in negotiating a war loan here in 1915 and which the French used in paying their indemnity to Germany after 1870. Our commercial banks have recently made a tentative arrangement by which a portion of the exchange bought by American tourists intending to travel in Germany will be applied to their frozen debts. There is ample opportunity, what with tourist expenditures and immigrant remittances, to work out exchange agreements which will not be unduly burdensome but which will furnish the funds to resume the service upon their debts to us.

(7) Adopt a national policy of selective imports and exports administered on the recommendations of the Foreign Trade Board or commission. We should, as a matter of policy, send abroad, preferably in manufactured form, those products we can best produce, particularly those agricultural products which are the backbone of our foreign trade and of our domestic prosperity, taking in return those raw materials we need. It seems clear that to secure payment for our exports we should import the commodities we need and do not produce, such as tea, coffee, rubber, silk, etc., and such other commodities, the importation of which will improve our standards of living and will not seriously affect our industries. We should not leave our doors open to unregulated imports.

It is quite possible that selective exports and imports may involve greater use of the two-column tariff and of import quotas on certain products from certain countries. I am of the opinion that such a policy would go far toward preserving the home market for both agriculture and industry and restoring a balance between them; and that it would reopen important foreign markets. It would establish a sound method for the exchange of goods on a mutually advantageous basis.

(8) Making the tariff effective for agriculture will go a

long way toward giving the farmer a proper exchange price for his products within a reasonable period. But because the farmer has been hurt by too much Government meddling and his condition is now artificial, it may be necessary in emergencies to make provision in connection with the removal of burdensome surplus products, through foreign trade, for the payment of benefits on these products through processing or other taxes. Or again it is argued that it is feasible to adopt a plan of setting a minimum price for domestic production sufficient to provide an exchange income. Under no circumstances should production control through acreage limitation be again attempted.

(9) Encourage the growing of such agricultural products as are now imported and further the industrial use of things that are grown. This is a big subject of itself and of the highest importance. Secretary Wallace has thus far blocked any considerable efforts in these directions, on the ground that thereby foreign purchasing power would be lessened.

The application of ordinary common sense to the facts will at least take us out of the mud of factless theory in which we are now mired. Then we can go ahead on our firm American ground.

An American point of view calls for one policy, the internationalist point of view for quite another. We have straddled long enough.

Shall we take advantage of our position of geographical and economic security and contribute to world peace and prosperity by developing our own country and by attending to our own affairs?

Or shall we toss our nation into a common pool in the management of which ours will be but one voice and not the controlling one?

Shall we dilute our strength with the world's weakness?

THE BOOK ENDS.